386

AF791724

DEVELOPMENT
A SAGA OF TWO WORLDS

About the Author

Vishwambhar Nath was born in 1923 and grew up in Lahore, now in Pakistan. His postgraduate studies took him to the U.S. during which he acquired a doctorate from Maryland University.

Trained as a Development Economist Dr. Nath has worked in the Planning Commission in Delhi and as Collector in Rajasthan. He went to the US first as a student and later as a teacher at Kentucky, Lexington. He went on to work as an Economic Planner in Kuwait, Sierra Leone and The Gambia on UN assignments. He lives with his wife Kamla and daughter Jyotsana in Vasant Vihar, New Delhi. His two sons Virendra and Arvind are permanently settled in the U.S.A.

DEVELOPMENT
A SAGA OF TWO WORLDS

VISWAMBHAR NATH

CONCEPT PUBLISHING COMPANY, NEW DELHI-110059

All rights reserved. No part of this work may be reproduced, stored in a retrieval system, or transmitted in any form or by any means, electronic, mechanical, photocopying, microfilming, recording or otherwise, without the prior written permission of the copyright owner and the publisher.

ISBN 81-7022-946-4

First Published 2002

© Vishwambhar Nath

Published and Printed by
Ashok Kumar Mittal
Concept Publishing Company
A/15-16, Commercial Block, Mohan Garden
New Delhi-110059 (India)

Phones: 5351460, 5351794
Fax: 091-(11)-5357103
E-mail: publishing@conceptpub.com

Introduction

This book is dedicated to the young people of today. Its object is to give them glimpses of the customs and life style of the people of my ancestral village and to contrast them with our and their present life styles. The values and life style of the people of my ancestral village can be considered pre-industrial. They did not have the artifacts that make our lives safe, more convenient and enjoyable. But all Hindus and Sikhs of the village knew one another. Marriages and funerals were occasions for all members of an extended family to get together, no matter how far some of them may be living. Their friends and neighbours joined the festivities in a marriage and shared their grief on the death of an elder. The families with which the affected family had such relations contributed to its expenses on marriages and funerals.

Today, however, our next door neighbour does not know and is not interested in knowing our joys or sorrows. Our lives are governed by the artifacts of the industrial and post-industrial age; the news and entertainment media, particularly television, not only inform but also amuse and entertain. They have taken the place of songs and dance in marriages or the kirtans in temples and gurudwaras (Sikh temples) that entertained our grandfathers and grandmothers.

My experiences of the U.S.A. and the other countries in which I have lived give the readers an inkling of what makes the people of these countries happy or unhappy. I have been lucky in having the opportunities of living in these lands; they have enabled me to observe better the human condition in them.

I have attempted in the following pages to tell the story of my life extending over a period of three quarters of a century which has seen revolutionary and accelerating changes in every area of human endeavour and human experience. I confine myself to changes in three areas – political, economic and technological that have affected my life in various ways.

I was born in 1923 in a village in Sargodha district and lived the first 23 years of my life in Lahore. Yet when I left Lahore in 1946 to study in the U.S.A., I had not dreamt that I would never return to it. My parents made their home in Delhi after migration from Pakistan to India in the wake of Partition in 1947. I have lived in Delhi for nearly three decades, although I first saw it only in 1946 on my way to the U.S.A. The Delhi of those days was unimaginably different from what it is today. It was so much smaller, uncrowded, more relaxed than the pulsating and heavily polluted metropolis of more than 10 million people that it is today.

Political Change

The British were firmly entrenched as the rulers of British India, which included the present Indian Union, Pakistan, Bangladesh and Burma (now renamed Myanmar). Britain had been the most successful among European countries in establishing an empire. British dominions (inhabited mainly by people of British descent), dependencies like India and colonies spanned the globe. The average Briton was proud of saying "The Sun never sets on the British Empire". This was no exaggeration, it was true. We were taught this in our schools and also that the British had brought peace and order where there was lawlessness earlier and had introduced the railways, post and telegraphs and built irrigation canals to bring prosperity to the people of Punjab.

The period of expansion of the British Empire had ended some years after World War I. However, the energies of the British government were devoted to administering the dependencies and colonies so that their agricultural and mineral resources were used to contribute to the enrichment of Britain and their manpower and that of the dominions was available for fighting Britain's wars. The empire contributed to Britain's prosperity, power and glory and made it a major player in international affairs.

India was the crown jewel of the British Empire. Indian soldiers, commanded by British officers, had helped the British to become the paramount power in India itself in the nineteenth century and helped them to extend their dominance in Africa and parts of Asia. India's agricultural and mineral raw materials and its large market had contributed to Britain becoming one of the richest industrial nations in the world. The Indian Army was the largest component of British forces fighting the Germans during World War I and the Germans, the Japanese and the Italians during World War II. India was too valuable a dependency for any Prime Minister of Britain to even think of granting independence to it.

As late as the summer of 1942, Mr. Winston Churchill, the Prime Minister of Britain during most of World War II had declared, "I have not become the King's first minister to preside over the liquidation of the British Empire". He said this a few months after signing with President Roosevelt of the United States, the Atlantic Charter, an important article of which was grant of the right of self determination to all people. Britain's power and glory were deeply ingrained in his psyche; he had begun his career as a soldier, fighting the Pathans in the North West Frontier Province (which now forms part of Pakistan) and the tribal lands located beyond British administered areas.

However, barely five years later, his successor, Mr. Clement Attlee, announced that:

India Would Become Independent Within a Year

Independence would be accompanied by partition of the sub-continent on the basis of religion. The areas located in the western and eastern parts of north India in which the Moslems formed the majority of the population would be included in Pakistan, while the remaining British administered areas would be included in the Indian Union. The rulers of the 600-odd princely states would be free to decide their future – to accede to Pakistan or the Indian Union or to remain independent.

A combination of circumstances had contributed to this *volte-*

face on the part of the British government. The decolonisation process which began with grant of independence to Myanmar in 1946, India in 1947 and Sri Lanka early in 1948 was completed by the mid–1960s, when the last British colonies in the Caribbean sea were given independence. After deciding to grant independence to India and failing to suppress the movements for independence in Ghana and Kenya in Africa, the British government concluded that discretion was the better part of valour and granted independence to all British colonies. The leaders of the government concluded correctly that the dependencies and colonies were more an economic burden than an economic asset. They believed correctly that:

Some of the most talented graduates of British universities were engaged in administering the dependencies and colonies instead of becoming executives in British companies;

Britain can obtain agricultural and mineral products from the dependencies and colonies or elsewhere, by paying prevailing prices for them, and

British manufactures would continue to sell in the dependencies and colonies if they were competitive in quality and price with those of other countries.

Although British manufactures do not dominate the markets of its former dependencies and colonies, the average Briton is today, richer, better fed, better clothed, better housed, better educated, healthier and has a much higher life expectancy than his or her parents or grand parents had half a century ago.

Meanwhile English has remained the language of the elite in all former British dependencies and colonies, and also the most important language of communication among nations. It is the first language of the United Nations. British institutions of parliamentary democracy and the right of all people to fair trial are regarded as ideals by the most despotic generals who rule some of the former British colonies in Africa. All this was unexpected.

The political leaders of my father's generation and those a few years older than them had struggled relentlessly for India's independence from British rule. Thousands who participated in the struggle died and hundreds of thousands spent varying periods in jails. We, the common folk, did not and perhaps many of those who participated in the struggle also may not have believed that independence would be achieved in our lifetime. The British were so firmly entrenched as the rulers of India.

We never thought that English would be retained as the link language of educated people of all parts of India, of communication between Indians and foreigners and also the principal language of business and finance. India and most other former British colonies have adopted the parliamentary system of governance and have chosen voluntarily to remain members of the British Commonwealth. The latter had not been formed when these countries became independent.

The attraction of colonies as sources of food and raw materials and markets of its manufactures was so great that Germany fought two wars in quest of them. During World War II, it lost millions of young men; its cities suffered heavy damage from air raids by American, British and Soviet bombers, and after the war, it remained divided into two for almost four decades. However, today, it is the richest and most powerful country in Western Europe. Japan is to-day among the richest countries in the world. Its citizens have among the lowest birth and death rates and have access to a comprehensive system of welfare services. It had such aspiration for colonies that it had occupied during the 1930s, the entire eastern, most populated and most productive part of China and sought political and economic domination over the whole of South, South east and East Asia. It lost all its colonies in World War II, millions of its youth died; its cities suffered heavy damage during the War and it was occupied by the U.S.A. for about two decades after the war. But it has recovered so rapidly that it has become an economic superpower.

The prosperity of the former colonial powers, Germany and Japan, and high level of living of their citizens are due to uninterrupted economic growth that the industrial countries have experienced for almost fifty years, and the benefits of the comprehensive systems of welfare that their governments have evolved for their citizens.

Economic Change

When I was growing up in the 1930s the world was experiencing the severest economic depression in living memory. Millions were unemployed in Europe, the U.S.A., Canada and other industrial countries. Industrial output is estimated to have declined by one third from its peak at the end of the 1920s to the depth of the depression in the mid-1930s. Unemployment among Hindu educated youth in Punjab was so severe that the newspapers carried reports every day of one or more young men committing suicide because they could not get a job. The leading economists and political leaders of the industrial countries did not know how to end the depression. It ended only with World War II, when the manpower and the agricultural and manufacturing capacity of the industrial countries was employed in producing food and armament for the soldiers. Many historians are of the view that World War II was fought partly to end the depression.

The depression contributed to my developing a pessimistic outlook. I worried that there would be no job for me when I graduated from college. Even when I was preparing for my M.A. examination in the winter of 1945 – 46, the only job prospect was of teaching in a small college in Punjab or an adjoining state. I had never dreamt that even before I passed the examination, I would be offered a fellowship for study in the U.S.A. We knew very little about the country and practically nothing about its educational institutions. The best students in Punjab went for post-graduate studies to London, Oxford or Cambridge in England and *Bauji* (my father) could not afford to send me to any of them.

However, when I went to the U.S.A., I found a country the like of which I had never dreamt of. It was rich and powerful; its average citizens had a standard of living which appeared fabulous to an Indian. At the same time, most of its people including most of my fellow students who had fought in World War II were friendly, curious to know about India and treated me with great consideration. My professional thinking was transformed. I learnt that it was essential to have a spirit of enquiry in order to be a good student. In India the best students were those who could reproduce best what they had learnt from their textbooks and teachers. Not so, in American universities. One was expected to think for one self and defend the position that one took on any issue. Madison, Wisconsin, where I went in 1946 was a very friendly city. Wherever I went, I was greeted with a smile. My spirit soared and although I was afraid that I would not keep good health in the bitter cold of the city, I have never been healthier. Prof. Baker, who was the adviser for my Ph.D thesis at the University of Maryland reminded me of an ancient Indian sage, because he embodied in his lifestyle, the ideals of plain living and high thinking. Children of farmers, he and his wife lived as farmers in an old wooden frame house which was situated amid three acres of pasture in which they kept cows and poultry and grew vegetables to meet their household needs. At the same time, I have yet to see two individuals who were so concerned about the welfare of Dr. Baker's students as were he and his wife.

I was among the first groups of students to go for higher studies in American universities. The Education Department of the Government of India, however, knew enough about the high quality of education in American universities and institutes of science and technology to send thousands of young men and women there as Government of India scholars.

On return from the U.S.A., as my ship was approaching Mumbai, I was worried. I was returning home with a Ph.D degree after spending three years in the U.S.A., but I had no job. My applications for jobs in two Universities in India and one in the University of Ceylon (now Sri Lanka) had elicited no response. Meanwhile, my parents had become refugees and had lost all they had in Lahore. However, the first thing, that I learnt on landing was that I had a job in the University of Ceylon.

What a relief, I would not be unemployed after all!

From there on I never looked back. A short stint in the Unversity of Ceylon at Colombo, followed by a fairly long period in the Planning Commission of India and as collector in a district of Rajasthan provided useful experiences. UN assignments in Kuwait Sierra Leone and The Gambia were pleasant and extremely lucrative interludes.

Technological Change

The rapidity of technological change and its effects on human life are mind boggling. A few examples illustrate the point. Computers began to be developed soon after World War II. Yet their use has already revolutionized techniques in manufacturing, education, medicine, surgery, communications and in many countries even in agriculture. They have enabled men to walk on the moon and to send unmanned space vehicles to explore distant planets or stars. I am a computer illiterate but I belong to a genre which is bound for extinction. Every child in the developed countries would be proficient in the use of computers by the time he or she graduates from high school. Projecting present trends in education in the use of computers in India it is safe to predict also that the same will be true of children of middle income groups in most cities of India in another two decades.

I am alive to write this story only because I underwent successfully coronary by-pass surgery at a Delhi hospital ten years ago. Thousands of such surgeries are performed every year in hospitals in India and on millions of patients round the world. The surgery has become possible with the development of the heart lung machine in the 1960s. It has been developed with the aid of computers. Some of the best cardiac surgeons already consider the technique too risky and are trying to develop techniques which are less risky but equally effective. Transplant of human organs began only in the late 1960s but advances in the field are so rapid that even in India with few hospitals equipped for such transplants thousands of patients benefit from them every year.

The radio receiver was a luxury in Indian cities in the 1930s and the television receiver was a luxury as late as the early 1970s. Today, there are hundreds of television receivers in every large slum cluster in large cities like Mumbai, Calcutta and Delhi and also in large villages in many states. The radio receiver is the proud possession of the poor in India's cities and villages. The news and entertainment provided by the radio and television receivers make living for the poor less boring. The manufacturers of consumer goods – soap, hair oil and other cosmetics or medicines such as aspirin for treatment of common diseases – have been quick to see the potential of advertising on radio and television to boost the sales of their products.

The most important lesson that I have learnt in my life is that the unexpected is a recurrent phenomenon in human life, as in the history of nations. There is light after every tunnel, joy after every sorrow, success after every failure, a period of health and well being after every sickness.

New Delhi VISHWAMBHAR NATH
March, 2001

ACKNOWLEDGEMENTS

For assistance in writing this story, I must thank first my wife, Kamla, and my elder son, Virendra, who have encouraged me to write it and have revised various drafts of it. For editing this book and bringing it to publishable size, I thank Mrs. Ramaswamy who has spent hours on the job. Finally, I am grateful to the publishers for bringing it out in record time.

V. Nath

Contents

1

Life in my Ancestral Village

Khaddar ke gole banaye jainge, golon se gore urae jainge [We will make cannon balls of khadi and blow up the British with them] *Sar faroshi ki tamanna ab hamare dil men hai dekhna hai zore kitna bazue katil men hai* [We want to sacrifice our lives for the independence of India. Let us see how much strength these murderers (British rulers) have to suppress us.]

As a bonny fair seven year old child, I was singing these jingles while walking from the bus stop to my grand-uncle's shop-cum-house which was in a bazaar, in my ancestral village, Jhawarian. As I entered the *bazaar,* I was picked up by the shop-keepers who were friends of my grandfather and grand uncle.

My mother, two younger sisters and I were visiting the village because my mother had to participate in the ceremonial mourning called *sayapa,* after the death of my grand uncle. Participation in death and marriage ceremonies was a primary obligation of all members of an extended family even though some of them lived far away. We had travelled to Jhawarian from Lahore, where my father had his small wholesale business of importing safety razors and blades from Germany.

Jingles like the ones above were very popular because they evoked nationalist feelings among the people during the civil disobedience movement launched by Mahatma Gandhi in the thirties. They expressed the determination of the people to struggle for independence of the country from British rule. For children like me, however, it was like singing a popular film song. Ours was one of the richest families in the village. My grandfather was also respected for his honesty and simplicity.

A few days before my visit to the village, on 31 December 1929, a resolution for *Poorna Swaraj* (complete independence) had been passed at the annual session of the Indian National Congress held in Lahore. The session was presided over by Pandit Jawaharlal Nehru.

We took a train from Lahore on a cold wintry night to reach Sargodha, which was 160 km from Lahore. From there we took a bus to Jhawarian another 30 km away. The ride was in a rickety old bus on a *kuchha* (unmetalled) road. It was around noon when we reached Jhawarian. Jhawarian was a village located six km from the river Jhelum. Excepting the bus service connecting the village with Sargodha, the principal means of local transport in big villages was the *tonga* – a one or two horse-drawn carriage. People going for short distances travelled on horseback.

From the bazaar we went to my grandfather's house, located in a lane about one km. from his shop. Our family had lived in this village for several generations. Although there is no historical record to support it, there is a traditional belief that we, the Aroras, had migrated from Sindh to West Punjab in the eighth century A.D. when Sindh was conquered by the Arab invader, Mohammed bin Kassim by defeating its Hindu ruler, Raja Dahar. There is some ground for the belief because our language *Lehnda* which is spoken all over West Punjab is linked through Multani (the language spoken in South West Punjab) with Sindhi, the language of Sindh. Further, the Aroras were found mainly in villages and towns located near the three rivers of West Punjab – the Sindh (Indus), Jhelum and the Chanab. The Aroras, originally soldiers of Dahar, had become traders and money-lenders after migration to West Punjab. They were along with the Khatris the richest and best educated group in West Punjab.

I was born in Jhawarian on 14 July 1923 at 2.30 p.m. the hottest time of the day, in *Asarh* (the hottest month of the year). It was *Amawas,* the darkest night of the lunar month. Although my father lived in Lahore, my mother had to go to Jhawarian because it was the custom that the first child in the family, must be born in the ancestral home of the husband. The custom was meant to prove to the parents of the pregnant woman that her husband's family were well off and could bear the expenses of the delivery. The rigour of the custom was such that *Bauji* my father, an educated and enlightened man, sent his wife to the village fully aware of the fact that the unhygienic traditional delivery practices followed by the untrained village midwife could lead to the death of either mother or child or both. All three subsequent deliveries of my mother were conducted, however, in our house in Lahore by a trained mid-wife.

My paternal granduncle, although younger than my grandfather was the decision-maker in the family. On hearing about my birth, he came to grandfather's house and said that I should be called Shamba, an acronym for Bishambar Nath. I changed my name from Bishambar to Vishwambhar, when I joined Government College Lahore, in 1938.

Jhawarian was a large village with a population of about 6000 in the thirties. Moslems constituted about three-fourths of the population; the rest were Hindus and Sikhs who were shopkeepers. The affluent ones among them like my grand parents used to lend money as a side business. Most of the Moslems were subsistence farmers and artisans. However, there were also a few big landlords among them. In our area, the biggest landlord was Sir Umar Hayat Khan Tewana, who lived in village Kalra, about 3 km. from Jhawarian. His word was law in the area. In 1941, the Moslems boycotted the Hindus because some shopkeepers had extra-marital relations with their Moslem women customers. This incensed the *mullahs* (Moslem priests) who called for a boycott of Hindu shops. When the boycott had lasted for more than a month resulting in the closure of Hindu shops, two representatives of the shopkeepers approached *Bauji* in Lahore to go to Jhawarian to settle the dispute. He agreed. On reaching the village he met Sir Umar Hayat Khan with two representatives of the shopkeepers, tendered an apology on behalf of the Hindus and requested him to intervene to end the boycott. Sir Umar called the leaders of the Moslems and told them that since the Hindus had apologized the shops should be reopened. They were reopened.

Money was lent generally on security of gold and silver ornaments. But often it was lent without any security, because of the relationship of trust between the borrower and the money lender. The farmers borrowed money to meet the expenses of planting their summer and winter crops, to get over a financial crisis such as the death of a bullock or a milch buffalo, or to meet the expenses of a marriage in the family. Artisans took loans mainly to meet marriage expenses.

Earlier, in the second half of the nineteenth century, when the British became the rulers of the Punjab after defeating the Sikhs in 1847, there had been considerable exploitation of farmers by the money lenders. Large areas of farmers' lands were taken over by money lenders when the farmers defaulted in repayment of the loans. These transfers caused much unrest among the farmers who had lost their lands and had become landless agricultural labourers. To prevent such transfers, the Punjab Government passed the Punjab Land Alienation Act in 1901. The Act had the desired effect of stopping the transfers of land. But money-lending continued because of the needs of the farmers and the artisans. Their dependence was indicated by the popular saying, *"Guru bina gat nahin; shah bina pat nahin* (There is no deliverance from the cycle of births and deaths, the goal of man according to traditional Hindu belief without the guidance of a *guru* (spiritual teacher) and there is no honour without the assistance of a *shah* (money-lender). Honour here means escape from penury owing to lack of funds to farm one's land or practice one's traditional crafts.

Before my grand uncle, Roop Chand, returned from Burma (now renamed Myanmar) our family was so poor that my grandfather, Devi Dayal, would carry a 16 kg tin of *ghee* (clarified butter), which was the principal medium of cooking in West Punjab on his head from a small village Boonga about 10 km away to Jhawarian to sell it for a meagre profit.

Enterprising Hindu and Sikh young men from our village began to go to small Burmese villages to become traders. Some took their families with them and settled down there, others, like my grand uncle, went alone and returned home after collecting some capital. The migration had started after the British conquered Burma in

1880 and made it a part of British India. Most of the migrants returned home during the Japanese conquest of Burma during World War II. Others returned after the country got independence in 1946 and its government started sending Indians back.

My grand uncle returned from Burma in about 1908. With his earnings there he opened a retail cloth shop in partnership with my grandfather. He married and had a son, Chooni Lal in 1910. But his wife died in childbirth and although he was in his mid-forties, he decided not to remarry and remained a widower for 19 years until his death in 1929. My grandfather also became a widower in 1923 when my grandmother succumbed to burns sustained by her while cooking. He too remained a widower for 11 years until his death at the age of 69 in 1934.

The decisions by my grand uncle and grandfather not to remarry were a departure from the prevailing practice of Hindu widowers, who invariably remarried. Since both were widowers, their household was managed by my *Bhua* (father's sister), who had herself been widowed after the death of her husband in the influenza epidemic of 1918-19 which swept the world after World War I and claimed millions of lives.

Granduncle had to start his cloth shop in partnership with grandfather because the joint effort of the two was considered essential for running a shop successfully. For their widowed sister, they financed the establishment of a provision store to provide a source of livelihood for her sons, Agya Ram and Chanan Mal. Agya Ram, the elder son proved to be such a good manager that the store soon become the largest provision store in the village. He built a house in which the two brothers lived along with their families and their mother. Chanan Mal did not do much because he was addicted to smoking *hashish* (marijuana) and *hafim* (opium). But the strength of the joint family system was such that Agya Ram considered it his moral duty to provide for Chanan Mal's family also.

The profits of the store were shared in mutually agreed proportions, between the financiers (my grand uncle and grand father), Agya Ram and Chanan Mal, and three other workers in the store; they received no salaries. Six per cent of the profit was earmarked for charitable purposes. After the death of grandfather and granduncle, their share in the profits of the store went to Chooni Lal, my father's elder brother and my father.

In our family cloth shop, the profit was shared equally between granduncle and grandfather although the former was the main financier and a much better salesman than my grandfather. On the death of grand uncle, his son, Chooni Lal, who was then 19 years old, became the successor to his share of the profits. Chooni Lal had studied for three years in Lahore to become a *Vaidya* (physician practising the ancient Hindu Ayurvedic system of medicine). After completing his training he returned to the village in 1929 and started working in the clothshop. He became its sole owner and manager when my grandfather died in 1934 and continued to manage it until August 1947, when he and his family had to leave Jhawarian as part of the migration of Hindus and Sikhs from West Punjab to India. He was also practising as a *vaidya* and a *homeopath;* he had learnt homeopathy by self study. He was greatly respected in the village for his competence as a physician and had a large clientele among both Hindus and Moslems. He did not charge any fees because he believed that he would lose his healing touch if he did. This added to his popularity because he was considered to be a benevolent man.

After migrating from Pakistan he settled down in Delhi and set up a small factory for manufacturing kerosene oil lamps in Jhandewalan in central Delhi. The factory is now being run by two of his seven sons. With the profits of his factory he built a house on Rohtak Road in Karol Bagh in which lived two of his sons along with their families. Three other sons have their own businesses and houses in Punjabi Bagh in West Delhi. Two of his sons are settled in the USA. One, a cardiologist, is married happily to an American and lives in Omaha, Nebraska. He facilitated the migration to the USA of his younger brother, who is now working as a computer programmer.

Chooni Lal was a hearty, overweight man who had a great appetite for good food, and was also very fond of travelling. Whenever he came to Lahore in early winter, he would spend several hours in *Papad Mandi,* the wholesale market for dry fruit, spices and provisions. He would buy enough dry fruit and nuts to last him and his family through the winter. A few years before his death, he travelled to the USA with his wife and stayed with his son for four months. On his way back, he spent two days in Moscow. He greatly enjoyed describing his experiences particularly about how he managed to see a part of central Moscow defying all Soviet government restrictions on such sightseeing by individual tourists.

His wife who died of the age of eight-two years age, was a self effacing, kindhearted woman who followed all her husband's wishes without question. In Jhawarian, his cloth shop's Hindu clients from neighbouring villages were invariably provided lunch or dinner and arrangements for staying in his house if they had to stay overnight. His wife was, therefore, used to cooking enough to cater to the needs of at least two extra persons. She also maintained a large store of utensils and bed linen which was enough for at least fifty persons. They were lent free of charge to other Hindus or Sikhs during weddings in their family.

Grandfather and granduncle lived in the same house and had a common kitchen. Later, granduncle built a three bed-room house on top of the cloth shop where he used to live. However, he continued to have his meals in grandfather's house where my widowed *bhua* (grand-father's daughter) lived along with her two daughters and managed the household. After the marriage of her daughters and the death of grandfather, *bhua* would lock her house and stay with Chooni Lal and his wife. She would also come to Lahore to stay with us for long spells or be with my father's elder brother who was a doctor, and as a member of the Subordinate Medical Service used to be posted in small towns or large villages in Punjab.

Bhua

Bhua was a cheerful old lady, who could not bear to live alone. She was also very fond of going on pilgrimages. She would go to Hardwar often. Once she went to the temples of Badrinath and Kedarnath, situated at an altitude of about 13,000 ft in the western Himalayas near the source of the river Ganga. Today, there is a bus service almost to the base of the mountain on which the temples are located, and the pilgrims have to walk only a few miles to reach the temples. But in the thirties when *Bhua* went there was no bus service beyond Rishikesh, a few miles upstream of Hardwar, and the pilgrims had to walk a long distance on a hilly road in order to reach the temples. Although she was more than fifty years old, *Bhua* undertook the trip cheerfully and spent a month doing it. Her expenses of living in Jhawarian and travels were financed from the profits of the provision store. My parents were quite fond of her, as were we children. We liked her for her cheerful manner and her genuine love for us. She was full of chatter, and would sing religious songs when she had nobody to talk to. She had great dignity and charm and must have been a beautiful woman in her youth.

Bhua lost her husband when she was only thirty years old; she had two unmarried daughters. Grandfather arranged their marriages; the younger daughter was happily married to a shopkeeper in a small village and had several sons, all of whom are now settled in their businesses in and around Delhi. The elder daughter was married to an engineer working in a sugar mill in U.P., but was deserted by her husband within a year of marriage because she was not good looking. After being deserted she lived with us in Lahore for three years to train to be a primary school teacher. *Bauji* filed a suit against her husband, to get her a maintenance allowance. He won the suit but the payments were never regular. After she got a primary school teachers' certificate, *Bauji* got her a job in a primary school in Lahore. After Partition she taught in several primary schools in villages of Saharanpur District of UP until her death in the seventies. I can never forget *Bhua* or her.

Udasi Sant

Our family maintained an Udasi *Sant* (holy man). He had been a wrestler in his youth. A two-room structure called *Sant ka chabara* (the residence of the *Sant*) was built for him by our family on the outskirts of the Hindu-Sikh area of the village. The *Sant* lived above a cowshed where fodder was also stored. The *Sant* was a heavy smoker and relished eating meat. Since Hindu women were strict vegetarians, many men who wanted to eat meat (invariably goat's meat) would go to the *chabara* to cook it. The *Sant* was celibate; women were not allowed to visit his abode. He developed cancer of the prostate and died a few months before Partition at the age of 70. Thus he escaped seeing the trauma of migration of his devotees.

Drinking and gambling were considered sinful by all — Hindus, Sikhs and Moslems. Smoking the *Hukka* (hubble-bubble) however, was common among men and women. Men smoked individually and in groups; women, however, smoked individually in their homes; it was supposed to relieve constipation. The *Sant's* abode was the popular meeting place for elderly men of the village to smoke in a group, discuss the news of the village, neighbouring villages, of India and the world. Most Sikhs and all Moslems were non-vegetarians. The *Sant* was a worldly wise man whose advice was sought in family and village problems by Hindus as well as by Moslems.

Later, in the early forties, a large three-room house was constructed known as the *Sant Ghar*, with contributions from our family and other families. The *Sant Ghar* was also used as a *Janj Ghar* (place for overnight stay of marriage parties).

Although illiterate, the Sant was very fond of listening to the news published in the Urdu daily, the *Pratap*. The news would be read out to him by one of the men who had come to his abode after dinner. It would then be discussed at length till about 10.30p.m. when the men would return to their homes. Most Hindu men of my grandfather's age were literate in Urdu; the village had a school up to the eighth grade run by the government. I attended the school for a few days during my first visit to the village. The school day would start about 10 a.m., and end by 4 p.m. Before the teaching started, all children would gather to recite one or two poems in praise of God and seek his blessings. It would end with recitation of multiplication tables in a sing song manner by all the students in a class. Slapping the students and beating them with a cane stick by the teachers was common.

All Hindu and Sikh males were literate in Urdu, which was the official vernacular language of Punjab and is now the national language of Pakistan. However, they maintained their accounts in *takare,* the traditional language of keeping accounts books in West Punjab. Most Hindu and Sikh women including my mother were educated only up to five grades. They were taught Punjabi in the Gurumukhi script so that they could read the Sikh scripture, Shri Guru Granth Sahib, in small schools run by Hindus or Sikh teachers. My mother, aunts and other female relatives of her age, as well as Kamla's mother had all studied up to five grades in Gurumukhi.

Death was common in the village and was taken in a stoic manner. It was considered to be the only certainty in life. During the thirties and the forties most of the deaths were caused by malaria, dysentery and diseases of the respiratory tract including tuberculosis. Malaria, which broke out in epidemic form after the summer monsoon was by far the greatest killer. In 1945, several hundred people died of malaria. Poor sanitation in the village was due to lack of drainage facilities for disposal of liquid waste. It led to breeding of mosquitoes and flies which led to the outbreak of diarrhoea, dysentery, trachoma and respiratory diseases including tuberculosis. The village *bazaar* and the streets had dirty water flowing through them, primarily because most houses were *pucca* (made of brick and mortar) and many had hand pumps without any provision for drainage. The water from the drains flowed into several ponds located outside the village. Solid waste including night soil was carried by scavenger women on their heads and dumped in several places on the outskirts of the village. These too were breeding places for flies and disease germs. Deaths of children were very common. Out of the nine children of my grandfather only three, *bhua,* my father and his elder brother survived. I remember that when one of the village *pansaris* (herb sellers) learnt that one of his children had died, he did not rush to his home but continued to work in the shop. He went home and buried the child only during the lunch break.

The death of an adult was followed by several rituals. After cremation, ceremonial mourning was observed for ten days. During this period women of the extended family and their friends congregated in the afternoons to beat their chests while chanting songs funeral. In these chants the good qualities and accomplishments of the deceased would be described and his 'early' death mourned. This ritual was called *sayapa.* The male relatives and friends of the deceased would assemble quietly in the afternoons to condole his death and console the sons on the loss of their father. There was no ceremonial mourning after the death of women. Three days after the cremation the men of the family would go to the cremation ground to pick up the bones of the deceased which were collected in an earthen pot. The bones, called *phool* (literally flowers) were immersed in the holy water of the Ganga in Hardwar, by the eldest son of the deceased or another male relative, if he had no son. Those who could not afford to go to Hardwar immersed the bones in the nearest river. The bones had to be carried directly from the cremation ground to Hardwar. Bringing them home before departure for Hardwar was considered inauspicious. The pilgrimage to Hardwar was followed by a visit to Kurukshetra for a purificatory bath by the nearest relatives, in case death had occurred in bed.

According to Hindu belief a person must die on the floor to be close to mother earth. Since the relatives were keen to avoid a pilgrimage to Kurukshetra, they would lay the dying person on the floor, while he/she was still alive with the had facing the east. An oil lamp was lit near the head. The dying person would quietly pray to God for freedom from the cycle of births and deaths. However this was a shocking experience for those who survived after having been laid on the floor. They never got over that shock. I saw this ceremony when my grandfather died in our house in Lahore in 1934. However, when my father died in bed in 1972 my mother, a younger brother of Kamla my wife and our elder son, Virendra all went to Hardwar and Kurukshetra. Virendra lit the fire for my father's cremation because both my younger brother and I were far away from Delhi. I was in Sierra Leone and my younger brother was in Secunderabad. Virendra has never forgotten this experience.

The visit to Hardwar was accompanied by a meeting with the family *panda;* the Brahmin who performs the religious rites for immersion of the bones in the Ganga. He also keeps the lineage records of the family. The *pandas* congregate at Har Ki Pauri (lit. Shiva's steps) the immersion spot for the bones. As soon as one or more members of a family reach Har ki Pauri the *pandas* crowd around him, identify the family *panda* among them and if he is not there he is called immediately by the others to perform the immersion rituals. At this time he updates the lineage record of the family. One can get lineage records going back several generations from the *pandas.* Similar records of Punjabi families were kept until very recently by Pandits living in village Martandam (commonly known as Mattan) in Kashmir. During our visit to Kashmir in 1987 we visited our family Pandit and were happy to see his record going back to my great great grandfather. These records were updated by the Pandits who used to visit Lahore and meet *Bauji* every winter.

Hindu or Sikh widows never remarried. But Moslem widows would remarry unless they were old. There was a common saying that a Jat woman is never a widow (*Jatti kabhi randi nahin rehti*). This was because the women worked in the fields and the artisans' wives invariably assisted their husbands in their craft. Thus by marrying a widow, a farmer or an artisan acquired a valuable worker besides a manager of his household. Later, during my work as a Collector in Sawai Madhopur district of Rajasthan I found that the taboo on widow remarriage was prevalent only among the three high castes - Brahmins, Rajputs and Mahajans (trader); and widow remarriage was universal among the farmers, artisans and the scheduled castes because the woman was a valuable worker. It would be interesting to conduct surveys in all states of India to ascertain the practice relating to widow remarriage among various Hindu castes.

Economic Conditions

Although most of the Moslems were subsistence farmers or artisans, every one had enough to eat. The same was true of Hindus and Sikhs. Poverty among the latter meant inability to keep a milch animal. The Brahmins were the poorest caste in the village because their priestly duties did not bring them much money. An old Brahmin woman would go daily to a few houses to get one or two freshly made *chappaties, lassi* (butter milk) and some butter. She would also bring to the women the gossip of the village. One or two *chappaties* and *lassi* were also given to the scavenger woman in exchange for her services.

During Second World War when prices of wheat and cotton, the main crops of the village, besides fodder (alfalfa, clover and sorghum sticks) increased rapidly, farmers with land holdings of 10 to 15 hectares or more became quite affluent. They invested their savings mainly in gold ornaments. The income of the subsistence farmers went up who also invested their savings in gold or silver ornaments. But they continued to borrow money for meeting marriage expenses and financial crises caused by the death of a bullock or a milch animal or prolonged sickness in their families. The Hindu and Sikh merchants also became more prosperous because the sales of their textiles increased. Chooni Lal and Agya Ram bought large quantities of wheat which they sold at a profit because its prices were increasing rapidly.

Public Service Facilities

Being a large village, Jhawarian had a police station, an 8-grade school and a small hospital which had a qualified doctor, and two paramedical personnel — a druggist and a nurse. The sub-inspector of police and the doctor were respected. The village had also two qualified medical practitioners. But most people sought the advice of herb sellers for treatment of common ailments.

Places of Worship and Religious Practices

The village had several mosques, a temple called Devi Dwara, devoted to the worship of Devi, the Hindu mother goddess Durga, a Gurudwara (Sikh temple) and a small building which housed the Arya Samaj. Large numbers of Hindu men and women visited the Devi Dwara, every day. Once a month or on an occasions like *Durga Ashtami*, night-long *kirtans* (prayers and songs in praise of the goddess) were held by the devotees.

All Sikh and many Hindu men and women went to the Gurudwara every day and listened to recitations from the Sikh scripture by the *granthis* (professional readers of the Sikh scripture) accompanied by music. There was also a small two-room *Dharmasala* maintained by a celibate *Mahant* (Hindu holyman). Here the Ramayana was kept in one room and the Sikh scriptures in the other. The *Mahant* would recite from both. I visited the *Dharamsala* once. The Arya Samaj had a weekly meeting in which *havan* (the ceremonial worship of fire) was followed by singing of songs in praise of God. I attended the meetings in the Arya Samaj regularly whenever I visited Jhawarian.

Marriages between Hindus and Sikhs were common. The eldest son in a Hindu family born after several years of marriage was made a Sikh according to the custom of that time. Children born after him remained Hindus however. After seeing these close relations between Hindus and Sikhs in West Punjab, I am distressed to see the increasing gulf between them created in recent decades by political parties. My father and uncle Chooni Lal were followers of the Arya Samaj, as were most educated men in West Punjab. The Samaj was a reform movement started in 1880 by a Gujarati preacher, Swami Dayanand Saraswati. He advocated education of men and women, remarriage of widows and opposed child marriage, practice of untouchability, worship of idols and various superstitious beliefs. Although started in Bombay, it became very popular in undivided Punjab, Haryana and Western UP.

The village had a number of mosques in its Moslem-dominated areas. Men would go to them every day but women were not allowed inside them. The Friday afternoon prayer, which was followed by a long sermon by the priest was the high point of the weekly worship. Moslems invariably observed fast during the month of Ramadan and observed the three *Eids* (feasts) prescribed by Islam. The few men who had performed the pilgrimage to Mecca were respected and called *Haajis* (lit. one who has performed the pilgrimage). The Ramadan fast caused great hardship when it came in the summer months of May to September. Thirst and the ban on smoking, rather than hunger caused the hardship, because those who observed the fast were not supposed to drink any fluid or smoke between sunrise and sunset. I was amazed to see a large crowd of Moslems around a shop selling a mixture of sweetened milk and water just before sunset during a visit to the village which came in Ramadaan. Their faces showed the extreme hardship they had suffered in enduring thirst for 14 hours (5 a.m. - 7 p.m.); summer days were long in Punjab. As prescribed by Islam prayers were performed five times a day only by the devout Moslems.

The practice of *purdah* was not common among Moslem women. Only women folk of the priests or of families in which one or more sons had joined government service after getting educated wore the *burqa* (the black dress which covers a woman from head to foot). Women of farmers and artisans did not wear it because it would interfere with their work. Hindu and Sikh women invariably covered their heads with their *dupattas* (long scarves) when passing through the village *bazaar*. They covered their heads, is show respect when talking to male relatives who were older than their husbands, and also to male strangers. Conversation with them was confined to the minimum; mentioning their husband's name was considered disrespectful.

Dress

All men - Moslem, Hindu, and Sikh wore a turban, a long shirt and a *tehmat* (a *dhoti* worn in the typical West Punjab style). In winter, Hindu and Sikh men would wear woollen sweaters and jackets on top of their shirts and *salwars* (slightly wide pyjamas). Moslem men and women would wear a knee or ankle length woollen or thick cotton shirt on top of thier *tehmats*. Silk garments were worn by the bride, the bridegroom and their close relatives during marriages in both winter and summer. Moslem bridegrooms wore a long shirt made of locally woven silk of mauve colour and a yellow *tehmat* called *lungi;* the women wore a long robe of deep pink colour and a deep green *lungi*.

Food was simple but wholesome. It included large quantities of milk products. Wheat was the principal cereal; rice was consumed only on festive occasions. In summer, breakfast would consist of *chappaties* (unleavened bread) left over from the previous night, spattered with butter and washed down with *lassi* (butter-milk) ; Hindu women were strict vegetarians but men who were non-vegetarians cooked goat's meat outside the home. Although all

Moslems were non-vegetarians the poor could afford to eat meat only occasionally. Moslems would eat mainly beef and lamb. Moslems ate large loaves of leavened flour cooked by baker women in large *tandoors* (earthen ovens).

Vegetables and fruit were sold in two shops in the village bazaar and by women of the *Arain* (vegetable grower) caste. They would come to the houses of their clients in the late mornings. Payment in kind was common in small villages. These women would accept grain from the farmers' wives and salt, oil or other provisions from the shopkeepers, in exchange for their vegetables. In summer large quantities of summer vegetables, melons and water-melons were brought by farmers. This was also the season for the arrival of the Balochis (lt. residents of Baluchistan) in south western Pakistan. They would sell some of their camels, which were used both for work on the farms and for riding. Sheep and goats were sold by *janglies* a nomadic people who grazed their flocks on grasslands located between the areas irrigated by wells or canals.

II

LIFE CYCLE EVENTS

Hindus and Sikhs, celebrated births, marriages and deaths. The Moslems celebrated circumcision of males, marriages and deaths. In the Hindu and Sikh families the birth of the first son was an occasion for rejoicing and was often celebrated by sending sweets to relatives and friends, giving alms to the poor and making contributions to the temple or gurudwara. Subsequently births were accepted as a matter of course . Every Hindu or Sikh couple wanted to have one or more sons. Many couples ended up with three to six daughters before they had a son. The birth of a son was keenly awaited so that he would keep the family tree alive. The birth of a daughter was considered by many families, to be a burden because a dowry had to be given on her marriage, besides gifts at the time of the birth of her children and also during religious festivals like Deepavali and Baisakhi. Among the Moslems, the preference for sons and the feeling of hardship at the birth of a daughter were not so strong. The birth of at least one son was keenly awaited by farmers so that he could inherit the property and work on the family farm.

Marriage

Moslem marriages were always performed during the mornings. Small subsistence farmers and artisans did not spend much on their marriages. The principal expenses were in making one or more suits of silk clothes for the bride and bridegroom and getting silver or gold ornaments. However, farmers with large holdings and big landlords spent large amounts on marriages.

Marriage was an occasion for great festivity among Hindus and Sikhs. Ten days before the marriage of a Hindu a sacred thread was tied on the wrists of the bridegroom and the bride. This would be untied only by the spouse after the marriage. This period was also the occasion for making large quantities of non-perishable sweets made of wheat flour and sugar or *gur* (jaggery) fried in ghee to be distributed by the bride's family to their friends and relatives and to the family of the bridegroom. Male relatives and friends of the bride's family would assemble in the afternoons to help the *halwai* (the hired cook); their women would sing and dance and exchange jokes among themselves in the bride's house after dinner.

The marriage party would be formally received by the father, brothers and other male relatives of the bride and their friends at a function called *Milan.* At this ceremony the father and male relatives of the bride and their friends would welcome the bridegroom, his father and brothers by embracing them and covering them with garlands. One or two songs were specially composed with the refrain that the newly wedded couple should have a long life and bear many children.

After the *Milan* ceremony, the bridegroom's party would enter the village. The bridegroom, mounted on a mare with a young nephew with him would go to the bride's house to the accompaniment of a hired band. He would be received by the relatives and friends of the bride. The bride was specially dressed and made-up by her friends to look her best. After this ceremony the bridegroom would go to the room where the bride and her friends were waiting for him. The bride's friends would tease the bridegroom. The food served included large quantities of *halwa* (a sweet pudding made of wheat flour fried in ghee). The helpings were so large that few guests could eat them. This was followed by chappaties and vegetables. Those who could not eat the food served to them, would be derided for their poor appetite. I cannot help recalling the contrast between this practice in our village and the practice in marriages of affluent Hindus in Delhi in which the guests have to queue up for their food.

The marriage ceremony among the Hindus was always performed during the early hours of the morning with a *Pandit* (priest) chanting hymns praying for a long, happy and productive marriage. At this ceremony only the close relatives would be present. The marriages of Sikhs were performed during the mornings to the accompaniment of hymns from the Sikh scriptures by a *Granthi.* (Sikh Priest). In the forenoon after the marriage, the dowry given by the bride's family would be displayed along with a description of its contents by a specially hired woman in a sing-song manner. The refrain of her description was that the bride's family had gone out of their way to give a large dowry for use by the couple. After lunch, the bride would depart for the groom's home accompanied by her younger brother. She would return to her house after a couple of days and then go back permanently to her husband's home.

While leaving her home, the bride would weep because she felt afraid of going to the home of strangers who might not treat her well. Her parents and siblings would reassure her. The usual age of marriage was 20 - 25 years for men and 16 - 18 years for women. Just before the departure of the bridegroom for the bride's home, his relatives would give a fixed amount of money to his father at a ceremony called *Sehra Bandi.* At this time, the groom would wear a silk turban and his face would be covered with garlands. This money was meant to assist his father in meeting the high expenses of marriage. They would be returned at the time of marriage in their homes. The bride's relatives, especially those of her mother would also make large contributions to lighten the burden of marriage expenses on her parents. Usually they would bear the cost of one meal provided to the marriage party.

Two days before the marriage a ceremony called *Nav Grah Pooja* (worship of nine planets) would be performed to get their blessings for a long and fruitful marriage. After this ceremony, lunch was sent to all the families with whom the family of the bride and bridegroom had close relations. This would be reciprocated during marriages in their homes. Thus marriage was a time of great festivity and co-operation between the friends and relatives of the bride and bridegroom.

III

LEAVING JHAWARIAN

All Hindus and Sikhs left Jhawarian a few days after Partition. An indication of the cordial relations between the three communities is provided by the fact that there were no casualities amoung the migrants. This is in sharp contrast to the situation in villages and towns of neighbouring districts of Gujarat and Jhelum where large numbers were killed or severely wounded, their women (wives and grown up daughters) were converted to Islam and married to men who would never be married otherwise.

The Moslems said to the Hindus and Sikhs, "We do not want you to leave because we have lived together for centuries; but we are caught in the fire of communal riots and are helpless. But in order to ensure that you reach the refugee camp at Sargodha safely, we shall provide an armed escort". As a result, all Hindus and Sikhs travelled safely to the refugee camp and from there to India. They could bring with them their valuables also including gold ornaments and cash with which they started their business in India. Most of them are now settled in Delhi and in towns of Muzaffarnagar and Saharanpur districts in western U.P. After a few years of hard work, they are now more prosperous than they were in Jhawarian.

2

Lahore, 1923-46

Jinhe Lahore dekhiya nahin, woh jammia hi nahin (One who has not seen Lahore is not born yet) was the title of a play which I saw some years ago. It concerns an old Hindu widow who refuses to leave the room in her house, even after the house has been occupied by a Moslem family after the Partition of India. The widow loves the children of the Moslem family. She makes sweets for them. They reciprocate by allowing her to celebrate her Hindu festivals in her own way. This play illustrates the intense attachment of the residents of Old Lahore to their city. The Moslem family in turn allowed her to live in her room. When she died, they cremated her instead of burning her, and mourned her death as if she was a member of their family.

Although I was born in Jhawarian, I lived in Lahore for the first 23 years of my life where my father had his business. He had come to Lahore in 1908 at the age of ten after his primary school education in Jhawarian to join the D.A.V. High School. After finishing high school he joined the D.A.V. college for his B.A. degree which he got in 1919. The eleven years in D.A.V. institutions, run by the D.A.V. College Managing Committee, the educational wing of the Arya Samaj, made him an ardent Arya Samajist. He was also an ardent nationalist. After graduation, he was persuaded by grandfather and granduncle to join the Law College. They had incurred considerable expenditure on his education and were keen that he should become a professional who could earn a decent living. But after a year at the Law College in Lahore father left, because he felt that in order to become a successful lawyer it was essential to lie for clients and he felt lying was a sin.

So he decided to become a businessman. After losing some money in trying to promote the sale of goods made in India such as buttons, he started importing safety razors and blades from Germany. As a nationalist he did not want to import and sell British goods. Also, German goods were superior in quality and lower in price than British goods. He was successful enough to accumulate the capital needed to build a three-bed room house in Sant Nagar in 1931, one of the new residential neighbourhoods in which Hindus and Sikhs lived. I lived in this house till 1946 after which I went to the USA. The family lived in it until they had to migrate to India in August 1947.

My earliest childhood memories are however those of our stay in *Gowalmandi* (lit. colony of milk sellers) where father had started his business in 1921, just before his marriage in 1922. We lived in two houses in this neighbourhood, but my memories of the house in Amritdhara street, where we lived from 1926 to 1931, are more vivid than those of living in the first house. Gowalmandi was a neighbourhood in which Moslems, Hindus and Sikhs lived in different parts. In Amritdhara street there was an orphanage-cum-*madrassa* opposite our house where Moslem boys lived and were taught the three R's and the holy *Quran*. The street was named Amritdhara, because it was close to the Amritdhara pharmacy, which manufactures Amritdhara, a remarkably effective medicine for stomach ache and indigestion. It is still being manufactured in Delhi by the family of the founder and is widely used in the north.

Lahore is now the capital of Punjab state in Pakistan and is the second largest city after Karachi. Its population has increased from 430,000 in 1941 to more than 8 million in 1991 i.e. about 20 times. Before Partition it was the capital of undivided Punjab, an area which is now divided into West Punjab in Pakistan, Punjab and Haryana and two districts of Himachal Pradesh in India.

More than half of the population of Lahore was Moslem; the rest were Hindus and Sikhs. The city is situated on the east bank of the river Ravi, which not only provides water but also defends it from invaders from the west. However, one of its suburbs, Shahdara, is located on the west bank of the river. There was a belief among the Hindus that Lahore was founded by Lava, the elder son of Lord Rama. There is however no historical record to support this belief.

The city was of strategic importance for the Pathan and Moghal rulers of Delhi because it was on the direct route from Delhi to Iran, Afghanistan and Central Asia from where the invaders came. It was also on the direct route from Delhi to Kashmir, the favourite summer holiday resort of the Moghal emperors, Jahangir and Shah Jahan. Jahangir's mausoleum, built of red sandstone and white marble by his son Shah Jahan is one of the most beautiful historical buildings in Lahore. The other important historic buildings are the Jama Masjid (the mosque for holding Friday prayers) and the Fort, which the Moslem and Sikh rulers of the Punjab used as their residence-cum-court.

Lahore has many gardens. The most popular are the Shalimar gardens built by Shah Jahan on the pattern of the Shalimar garden which he had built in Srinagar and Lawrence garden built by the British. In the forties the Principal of the Government College, G.D. Sondhi had constructed an open air theatre in Lawrence Garden on the model of the classical Greek theatres, in which plays were staged by students of his college in early summer before the college closed for the vacation.

The city was an important railway junction for trains going west from Delhi, Calcutta and Mumbai to the North West Frontier Province on the border of India with Afghanistan and south west to the port city of Karachi from which the agricultural produce of the Punjab (mainly cotton) was exported and consumer and producer goods needs of north western India were imported. There was a large facility for servicing and repair of steam locomotives and other railway equipment in one of the suburbs of Lahore.

Like most historic cities, the city had two divisions, which were separated by a boundary wall around the old city. The old city dated back to the Moslem period; the new city had developed during the British period. Most of the Moslems lived in the old city and in two residential colonies in the new city. The Hindus and Sikhs lived mainly in the new city, and in one part of the old city.

British officers and other Europeans lived in large bungalows to the west of Lawrence garden. The Anglo Indians, most of whom worked in the railways, the posts and telegraph department and in junior positions in the Punjab Government, lived mainly near the railway station. Thus, there was residential segregation in Lahore.

The wall around the old city had 11 gates which were the outlets for the bazaars and side streets in which the people lived. Hindus and Sikhs lived mainly in the bazaar and side streets of Shah Alami gate.

Since the Hindus and Sikhs were mainly traders, Shah Alami gate and its side streets housed the principal wholesale and retail markets of the old city. One of these streets named *Papadmandi* was the principal market for dry fruit, medicinal herbs, condiments and other provisions. Another street called, *Sarafa Bazaar* was the street of goldsmiths. A third called *Dabbi bazaar* was the principal market for textiles and sundry goods- from toiletries to needles. The Moslem-dominated areas did not have any important markets. The most famous quarter in it was *Heera Mandi* (lit. the market for diamonds) in which lived dancing girls and prostitutes.[1] Incidentally, these women were highly respected for their skills in dancing, vocal and instrumental music and polite conversation.[2]

Immediately outside the wall, were lawns in which there were several *akharas,* where wrestling and body building were taught by *ustads* (lit. teachers) who had themselves been wrestlers. Moslems and Hindus had their separate *akharas.* Wrestling was a popular sport and contests between famous wrestlers were watched by thousands.

The new city was located beyond these lawns. It had two shopping areas. The principal shopping area for Indians was the Anarkali bazaar, named after Anarkali, a dancing girl in the court of the Moghal emperor Akbar. His son, Jahangir, fell in love with her and wanted to marry her. But since emperor Akbar was against this, he had her murdered.

The principal shopping centre for the British and other Europeans was the Mall. Indeed, it was the principal road of the new city, along which were located the High Court, the General

Post Office, the Punjab University, the chamber of the Punjab Legislative Council, two cinema houses which showed British and American movies, showrooms of automobiles, local branches of British banks and other companies as well as stores selling imported provisions, liquor and other needs of the Europeans.

Lahore was an important educational centre. Besides numerous high schools, it had 12 arts and science colleges, eight for men and four for women. There were also several colleges for training professionals including a medical college with a hospital attached to it, and colleges in engineering, commerce, law, veterinary science, the fine arts, training of teachers and training of *Vaidyas*, practitioners of *Ayurveda,* the ancient Hindu system of medicine. Two colleges, one for men and the other for women and all the professional colleges, except the college for *Vaidyas* were run by the government. An American Presbyterian mission managed two colleges, one for men and the other for women. The D.A.V. College Management Committee administered three colleges - an arts and science college for men, an arts college for women and the college for training of *Vaidyas.* All the other arts and science colleges were run by denominational institutions of Hindus, Moslems and Sikhs.

I was a student of the D.A.V. High School and the Government College, while my two sisters were students of the Deva Samaj school, run by the Samaj and located near our house in Sant Nagar. They took their B.A. degrees from the college for women run by the D.A.V. College Managing Committee. All the colleges were affiliated to the Punjab University which had jurisdiction over the whole of undivided Punjab, the princely states located within and adjacent to Punjab including present day Himachal Pradesh and Jammu and Kashmir, the North West Frontier Province and Baluchisthan. Today there are 15 universities; seven in India and eight in Pakistan in the area covered by the Punjab University. It was primarily an institution for conducting examinations, but it also conducted post-graduate teaching in the humanities and the sciences.

The cultural and recreational institutions in Lahore included an excellent museum and several libraries, the largest of which was the Punjab Public Library. The D.A.V. college library had a large collection of rare Sanskrit manuscripts most of which were written on palm leaves. There was also a zoo, about a dozen movie houses and a broadcasting station of the All India Radio.

Lahore had extremes of both summer and winter; the temperature would shoot up to 110-115°F (43-45° C) for weeks in June and would go down to 3° C in winter. There would be frost on the lawns. But it never snowed. There were no air conditioners to keep us cool in the summer or electric heaters to keep us warm in the winter. Only a few houses had ceiling fans. We had fans in all our rooms and relied on thick cotton-filled quilts to keep us warm in the winter. I remember that during our annual examinations which were held in March, it was so cold that I had difficulty in writing; my fingers would be numb with cold.

In the summer we slept on the terrace under thin muslin sheets, worn in order to ward off mosquitoes, keeping ourselves cool with reed fans and drinking cool water from earthen pitchers. On some nights in June when there was no breeze, it was so uncomfortable that we (my two younger sisters and I) would get very little sleep. However in winter we were quick to sleep as soon as we entered our beds after dinner. Summer was also the season for dust storms; the sky would be covered with a dusty haze for days. July and August were the months for rains. When it rained, we loved to bathe in it, singing *Rabba Rabba meenh vasain, saadi kothi dane paein, khakharian, kharbooze lain, auran di kothi daddu vasain* (God give us rain, so that our granary is full and we have cucumbers and melon that we enjoy eating. But let there be no grain but only frogs in the houses of our enemies). This little jingle is a good illustration of wry Punjabi humour.

Lahore received about one-third of the total annual rainfall of about 50 cm in the winter and early spring months of January to April. The rainy days and nights in the winter were very cold and we would shiver through them despite the fact that we were heavy woollens.

Winter was also the season for eating dry fruit : almonds, pine nuts, pistachios, raisins and walnuts. They were imported from Afghanistan and Iran and were quite cheap. Like most of my fellow students in school I was very fond of munching pine nuts. Thus, when the janitors came for cleaning our classrooms after the school closed they would find the shelves in our desks full of husks of pine nuts and ground nuts. Many of my classmates were fond of eating ground nuts; they were very cheap but *Bauji* and *Beji* never allowed us to eat ground nuts and walnuts because they were supposed to cause cough. Cough and colds were very common during winter despite all the precautions that we took to prevent them. *Beji,* one of my sisters, and I were particularly prone to catching colds.

Winter was also the season for eating a delicious and highly nutritious sweet, called *pinnies* made of wheat flour fried in *ghee* and spiced with raisins, bits of almond, pistachios, pine nuts and cardamom seeds. They were invariably eaten after dinner because of their nutritive value and the fact that they would keep without spoiling for several weeks. College students who lived away from their parents in hostels would be sent boxes of these by their parents. Whenever one of the students received a box, he would share the *pinnies* with his friends. Another favourite sweet was a pudding made of carrots and milk spiced with bits of almonds, seeds of melons and cardamoms. It was the favourite dessert for dinner in winter.

Since *Bauji* was a strict vegetarian, we did not eat meat or eggs. But he was very fond of milk, milk products, green vegetables and fruit in season. Before going to school in winter I had my brunch of freshly baked *chapattis* cooked vegetable and curd. In the lunch break in the school, I would eat a cold *chapatti* and dry *curry* brought from home. Vendors sitting outside the school campus sold a highly spiced *curry* and a small loaf of leavened bread called *kulcha.* But I was not allowed to buy these because chillies were supposed to be bad for digestion.

My parents did not drink tea or coffee. In the late thirties when there was overproduction of tea, the Indian Tea Board employed hundreds of young men to make tea just outside people's houses and give them a cup for every member of the family along with a bun free of cost. This was done in order to popularise drinking of tea among the Punjabis who used to drink only *lassi* (butter milk) earlier. I had my first cup of coffee in 1945, soon after the opening of the India Coffee House on the Mall. I did not like its bitter taste and began to drink coffee only when I went to the US for my post-graduate studies.

Despite its importance as the capital of one of the most important provinces of British India, which provided more than half of the recruits to the Indian army and was an important commercial and educational centre, Lahore was a dirty city. There was no underground sewerage; the sullage water flowed in drains on both sides of the *bazaars* in both the old and the new city. They discharged their contents into open drains which carried the water to the river. Solid waste including night soil, was carried out of the old city and dumped in places designated for it. Conditions were similar in most of the new city. The bungalows of the European and affluent Indians had soakage pits for disposal of solid and liquid waste and were quite clean. In the late thirties, a well planned township called Model Town was developed by affluent Hindus and Sikhs about 10 km. to the south east of the new city. It was quite clean because all the bungalows had soakage pits for disposal of waste.

Municipal water supply too was not adequate for the needs of the rapidly growing city. As a result, Sant Nagar and most of the other neighbourhood which had been developed in the thirties, did not have municipal water supply until 1946. The residents depended on shallow (15-30 ft deep) handpumps for their needs for drinking water. Further, because of lack of surface drains, the solid and liquid waste was dumped in small tanks located just outside the houses. These were emptied every morning by a sweeper, who would carry the waste a small distance from the house and dump it in the nearest available open space, to be absorbed in the ground and dried in the sun.

Owning to insanitary conditions near our house I fell sick in the late thirties. I probably had amoebic dysentery. I argued with myself that it was impossible to be well when one lived in such insanitary conditions. Later in 1945, when I was well with the help of homeopathic medicines prescribed by my uncles, I heard a lecture by a Professor of Psychology of the DAV College who described that most of the coal miners in Britain and other European countries were quite healthy despite working constantly in underground mines which were full of coal dust. This lecture assisted my recovery because it convinced me of the ability of the human body to acquire immunity to adverse environmental conditions.

My First Day in School

It was a cold morning in March 1928 when I joined the newly established primary school branch of the D.A.V. High school located in Gowalmandi. Contrary to the attitude of most five to six year olds, who dread going to school, I had looked forward to it. It would mean an end to the boredom of sitting at home doing nothing and an opportunity to make new friends. Therefore, I was disappointed when the teacher announced a few minutes after I had sat down in my class room that the school would be closed for the day as a mark of respect for Lala Lajpat Rai, the foremost leader of the Indian National Congress in Punjab. He had been severely wounded by *lathis* (long bamboo sticks used by the police) while he had been leading a black flag procession, protesting the visit of the Simon Commission to Lahore. He succumbed to his injuries a few weeks later.

The Simon Commission, led by Sir John Simon, a leading member of the British Parliament had been appointed by the Parliament to recommend to it, the nature and extent of powers of governance of the country to be transferred from the British to the Indians.

The Indian National Congress, the political party, which was leading India's struggle for independence had decided that the Commission should be greeted with black flag processions wherever it went, because its recommendations were not expected to go far enough in meeting the Indians' aspirations for transfer of power.

When I reached home, I found that Raja Ram, the peon (messenger) whom *Bauji* employed for running small errands, was lying on a *charpoy* (knotted rope bed used in most of north India) writhing in pain, in the courtyard behind *Bauji's* office. He too had been in the procession.

It was too early in the day to start playing with children of my age in the neighbourood. So I decided to mount a small bamboo stick to come slowly down the staircase of our house. But instead of coming down slowly, I fell to the bottom of the stairs, as soon as I mounted the stick. *Bauji* who was in his office, heard me fall and although I was not injured, he he slapped me to teach me a lesson not to attempt such foolish pranks again.

Unlike the students of today who have to carry a load of text books and notebooks from their first year in school, we had only one thin primer for learning Hindi,which was taught in the DAV school from the first grade (in all other schools, Urdu was taught from the first grade) and another thin book for learning arithmetic. There were no note books; we wrote in black ink with reed pens on a *takhti* (rectangular wooden board) and did sums on a rectangular piece of slate held together by a wooden frame. The *takhti* would be smeared with a yellow clay paste on both sides before writing on it, the paste would be washed off after the teacher had seen our writing.

Smearing the *takhti* with the yellow paste and drying it in the sun was a pleasant pastime. Thus the expense of sending a child to school was minimal, unlike today when the expense is quite substantial. As a result despite the provision in the Indian Constitution for free and compulsory education for all, a large proportion of poor parents do not send their children to school.

Sant Nagar

All the residents of Sant Nagar were either Hindus or Sikhs. It had been developed in the early thirties along with three other Hindu and Sikh colonies; Krishna Nagar, Ram Nagar and Ram Nagar *Chauburji* which was located near *Chauburji,* (a structure with four minarets) built in the Moghal period. Our house was in an unpaved lane off a narrow paved but poorly maintained road which connected it to the city. The Punjab Secretariat, the Government College, the D.A.V. High School, the Punjab University, and the museum were all located within 2 km. of our house.

The D.A.V. High School was one of the best high schools in Lahore. Its campus had a small library, laboratories for experiments in physics and chemistry, a well equipped gymnasium, a small swimming pool and a large hall in which all students assembled on

Saturday mornings for debates on various issues by the students or to hear speeches by distinguished visitors to Lahore or leaders of the Arya Samaj. One visitor was Rabindranath Tagore. He was touring various Indian cities to collect funds for Vishwa Bharati, the model University, which he wanted to establish near his home town in West Bengal. He was a tall, handsome man in his early seventies with long gray hair and a flowing beard, who wore a saffron robe and a black woollen cap. Thus except for the saffron robe, he appeared to be a Moslem holy man. He did not speak to us, but the headmaster explained the purpose of his visit.

Students of the school and the D.A.V. college had access to large playgrounds located about 3 km. from their campuses.

The school prided itself on the high standard of academic teaching and producing a number of students who won scholarships in the matriculation examination conducted by the Punjab University. In 1938, when I passed the examination, students of the school won 13 out of the 40 scholarships given by the University. I was one of the recipients. I had secured the second highest position among about 30,000 students who had appeared in the examination. The teachers, including the headmaster worked hard with the best students by holding special classes for teaching various subjects. In winter, these classes were held immediately after the school closed at 4 p.m. and in summer, in the evenings. The teachers did not get any extra payment for this work; their only reward was the satisfaction of producing a large number of scholarship holders.

The school day started with an assembly in which one or two religious or patriotic songs were sung by all students. This was followed by announcements for the day by the headmaster. There was great emphasis on punctuality; those who came late were severely reprimanded by the headmaster. Religious teaching was emphasized and one 45 minute period was devoted to it every day. One of the senior teachers had spent many years studying the Quran, and was very fond of telling stories about the life of Prophet Mohammad and reading extracts from it.

Hindi was the medium of instruction in the D.A.V. school. Urdu, English and Sanskrit were taught from the fifth grade. Teaching of Urdu and Sanskrit was discontinued after the eighth grade, but

English was taught up to the tenth grade because it was a compulsory subject for taking the matriculation examination. Teaching English continued for four years in college also because it was compulsory for passing the B.A. or B.Sc. examinations.

I had selected Sanskrit as an elective subject for my matriculation examination and for two years in college, so that I was proficient enough to read the *Bhagvad Gita,* the most widely read holy book of the Hindus in Sanskrit. I was also such a good student of Hindi that I was appointed co-editor of the Hindi section of *Ravi,* the quarterly magazine published by the Government College. The other co-editor was Mr. M.K. Rasgotra, who later joined the Indian Foreign Service and rose to be Foreign Secretary and India's High Commissioner in London. The editor of the English section was the Nobel Prize winning physicist, Abdus Salaam. Because of lack of emphasis on teaching Urdu in our school, I have not learnt it well. I cannot write it, and although I greatly enjoy listening to Urdu *ghazals*. I do not understand many words in them.

My generation was passionately interested in the freedom movement. However everything we read - newspapers, fiction and our course books—was in English. The best students in the matriculation examination prided themselves on writing their answer papers in English although they could easily do so in Hindi or Urdu. There was no such choice in college. The answers to all subjects except the languages had to be written in English. As a result, acquiring proficiency in English became a *sine qua non* of being a good student. The language of conversation among the students remained Punjabi but conversation with the professors had to be in English. As a result I have developed an ability to speak three languages – Punjabi, Hindi and English.

Friends in School

Among my friends in the D.A.V. school, I shall mention first Deena Nath Malhotra whose father had a publishing house in Lahore. He published a book in the late twenties called *Rangilla Rassool* (lit. the profligate prophet) written by Pandit Chamu Pati which described the love life of Prophet Mohammed. The book so enraged the Moslems that both the writer and the publisher were murdered by them. Deena Nath now runs a successful publishing house in Delhi called Hind Pocket Books which specialises in publishing paper backs in Hindi. A few years ago he received a UNESCO award for making a distinguished contribution to publishing in the native languages of the developing countries.

Another good friend, Madan Mohan Mehta, became a dentist,worked in the Irwin Hospital (now known as the Jai Prakash Narain Hopsital) in Delhi for a few years after graduation from the Dental College in Lahore. Thereafter, he went to Canada in the early fifties on a Commonwealth Scholarship, married a Canadian woman and became a Canadian citizen. He established a highly successful practice as a dentist in Brampton, a small town in Ontario. He visits India every year and makes a special effort to see me.

Among my playmates and friends in Gowalmandi, and class mates in school, I shall mention three—Sudarshan and Tribhuvan Chawla and Krishan Dev Madan. The families of all three had come to Lahore from Dera Ghazi Khan, a district in extreme south west Punjab. Sudarshan was my first playmate because our families lived in the same house in Gowalmandi. The relations between the two families were so good that his mother requested *Beji* to accompany her on her visit to Gujranwala—a town about 60 km from Lahore, to approve the selection of a spouse for her elder daughter, Vidya Vati. Now in her eighties Vidya Vati is the executive secretary of the National Association for the Blind which works for the welfare of blind children in various Indian cities. Sudarshan went to the US after graduation from college, married an American, became an American citizen and settled down in a suburb of Los Angeles. I have heard this from Vidya Vati but I have never heard from him.

Tribhuvan Chawla, whose father worked in the railways, became my friend in school. After two years in college, he joined the Dental College in Lahore. He was a good student, won the first position in the BDS (Bachelor of Dental Science) examination, and was awarded scholarships by the Government of India for post-graduate studies in London and the U.S.A. The last time I saw him was in Lucknow in 1954. I had gone there to attend a seminar. He was the Principal of the Dental College in Lucknow; I had dinner with him one evening during which I met his wife, two children and his parents who were living with him. I never saw him again, because he died of a heart attack in the 1960s. But I can never forget his unassuming and genuinely affectionate manner.

Krishan Dev Madan, whose father was an officer in the Accounts Service was my next door neighbour in Amritdhara Street. We were classmates in primary school and used to consult each other while doing our home work. We remained class fellows in high school. After passing his matriculation examination, he joined the Forman Christian College established by the Presbyterian Mission. He did his M.A. in Economics from there. He was a good student, and was selected for the transportation service of the Indian Railways in 1948 when recruitment to All India Services was restarted after formation of the Indian Union. I had dinner with him and his wife, Sarla, in 1954 in Lucknow where he was posted. Now retired from service, he is living in Vasant Vihar about 1 km from our house.

Another friend of my school days is Dharam Prakash Sharma who is now settled in Mumbai and works as a journalist reporting on the stock and commodity markets for various journals. Although we were together in school for only two years, we became close friends. He took an M.A. degree in Economics in 1944. He was awarded a Research Scholarship by Punjab University for three years. His ambition was to become an Indian David Ricardo.

My elder sister, Savitri, was engaged to be married to Dr. S.P. Varma, a doctor who was practising in Ferozepur early in 1947. But two months after her engagement, Hindu Moslem riots had assumed such fury that it was difficult to celebrate her marriage in Lahore. So my father travelled with Savitri and Dharam to Ferozepur where they stayed with a cousin of my mother's who was posted there. It was an odd way of celebrating a daughter's marriage without a marriage party or the traditional *barat* (marriage party) with the bridegroom arriving at the bride's home, mounted on a mare and accompanied by a band. Many Hindus performed such marriages to reduce the burden of keeping young unmarried daughters in their homes under constant fear of their being abducted by the Moslems. Dharam Prakash was the one who received me on my return from the USA in September 1949.

The Government College, Lahore

My decision to join the Government College was based on my aspiration to join one of the all India services like the Indian Civil Service or the Indian Audit and Accounts Service. It was also influenced by *Bauji*. Although an ardent nationalist himself who had refused to join government service, he wanted me to become a high ranking government official.

The college had the best teams in the Punjab in field hockey, cricket and tennis. Some of its students got selected for all India teams in these sports. Its students were among the best performers in Punjab in athletics and swimming also.

The campus consisted of a main building built in the Gothic style of architecture and located about three metres above the surrounding plain; several small buildings which housed the lecture rooms and laboratories for experiments in physics, chemistry, botany and zoology, a well stocked library, two hostels, a large swimming pool and the residence of the Principal. Its playgrounds were located about four km from the campus. Later when I visited Oxford in 1949 on my way back from the U.S. I was stuck by the similarity in the style of architecture between the buildings of colleges and the Government College. Most of the teachers in the college had taken their bachelor's or master's degrees from Oxford, Cambridge or London. One of them, Mr. E.C. Dickinson, Professor of English, was an outstanding art critic, who had written extensively on the Bundi School of Rajasthani paintings. However they were government servants and did not concern themselves with their students' welfare to the same extent as some teachers in the DAV High School did. I greatly missed this personal contact between teacher and student.

My first two years in College were not happy. I suffered from mild pains in my joints which were never diagnosed and eventually disappeared as suddenly as they had begun. When the pains did not disappear after treatment by two of the best physicians in Lahore and a renowned *Vaidya, Bauji* persuaded me to leave college and rejoin it when my health was better. Second World War had started in September 1939 and by the summer of 1940, German armies had occupied almost all of Europe. *Bauji* was elated by German victories. He was convinced that Germany would win the war and that India would either be free from British rule or be under German occupation. In either case, education in English was not of much use. He was also keen that I should join his business so that he could expand it. I followed his advice, but soon found that he had no work for me. I was bored staying at home doing nothing.

Bauji reluctantly agreed to my decision to rejoin college because he had seen the deterioration in my health during the two years that I stayed at home.

As soon as I rejoined college, my health began to improve steadily. I passed the B.A. (Hons) and M.A. examinations with distinction. I secured the first position in the University in B.A. (Hons) in geography and M.A. in geography which I passed in 1946 before going to the U.S.A. in August 1946 on a Whitbeck Foundation Fellowship awarded by the University of Wisconsin in Madison.

The thirties was a decade during which India made steady progress towards achieving independence from British rule; the world experienced the severest economic depression in living memory and was moving steadily towards World War II which broke out in September 1939.

Steady Progress Towards Independence

On hearing about Lala Lajpat Rai's death three young men, Bhagat Singh, Rajguru and Sukhdev took a vow to avenge his death by killing Mr. Saunders, the Asst. Superintendent of Police. He had ordered the lathi charge on the procession led by Lala Lajpat Rai. They watched his movements for several days and noted that he would leave his office at 10 a.m. every working day on his motor bicycle for inspecting various police stations. On one such morning, they shot him dead and tried to escape arrest by fleeing through the large campus of the D.A.V. College. However, they were arrested by the police and sentenced to death by the trial court. This decision caused so much resentment among the people of Lahore that the Government of the Punjab was in a dilemma. The people argued that the young men had done nothing wrong by killing the man who was responsible for the death of their beloved leader. The Government did not want to inflame the feelings of the people by executing the young men publicly. On the other hand, the verdict of the court had to be respected. Accordingly they were kept in jail for several months and executed one night in Ferozepur jail, about 100 km. from Lahore. Incidentally, notes from Bhagat Singh's diary which he had written in jail were edited and published in 1994, by Mr. B. Hooja who edits a monthly journal, the *Indian Book Chronicle.*

Civil Disobedience Movement 1930-32

Gandhiji launched the Civil Disobedience Movement in 1930, soon after the Indian National Congress passed the resolution for achieving *Poorna Swaraj* (complete independence). The movement lasted for two years and was suspended in 1932 after an agreement between Gandhiji and the Viceroy of India, Lord Irwin. It was called the Gandhi-Irwin Pact. During the movement thousands of people went to jail, and hundreds were killed or severely wounded by the police while defying the Government's order prohibiting processions to express their resolution for achieving independence. Gandhiji had also given a call for boycott of British goods and for making bonfires of foreign clothes worn by the affluent . I remember seeing several such bonfires in Lahore.

The agreement between Gandhiji and Lord Irwin provided for holding one or more meetings called Round Table Conferences in London between the leaders of the various political parties in India, the President of the Chambers of Princes of Indian States, and British M.P.s to determine the nature and extent of powers of governance of India to be transferred from the British to the Indians. Three such conferences were held during 1932 and 1933. Gandhiji participated in the first conference. Other important participants were: Mr. Mohammad Ali Jinnah, President of the Moslem League the political party which claimed to be the sole representative of the Moslems; Dr. Ambedkar, a very able lawyer who belonged to a scheduled caste; the President of the Chamber of Princes; and His Highness Sir Agha Khan, leader of the wealthy and influential Khoja Moslems of Mumbai. As a result of these conferences, the British Parliament passed the Government of India Act 1935. The Act provided for elections to legislatures in the British provinces to be held in 1937. The Ministries formed by the parties winning the elections would have full powers of governance in the provinces. It also provided for the formation of a Federation of British provinces and Indian princely states at the Centre.

The Central Government would have responsibility for defence, external affairs, communications including railways, posts, telegraphs and telephone and finance. The latter included collection and disbursement to the provinces of taxes such as income tax, and customs and excise duties collected by the Central Government and formulation and implementation of economic policies. In the council of ministers formed at the centre after the elections, the four portfolios mentioned above would be under the British; all the others would be under Indians. The Viceroy would have the responsibility for external affairs and relations with the princely states; the Commander in Chief of the Indian Army would have responsibility for defence while the other two portfolios would be under senior British officers.

The principle of separate electorates for different communities (religious groups) which had been introduced in 1906 and carried further in 1919 was extended still further. At the Round Table Conferences Dr. Ambedkar argued that since the high caste Hindus had oppressed the scheduled castes, a separate quota for their representation should be provided in the act. Appreciating his argument and realising that a separate quota for them would alienate them from the Hindus, Gandhiji assured Dr. Ambedkar that representation in proportion to their population would be provided for them within the quota for the Hindus. Dr Ambedkar agreed to this. The Constitution of India provides for reservation of 25 per cent of the seats in Parliament and state legislatures, and jobs in the

Government for persons of the scheduled castes and scheduled tribes. The practice of untouchability was declared a criminal offence and special measures are being taken to educate the children of these groups in order to raise their economic and social status.

The princely states were approximately 600 in number. Some of them, such as Hyderabad and Mysore were very large and had populations of several million; others were tiny bits of land of a few square miles. The small states were concentrated in the Western Himalayan region (adjoining Punjab and Uttar Pradesh), in Rajasthan, Saurashtra in western India, in central India and in Orissa. A popular joke in the thirties and forties was that a European travelling through the Himalayan region asked a man ploughing a field that he wanted to meet the ruler of the state. The man told him to see the ruler in his court in one hour. When the traveller reached the court, he found that the same man was the ruler: The governments of some of the larger states like Mysore and Travancore in the south and Baroda in western India were more progressive than those of the British provinces. But in tiny states the whim of the ruler was law.

Within a year of the end of British rule and formation of the Indian Union and Pakistan, the princely states located within their territories were integrated with the two countries. In India the task was masterminded by Sardar Patel who was then the Home Minister. The accession of most of the states was peaceful, but in the case of Hyderabad, the largest state within the Indian Union, accession was achieved only after the Indian Army occupied the state by defeating the forces of the Nizam (ruler) of the state. The second largest state, Jammu and Kashmir, which borders India, Pakistan, Afghanistan, China and the former Soviet Union, has been divided between the two countries, and remains the bone of contention between them. About two-thirds of it is occupied by India and one-third by Pakistan. Four wars have been fought over it, in 1948, 1965, 1971 and Kargil in 2000. The agreements reached after the wars have not been respected.

The Congress party secured the majority of seats in seven out of eleven British provinces in the 1937 elections and formed the governments in them. In an eighth province, the NWFP (North

West Frontier Province) which borders Afghanistan the majority of seats went to a party headed by Dr. Khan Sahib, younger brother of Khan Abdul Ghaffar Khan, who was an ardent follower of Gandhiji. He was popularly called Frontier Gandhi. Thus the Congress party with its ally in NWFP was in power in eight of the 11 British provinces. In the remaining three Moslem majority provinces — Punjab, Bengal and Sindh — the ministries were formed by parties representing the interests of the *kulaks* (middle sized and large farmers). Thus the Unionist Party which formed the Ministry in the Punjab represented the interests of Moslem, Hindu and Sikh kulaks. The Moslem League, led by Mr. Mohammad Ali Jinnah, was routed in the elections and could not form the government in any province.

The Chief Ministers of the provinces in which the Congress party formed the governments were all greatly respected leaders and able administrators. Perhaps the best among them was Pandit Govind Vallabh Pant, Chief Minister of U.P. who became the Home Minister of India in the early fifties. They were in power until the outbreak of Second World War in September 1939 when they were forced to resign by Gandhiji on the ground that the Government of India had not consulted the Congress party before deciding that India would join the War. This decision, according to me was one of the biggest mistakes made by Gandhiji. The British government took advantage of it by encouraging Mr. Jinnah to press for the formation of Pakistan. It is ironical that the resolution for its formation was passed by the Muslim League in 1940 at the same place i.e. on the bank of the river Ravi in Lahore where the Congress had passed the resolution for *Poorna Swaraj* in December 1929.

During the two years that the Congress ministries were in office, they initiated several measures for the welfare of the peasants and the poor - mainly members of the scheduled castes and the scheduled tribes. The ministries in U.P., Bihar and Madhya Pradesh, where there were big *zamindars* (non-cultivating landowners who exploited the peasants), legislation was initiated for abolishing them. In Punjab, the Unionist Party and the ruling parties in Bengal and Sindh passed a number of laws to promote the interests of the *kulaks*.

My First Glimpse of Jawaharlal Nehru

One evening in March 1937, *Bauji* and I were part of a gathering of perhaps 50000 people, who had assembled in a large field about three kms from our house, to hear Pandit Jawaharlal Nehru who was travelling throughout India to exhort the people to vote for Congress candidates in the elections to the provincial councils due to be held in May. He was travelling by plane as travel by rail and road would have been too slow to enable him to cover the whole of India in the limited time available for the election campaign. The meeting had been arranged by the leaders of the Congress in Punjab who had assured the crowd that Panditji would reach Lahore by 8 p.m.

The crowd had started assembling from five p.m. To keep them occupied while they were waiting for Panditji, various local leaders made speeches in support of Congress candidates and several volunteers led people in singing patriotic songs.

The crowd roared with delight when they heard Panditji's plane hovering in the sky around 11 p.m. Panditji arrived about midnight. When the crowd broke the cordon made by the volunteers to separate the crowd from the speakers on the dais in order to have a better view, he jumped into the crowd and asked them to get back and restore the cordon. He was a fair, slim man in his late forties. He was wearing a long shirt (*kurta*) of *khadi* (hand spin cloth) *churidar* (narrow pyjamas), woollen waistcoat which was named after him Jawahar jacket, and a cap called a Gandhi cap after Gandhiji who had popularised it in the twenties. Wearing clothes made of khadi and a Gandhi cap was a must for every member of the Congress Party.

Panditji spoke for about an hour in Hindustani, a mixture of Hindi and Urdu. Gandhiji wanted it to become the national language of India. He described at length the civil war in Spain, the occupation of about half of China by Japan, the gathering clouds of Second World War and the enormous progress being made by the Soviet Union under its five year plans. The main thrust of his speech was that enormous political and economic changes were taking place in the world and that independent India would be free to make major economic and social changes and be part of the change process. I expected him to be a fluent speaker, a great orator. But I was disappointed because he spoke haltingly, and it appeared that he was thinking in English and then translating his thoughts into Hindustani.

After his hour-long speech Panditji drove to the house of Mian Iftikhar-ud-Din, a rich lawyer and a prominent leader of the Congress Party in Punjab, who had been his class fellow and friend when both were students in Cambridge. He left Lahore the next morning.

My Glimpse of Gandhiji

It was in the same open field, on one afternoon in the autumn of 1935 when *Bauji* and I were part of a large crowd which had assembled to hear Mahatma Gandhi. We had reached the field at around 4 p.m. and waited an hour listening to patriotic songs and speeches by local Congress leaders. Gandhiji arrived at 5 p.m. sharp — he was always extremely punctual — and began his hour long speech. He was a thin dark, short man with large protruding ears wearing old fashioned horn-rimmed glasses. I was disappointed to see his ungainly appearance. But he was a fluent speaker in Hindustani, and asked the people of Punjab to join the Congress party and work for the independence of India.

I have mentioned these incidents because they are my most vivid memories of the movement for the independence of India. I saw Pandit Nehru several times in the fifties and early sixties after return from the U.S. because as Prime Minister, he was the Chairman of the Planning Commission where I worked for about 13 years. But I never saw Gandhiji again; he was assassinated in January 1948 when I was in the U.S.

Gandhiji never went to Punjab again, not even at the time of the Partition of India when millions of Hindus and Sikhs were fleeing their homes in West Punjab, NWFP and Sindh where they had lived for centuries; tens of thousands were being killed or severely injured by frenzied Moslem mobs, and their wives and daughters were being abducted. His visit might have provided some succour to the fleeing people. Gandhiji's visit might have helped cool the frenzy of the Moslem mobs and saved thousands of lives as it had done at the time of Hindu-Moslem riots in Calcutta in 1946. But Gandhiji was away in Noakhali in Bengal spreading his message of peace and non-violence.

The Economic Depression 1930-39

The economic depression started with the crash in the prices of stocks and shares in New York in September 1929 and quickly spread all over Europe, North and South America, and countries in Asia and Africa which had a large proportion of their foreign trade with these countries. During the depth of the depression during 1933-35, industrial production declined by one third, output of crops declined so steeply that farmers in America and Canada were burning their stocks of wheat and maize, in Brazil, the largest producer of coffee in the world, accumulated stocks of coffee were burnt in a vain attempt to hold up their prices. Millions of men and women were unemployed in these countries.

The depression ended only with the beginning of Second World War when the industrial countries devoted a large proportion of their industrial capacity to producing arms and equipment and their agricultural resources to producing food and fibre for feeding and clothing their armed forces. The economic depression can be said to have been one of the causes of Second World War, because it led to the rise of fascist dictators in Germany, Italy and Japan which had been severely affected by large scale unemployment and fall in industrial output. There is a wealth of economic literature available on the causes and history of the depression and how such a depression could be avoided. I shall confine my observations to its effects on India, my family and on me.

Manda Hai (there is a depression) and I have been able to get very few orders for our goods because the merchants are not buying much because of poor sales was the daily refrain of the salesman-cum-assistant whom *Bauji* had employed. He had imported a large stock of German safety razors and blades in the early thirties because of brisk sales of these in the twenties but could not sell them because of the depression. The salesman's report did not visibly affect *Bauji,* because he was a born optimist. He would invariably reply, "Never mind, you continue doing your job and you will have better results when the depression ends." But *Beji* and I would worry a great deal. My sisters were growing up and *Beji* would worry that she would not be able to get good matches for them because she would not be able to give substantial dowry with *Bauji's* modest income. Although still in high school, I would worry that if the depression continued, I would never be able to get a good job after finishing my college education since there was such acute unemployment among educated Hindu youth in Punjab that the newspapers would carry reports every day of one or more graduates committing suicide because of their inability to get a job.

Because of the depression, prices of goods and services fell so steeply that the family of a clerk with 4-5 children could live comfortably on a monthly salary of about 100 rupees if he had his own house. Most of our neighbours in Sant Nagar belonged to this class. A middle to high level government official with a salary of between 250-1000 rupees a month could live extremely well and accumulate large savings. Kamla's father, a doctor and a member of the Punjab Medical Services belonged to this category. Members of all India Services, like the Indian Civil Service who started with a salary of Rs.350 and earned Rs.3000-4000 at the end of their service career could live like princes. In fact some of them married the daughters of princes, big landlords or big businessmen.

The depression ended with the start of Second World War. The first economic effect of the war was that unemployment among educated youth ended. Large numbers of them joined the armed forces; others secured employment as clerks or middle level officials in the Government of India or the governments in the provinces. In the second year of my stay in Government College about half of my classmates joined the armed forces as officers. The starting salary of Rs. 425 per month for the junior most officer in the Indian Army was an irresistible attraction for a young man who could not hope to get even one-third of this amount after getting a post-graduate degree. Unless the young man suffered from a physical defect like poor eyesight or short stature, the very fact of his being a student of Government College was enough to qualify him for recruitment as an officer. Many of those who joined the armed forces were killed or seriously injured in various campaigns. The weekly news bulletin published by the College would be full of their names during 1942-46 when I rejoined the College after my sickness. However, those who survived rose to the highest positions in the armed forces. Among them was Sardar Arjan Singh, a champion swimmer who joined the Air Force in 1939, and retired as the head of the Indian Air Force in the eighties.

Second World War

In the late evening of 31 August 1939, I was lying in bed when Mr. Anand Prakash a customer and friend of *Bauji,* who had a shop of sundry goods in Rawalpindi, a town in north west Punjab, which is about 15 km from Pakistan's capital Islamabad told me "Bishambar, Hitler has invaded Poland despite the warning of Britain and France against the invasion and I expect that these countries will declare war against Germany in the next few days." They did on September 3. We had gone for a fortnight to Abbotabad, a hill station in the extreme north west of Punjab and a base for training army officers of the Corps of Gunners, After the visit, *Bauji* returned to Lahore, but the family was living for a month in Mr. Anand Prakash's house. I was not at all surprised by Mr Prakash's words because throughout the summer the newspapers had been full of reports that Second World War could break out any day.

The first effect of the War on our family was that all *Bauji's* unsold stock of safety razors and blades was sold at a profit within a year. Since further imports from Germany were not possible he switched to buying and selling combs and other sundry goods made of a plastic called celluloid manufactured by a company located in Jessore, a town in Bengal. But when the factory closed for some reasons, he started buying and selling buttons for jackets and trousers made of Brazilian cola nut. He did well enough in his business to finance the cost of my travel to the USA in 1946.

Beji was also greatly reassured by the turn-around in his business and began to accumulate a dowry for the marriage of my elder sister, Savitri.

Bauji being an ardent nationalist was very much in favour of Germany winning the war; his favourite phrase was, "Enemy's enemy is my friend". He was elated when during the first year of the war German forces occupied most of western Europe and the Soviet Union occupied most of eastern and south eastern Europe. Only Sweden, Switzerland which had declared their neutrality, and Spain whose dictator, General Franco was friendly with Hitler and Mussolini, the dictator of Italy, remained neutral. Spain's neutrality was important for Germany because Germany could import the raw materials needed by it to conduct the war through its ports.

I did not share *Bauji's* enthusiasm that Germany and its ally in Europe, Italy, should win the war. I hated dictatorship. Furthermore, I felt that the USA with its vast manpower and agricultural resources and industrial production would join the war and support Britain (France was already under German occupation) as it had done in First World War.

So when in the summer of 1941 the newspapers reported that German forces had invaded the Soviet Union, I told *Bauji* that Germany had lost the war. Hitler had written in his autobiography, *Mein Kampf* (My Struggle), that the Soviet Union, with its Communist Government, was the real enemy of capitalism and western civilization and its defeat was essential to save them. He coveted the agricultural, mineral and industrial resources of the western part of the Soviet Union and the vast thinly populated lands of Siberia for the settlement of Germans. He believed that with the Soviet Union under its control, Germany would become a great world power. Ironically Second World War had begun with an agreement between the Soviet Union and Germany to conquer and divide Poland between themselves, and further that the German forces would occupy western Europe while the Soviet Union would occupy eastern Europe where the Slav population was of the same racial stock as the Russians. I told *Bauji* that German forces would be bogged down fighting the Russians, as Napoleon's had been when he invaded Russia in 1812, while Britain and the USA would be busy rearming themselves and getting ready to invade and conquer Germany to free Western Europe from its occupation. Britain's own industrial capacity was not much lower than that of Germany. Besides it could draw upon the vast resources of manpower and agricultural raw materials of its colonies such as India and its dominions notably Canada, Australia and New Zealand.

The USA entered the War in December 1941 after the Japanese air force bombed and destroyed its principal naval base in the Pacific, Pearl Harbour in the Hawaiian Islands. At the same time, the Japanese destroyed and captured the British naval base in Singapore. During 1942, the Japanese conquered the whole of South East Asia and were knocking at the borders of India and Myanmar. In the thirties they had already conquered the whole of Eastern China and Manchuria, which contained most of China's population and its agricultural, mineral and industrial resources. After the USA joined the war, it joined Britain and the Soviet Union to defeat Germany and Italy and to free western Europe from their control, and to free China and the countries of South East Asia from the control of the Japanese. With its vast industrial resources, the USA quickly rebuilt its navy and air force in the Pacific and began the assault on Japan. It supplied huge quantities of food and armaments to Russia to relieve starvation and enable it to re-equip its armies. The assault on Germany from the west started in June 1944, and despite heavy casualties suffered by both sides ended with the unconditional surrender of Germany in May 1945. Hitler committed suicide along with his girl friend Eva Braun, in order to escape capture by the allies. Mussolini, the Italian dictator was hanged by the Italians themselves, after the allied forces had occupied the whole country. The war in the Pacific however ended only in August 1945 with the surrender of the Japanese forces to the American forces after the Americans had dropped atomic bombs on two Japanese cities, Hiroshima and Nagasaki, which were burnt to ashes and tens of thousands of their residents were killed or severely injured. The retreating Japanese had fought so bitterly and both the Japanese and the Americans had suffered such high casualties in battles in two islands, Okinawa and Iojima, to the south of the

Japanese mainland, that the American President, Harry Truman, saw no alternative to using these dreaded weapons of mass destruction to bring a speedy end to the war and save further loss of American lives. The dropping of the atomic bombs shocked the whole world because the people realised that the use of science and technology had enabled man to develop weapons of such power that they could destroy human life on earth.

Black-out and Rationing

During the summer of 1945, after the Japanese had conquered Myanmar and were fighting the Indian forces at the Myanmar-Assam border, the Government of India imposed a black-out in all Indian cities. The head of any household in which an electric light or a kerosene lamp appeared to be burning, was liable to be arrested and sent to jail. The residents of all houses covered the panes of their glass windows with black paper in order to ensure that no light showed outside. I remember walking through the dark nights with *Bauji* seeing our way with an electric torch to the house of a neighbour who had a radio receiver - there were very few receivers in those days and we did not have one - to listen to a news broadcast in Urdu from Berlin at 9 p.m. The broadcaster would describe the progress of German forces in various theatres of war and repeatedly assured the listeners that after Germany had won the war, India would be free of British rule and would make rapid economic progress through cooperation with Germany. *Bauji* was very fond of listening to the broadcasts and discussing the news with the few men who had gathered there.

During the thirties and the first three years of the war, food and all consumer goods were available in plenty and at low prices. But from 1943, as large quantities of food, cloth and other consumer goods began to be sent to meet the needs of the armed forces fighting the German and the Japanese forces, the Government of India introduced rationing of cereals, sugar, cloth, kerosene and petrol in order to ensure that the available supplies were equitably distributed. The prices of these goods increased rapidly. Thus good quality wheat which was available at Rs. 2.50 per maund (37kg) until 1942 was being sold at double the price by the end of the War. Prices of cloth and other essential consumer goods similarly rose steeply. Since a distribution system organised by the Government is always inefficient, in Lahore, a wheat eating city, the ration shops often supplied both wheat and rice. In our family only *Beji* ate rice while all others ate only wheat. Another new experience was to stand in long queues to meet our needs of wheat and rice. Fortunately, cotton cloth was available in plenty throughout the war, but woollen cloth and blankets became scarce as the available stocks were exhausted by the dealers, and the production of the two woollen textile mills in Punjab was devoted to production of woollen uniforms and blankets for the armed forces. Towards the end of the war when the needs of the armed forces had been met, the mills began to supply utility woollen cloth and blankets. This cloth had few designs or shades of colour in order to keep prices low. People heaved a sigh of relief when it became available.

Coming Events

When Second World War ended, it was clear that major political changes were in the offing. The Vicerory, Lord Wavell, called a conference of leaders of all political parties in Simla in the summer of 1945 to ascertain their views on the nature of the political changes that should be made in India. The conference ended in failure because the leaders of the Indian National Congress and the Moslem League had fundamental differences on the political future of the country. The Moslem League pressed its claim of being the sole representative of the Moslems and its commitment to the formation of Pakistan. The leaders of the Congress did not recognise the Moslem League's claim to be the sole representative of the Moslems because there were many Moslems among its leaders. Furthermore, they were opposed to the partition of the country and the formation of Pakistan. In 1946, the British Parliament sent a mission headed by Lord Pathick Lawrence to ascertain the nature of the political changes to be made in India.

The belief that major political changes were unavoidable spread both among the people and the government because of two events in 1946. The Government of India had planned to try for treason officers and men of the Indian National Army *(Azad Hind Fauj)* raised by Subhash Chandra Bose who had fought against the Indian Army along with the Japanese in Myanmar and along the India-Myanmar border during 1943 and 1944. However, there was such a wave of anger among the public against the proposed trial that the government abandoned its plan to try the members of the I.N.A. granted them amnesty and freed them from prison. Second, there was a mutiny on a ship of the Indian Navy in early 1946. It convinced the Government of India that it could no longer rely on the loyalty of the armed forces to defend British rule in India. Finally, the riots in Calcutta in August 1946 in response to a call by Mr. Jinnah as part of his direct action plan to achieve his goal of formation of Pakistan set in motion a process which eventually led to the partition of the country in August 1947.

NOTES

1. The dancing girls called *Vaishyas* were highly respected for their skills even in the Hindu period of Indian history. The Hindu classic on the art of love-making, *Kama Sutra* is full of references to the Vaishya's role in teaching the art of love making to a young man.
2. For a detailed description of *Heera mandi* see, Prakash Tandon: *The Punjabi Century,* Chatto and Windus, London 1963.

3

To the U.S.A. and Back (1946-49)

I

In the winter of 1945, when I was in the last year of my studies for M.A. in Geography, there appeared a notice in my College that the University of Wisconsin, U.S.A. would offer during 1946-47, five Whitbeck Foundation Fellowships of $725 each to outstanding foreign students for post-graduate studies. The amount of the scholarship was small, barely adequate for meeting living expenses in Madison; the cost of travel to and from Madison had to be borne by the fellow. When *Bauji* assured me that he would meet the travel cost, I applied for the fellowship enclosing with the application a paper on the economy of a small farmer in Jhawarian. Qazi Sayed-ud-Din Ahmed, the Head of the Department of Geography read through the paper and helped me correct and refine it before submitting it. I was a good student and he was quite fond of me. Several of my class fellows and Mr. O.P. Bhardwaj the University Lecturer in Geography, also applied for the fellowship.

I was keen to go to the U.S. During the closing year of World War II, we had read a great deal about the economy of the U.S. and the high standard of living of its people. The alternative of teaching in a small college in some town of Punjab or U.P. after passing my M.A. examination was rather unattractive.

A few months later, in March 1946 one evening my sister Savitri said excitedly "*Bhapa* (brother) you have been awarded the fellowship and you must go to America. Amrit (my younger sister) and I shall persuade *Bauji* to allow you to go". She then showed me the telegram from Prof. Trewartha, Head of the Department of Geography in Wisconsin, indicating my selection. I was both excited and apprehensive. The apprehension was due to the fact that Wisconsin was very cold and I wondered whether I would be able to bear the cold with my frail health.

Bauji and *Beji* had seen the telegram already. *Bauji* needed no persuasion to allow me to go because he had already assured me about bearing the travel cost. But he too shared my fear about my ability to maintain good health in the bitterly cold winter of Wisconsin. Accordingly both of us decided to consult Prof.A.N. Kapur, one of my teachers in college, who had returned a few years earlier after studying for two years in London and had borne the rigour of the English winter. On hearing about my apprehension he said "Don't worry about your ability to withstand the cold because all buildings in the U.S.A. are centrally heated and it is more comfortable in them than here where we are constantly shivering with cold. Besides, we Punjabis are hardy people and can withstand the rigours of any climate. Don't be afraid, just go!"

On Prof. Kapur's assurance, I telegraphed my acceptance. The next day *Bauji* and I went to the local office of Thomas Cook, the only foreign travel agency in Lahore, to enquire about getting a berth in a ship going to the U.S. The manager, told us that it was extremely difficult to get a seat as all ships were full of American soldiers posted abroad and American missionaries and businessmen returning home. But he had just received a cable announcing that a large unconverted troopship, *S.S. General Gordon*, would pick up 1500 Indian passengers on its journey in mid-August from Mumbai across the Pacific to San Francisco in California. The travel cost would be Rs. 1,000. He told us that the visa for the U.S. would have to be obtained in Mumbai as there was no American consulate in Lahore. We agreed, and he booked the seat.

On 11 August, ten days before the sailing date of the ship, *Bauji* and I travelled to Mumbai via Delhi where we stayed for three days with Mr. J.C. Manchanda, a distant cousin of mine who was in business there. His house was located in a newly established extension of Karol Bagh, an old residential neighbourhood. The area is so crowded now that it is difficult for a vehicle to pass through its streets. But in those days it was so thinly populated that its roads were lined with trees with few houses or shops in them.

An old friend of my school and college days, Lakshman Yati Chandhoke, who was working then in the All India Radio showed me around New Delhi. I remember that along Sansad Marg (then called P ırliament Street) that connects the Secretariat of the Government and the Parliament House with Connaught Place, the principal shopping centre of New Delhi, there were only four or five buildings including those of the All India Radio and the State Bank of India, then called the Imperial Bank of India

In the area around the Central Secretariat there were large bungalows in which senior officers of the Government lived. As in Lahore the principal modes of travel were bicycles, *tongas* and motor cars; there was no bus service.

I liked New Delhi very much because of its broad tree-lined roads, huge area of green in the bungalows and a sewerage system in the entire area outside the old city of Shahjahanabad. Thus it was quite clean, in contrast to Lahore, which was quite filthy. I decided that on my return from the USA, I would try to get a job in the Central Government and live in New Delhi.

During the three days in Delhi, *Bauji* did some business with his customers in Old Delhi. The main artery of old Delhi, Chandni Chowk was not too crowded. Fountains played in its shallow canals and there was an electric trolley service running along the covered shopping arcades. Thereafter, we travelled to Mumbai. August is about the rainiest month in the city. It poured and poured and it was possible to stir out of the hotel only briefly in the evenings when it stopped raining. *Bauji* could not withstand the damp weather and developed an ulcer in his left leg. The physician whom he consulted gave him some medicines and advised him to return home immediately because his ulcer would heal completely only in the dry climate of Lahore. Following his advice *Bauji* left. We had no difficulty in obtaining the visa for the US. Indeed *Bauji* and I were greatly impressed with the quiet efficiency of the staff, mostly women in the Consulate. However the Gujarati clerk in the office of Thomas Cook who was to issue the ticket gave me a hard time. I had to go to his office several times before he issued the ticket. In retrospect, I think that he wanted a bribe of Rs.10-15 before giving me the ticket but gave it to me when he found that I would not oblige him.

The four days that I spent in Mumbai between *Bauji's* departure and boarding the ship were among the most uncomfortable in my life. I too did not like the constant rain and dampness. I had no friends whom I could visit. Besides the hotel proved to be quite uncomfortable. The food was spicy and the sanitary arrangements and the general upkeep of the place were poor. On 16 August, Hindu-Moslem riots broke out in Calcutta in response to Jinnah's call. During the three days that the riots lasted, thousands of Hindus and Moslems were killed or severely wounded. The newspapers forecast that similar riots would break out any day in Mumbai; they did on 22 August the day after the ship sailed from Mumbai. The hotel was located at the junction of Hindu and Moslem dominated neighbourhoods and I was afraid that if riots broke out before the ship sailed it would be difficult for me to reach it.

II

THE VOYAGE—MUMBAI TO SAN FRANCISCO

Thus it was with great relief that I boarded the ship on 21 August. Most of my fellow travellers were students who were being sponsored by the Government of India, the Tata and the Wattumul[1] Foundations for studies in engineering, technology, physical and social sciences and teaching. All the male students were lodged in large halls with four-tiered bunks. It had also a large number of cabins which were allotted to female students and families of American missionaries and businessmen.

I chose the top bunk to avoid sea sickness. When dinner was served I threw up immediately. But I felt better when I walked on the deck of the ship and was refreshed by the sea breeze. I developed the practice of spending most of my day and a good part of the evening on the deck, walking or reading a book, sitting on one of the deck chairs or just watching the movement of the ship through the ocean. This practice paid off, and I was never sick in my entire month-long voyage.

Within a couple of days in the ship, I became friendly with Ashok Varma and K.L. Khandpur. Ashok, son of a wealthy physician in Jamaica, was returning home after being held up in his home town of Gujranwala because of the war. He told me that his father owned several sugarcane plantations and urban property in Kingston, the capital of Jamaica but he was expecting to lose them because there was a move to nationalise the plantations. They were nationalised but he sold the urban property at a good profit and settled down in Canada in the 1980s. K.L. Khandpur had been selected by the Government to learn sound recording for films at the University of Southern California in Los Angeles. We had adjoining top bunks and spent a lot of time together.

In its voyage from Mumbai to San Francisco, the ship made two stops. The first was at Manila, the capital of the Philippines. The Philippines which had been an American colony before and during Second World War had been granted independence soon after the war. The ship stopped for three days in Manila to pick up about 1,500 Filipinos. The second was at Hong Kong where 1000 Chinese boarded the ship. The passengers of different nationalities were lodged in different decks. The Filipinos were on the deck immediately below us and the Chinese were in the lowest deck. Thus there was little interaction between the people of different nationalities except at the gambling tables during the night. The Chinese were great gamblers and would think nothing of winning or losing $ 1000 during the course of a night.

Manila

Manila was a ruined city in which there was feverish activity to rebuild it. It had been partly ruined by bombing by the Japanese planes before they occupied the Philippines in 1942, but mostly by the American bombers when they recaptured the islands from the Japanese during 1945.

Manila had a large number of Sindhi merchants selling silk, rayon or other textiles. They were very friendly to us, and invited us to attend the service on Sunday morning which was the day after our arrival, in their *Gurudwara* (Sikh temple), which would be followed by an Indian lunch. We gratefully accepted the invitation and attended the service. There I noticed that while most of the Sindhi men had wives of their own community, others had married Filipino women and converted them to Sikhism. These women and their children formed a part of the congregation.

Besides the bus service in central Manila, the only means of public transport were unconverted jeeps left by the American army when they returned home. We would travel by one of these whenever we went from the ship to the city. We had been allowed to go to visit Manila, in the early evening of the arrival of the ship there. As soon as the three of us got into a jeep, the driver asked us "Want a girl; a dollar a shot". We were shocked and politely declined his invitation. But his remark revealed the extent of prostitution in the city.

Hong Kong

The next stop was at Hong Kong. Hong Kong is today one of the richest cities in Asia. But in those days, it was so poor that a number of urchins would crowd around every ice cream booth in order to lick the empty container after the customer had thrown it away. In contrast to Manila, Hong Kong had not suffered much damage during the war. But there was hectic construction activity to house its rapidly increasing population, caused by the influx of people from mainland China, and to house offices of commercial institutions. The British presence was strong. Being a British colony, most of the high and middle ranking officers of the Government were British. Furthermore, most of the big trading, insurance and banking companies were owned by the British. I also noticed that there was feverish activity in stitching garments for export. The industry was located in thousands of homes where men, woman and children were working in it. As soon as an American or a European landed in Hong Kong, a tailor would greet him and offer to make two to three suits and shirts for him and dresses for his wife. These would be delivered to the traveler before the end of his stay of two to three days.

On our first visit to the city, we were accosted by a tall Sikh who was working as a doorman in one of the big hotels. Noticing that we looked like Punjabis, he began to talk to us in Punjabi. He told us that there were a number of Sikh doormen in Hong Kong hotels. Their parents or grandparents had been brought to Hong Kong from Ludhiana by the British because they did not trust the Chinese for this duty. Another vivid memory of Hong Kong is of my train journey to Mount Victoria, the hill from which there is a magnificent view of the city and the ocean around it. Today, there is a good road from the city to the peak, and travel to it in taxis to have a good view of the city is popular with the tourists. But in 1946, the narrow gauge railway, similar to the one from Kalka to Simla was the only means of transport.

Food

Being an unconverted troopship, we were served our meals on steel trays, which were divided into several compartments for bread, meat, vegetables, tea or coffee etc. All the food was canned. The only fruit that we got was one apple or one orange taken out of the deep freeze of the ship and served with our dinner. We had grown sick of eating the canned food, and wished that we got more fruit. Furthermore, being a vegetarian I would not eat meat (mainly beef). Ashok being a smart fellow would offer a few dollars as bribe to one of the stewards serving the food and obtain half a dozen oranges, or apples which the three of us relished eating.

When we reached San Francisco, after three weeks of travel across the Pacific, the immigration officials took a day and a half to clear the passengers for landing on American soil. However American newspapers were delivered to us on board the ship. The first newspapers that I saw announced that Mr. Wallace, Vice President of the USA had resigned because he did not want to be a party to (i) the growing hostility between the USA and its West European allies on the one hand and the Soviet Union on the other that could lead to war between them, and (ii) the tendency in the U.S. Congress to brand a large number of officials in the State Department (Department of Foreign Affairs) who had dealt with the Soviet Union during World War II as communists. The feeling in the Congress was that as a result of the negotiations between the USA, Britain and the Soviet Union held during the closing years of Second World War, these officials had advised the ailing American President Roosevelt to allow the Soviet Union to occupy all the countries of Eastern and South Eastern Europe except Yugoslavia and Greece , while the Americans and the British occupied all the West European countries. I was a witness to this hostility, subsequently called the Cold War, increase rapidly during my three year stay in the U.S.A. It lasted from the 1950s to the mid-1980s when the Soviet Union broke up into several communist republics.

From San Francisco, Krishan Khandpur went to Los Angeles to join his University, but Ashok and I travelled together to Chicago. From there I went to Madison and Ashok went to New York where he boarded a ship to go to Jamaica. The train journey from San Francisco to Chicago took two and a half days. There was no air travel in those days. This gave us an opportunity to see the American West and mid-West. I was greatly surprised to see that the American West was an almost uninhabited desert. One could not see a man or beast for tens of miles. However as the more moist areas of the mid-West approached, one saw huge areas of grasslands on which cattle grazed, and large farms growing wheat, maize and other crops. In these areas, there were a large number of small towns and a few large cities. I was impressed by the neatness of the towns. There was not an open drain, or any other sign of filth which was such a familiar sight in Lahore and even in Mumbai.

Our bunks in the train were looked after by black stewards One afternoon, one of them came to me and asked, "Who is this fellow Gandhi and why does he starve himself from time to time?" I told him that Mr. Gandhi was the foremost leader of the Independence Movement. He fasted occasionally to achieve some political or social objective. This satisfied him but his question gave me an idea of how an American who read newspapers felt about Gandhiji's fasts.

III

MADISON

From Chicago I took a train to Madison, a distance of about 190 km. It was about 9 p.m. when I arrived in Madison. While I was looking for a taxi to take me from the station to the city YMCA, where I was to stay for two to three days before getting permanent accommodation, a middle aged lady came forward and said to me, "I am Mrs. Rothe. I have overheard you telling your fellow passenger on the train and that this is the first time that you have left home and you are to go to the city YMCA. My husband, Earl, will come here in a few minutes and we shall take you to the YMCA." I was surprised by her offer but gratefully accepted it. At the YMCA, I showed the desk clerk the letter from Prof Rice, Principal of the Forman Christian College, Lahore to Rev. Zimmer, pastor of a Presbyterian church requesting him to arrange accommodation for me at the city YMCA. When the clerk showed some reluctance in giving me a room, Mrs. Rothe told him, "He is a decent young man and I can assure you that you will have no trouble with him." At this, the clerk gave me a room in which I stayed throughout my one year stay in Madison.

The city YMCA was one of the most convenient places to stay in Madison. It was centrally heated and was kept comfortably warm through day and night in a city which was bitterly cold. Most landladies who had students as boarders did not keep their houses warm enough in order to save on fuel. The next morning I went to the Department of Geography and met Prof. Trewartha and other faculty members of the Department. They were happy to see me because I was the first Whitbeck Fellow to reach Madison and my arrival assured them that the other four would arrive soon. They did. Prof. Trewartha advised me to get the admission formalities completed so that I could attend classes which had just begun.

Madison was a city of about 100,000 people. It was situated on a narrow strip of land between two lakes. It was a beautiful and very friendly city in those days. Wherever I went, I was greeted with a smile. There were about 45 Indian students at the University.

Most of them were Government of India scholars; others were children of rich businessmen of Mumbai. The campus of the University was located on a low hill overlooking the city. It consisted of a large number of buildings, each of which housed one or more teaching departments or laboratories for research in physical or biological sciences. Since Wisconsin was primarily an agricultural state with specialisation in dairying, it was strongest in teaching and research in these subjects.

The campus also had a University Union, which housed a cafeteria serving food at subsidised rates. Wisconsin was one of the few Universities in which beer was sold on the campus. This was because Milwaukee, the largest city in the state, was the brewing capital of the USA in those days and the owners of the brewing companies made large contributions to running the University. The Union had also a movie theatre, rooms for several indoor games and a small auditorium for holding lectures on current political, economic or social problems by professors of the University or by visiting scholars.

On my second day at the University, a fellow student in the Department came forward and said to me "I am John Brush. My father was a missionary in Kharagpur in Bengal, I spent the first 12 years of my life in India, and had my primary education in Woodstock school located in Mussoorie". John and I became good friends and have remained so to this day. We exchange Christmas or New Year cards and during my service with the United Nations, I made it a point to meet him and sometimes stay a day or two in their home in New Jersey, located about 70 km from the UN office in New York.

After taking his Ph.D degree from the University of Wisconsin, John joined as a lecturer in the Department of Geography of Rutgers University in New Jersey. He retired as the head of the Department and was subsequently appointed Professor Emeritus, a retired professor who had a room in the building housing the Department for his personal research. The last time I saw him was in 1990 when I was on a short-term consultancy mission for the United Nations. I may never see him again because I have no wish to travel to the US and he has no plans to visit India. John has written two excellent papers on Indian cities and visited India once in the early 1960s in order to collect data for them.

During my year at the University, there was a great shortage of housing for students. This was because the University, which had approximately 6,000 students before and during Second World War, had about 17,000 students in that year. Most of the students were veterans—young men and women who had served as soldiers or officers in the American armed forces during Second World War. They had come to study in Wisconsin and other Universities because the American Congress had passed a law immediately after the war under which all expenses of going to University and most of the expenses of living as a married student were paid by the Government. Most of my classmates were veterans. Since the city did not have enough accommodation for this flood of students, most of the veterans lived in quonset huts (army barracks converted to house families of veterans) about 50 km. from the University campus.

Autumn (Americans call it fall because leaves of many trees fall off before the beginning of winter) is the time when states like Wisconsin in which the winter is long and extremely cold are at their colourful best. I remember a picnic arranged by students of the Department of Geography in the woods north of Madison where I saw the falling leaves at their colourful best. Every shade of pale green, yellow, brown, rust and deep red could be seen among them. This colour was nature's parting gift to man before it went to sleep, as if, under snow and ice during the long winter. I remember that when I went to attend the annual meeting of the Association of American Geographers (AAG) held immediately after Christmas, there was no snow in Madison. But when I returned on New Year's day, I found that there was snow and ice everywhere; the two lakes were frozen and a few adventurous young men and women had started skating on it. The University campus had a snow-bound low hill which was very popular with skiers. I never dared to ski for fear of falling and suffering serious injuries but I greatly enjoyed seeing the skiers on the hill. During severe snowstorms, it was difficult to walk or drive on the snowbound roads. The schools, the University and most offices would be closed on these days.

The last snowstorm was in mid-May and it was only then, that nature came to life again. The trees which had shed their leaves in the fall began to grow new leaves and green grass appeared on the ground. It was a beautiful sight to see the rebirth of nature .

During the meetings of the AAG, I met Prof. O.E. Baker, a very well respected agricultural geographer, who had recently retired from long years of service with the US Department of Agriculture, to head the newly opened Department of Geography of the University of Maryland located about 15 k.m. from Washington D.C. Prof. Baker told me that he had received a large grant from the US Department of Agriculture to prepare an Atlas of World Agriculture and that I could join his Department as a graduate assistant (a post-graduate student who receives a salary from the University for teaching undergraduates or research on some project of the Department), on a salary of $ 1,000 per academic year to complete my studies for obtaining a Ph.D. degree. I was very happy with his offer and told him that I would write to him after completing my year of study at Wisconsin.

IV

SETTLEMENT OF WISCONSIN

Wisconsin had in the mid-1940s a population of about three million, most of whom lived in the southern quarter of the state. The rest of the state consisted of very thinly populated forest. Most of the people of the state are of German or Scandinavian origin, who had come to the state to settle down as farmers after the Civil War (1861-1865). The US Congress passed in 1865 a law that any farmer family which undertook to develop a farm in the empty lands of central and western United states would be allotted 160 acres of farm land free of cost. I was amazed to know about this provision of the law because I had never heard of farm land being given free; it is such a valuable commodity in India. Coming from a country which had been inhabited for more than 5000 years, I was surprised to learn how recent the settlement of central and western U.S.A. was.

The settlers suffered great hardship in developing the land for farming.They had to keep themselves ready to fight wild animals and groups of American Indians who saw the lands in which they had lived for centuries grazing their horses and hunting wild animals of which the American bison (a large horned buffalo) was the most important, being taken away by strangers. Every farmer family had to live in isolation and face the rigours of the severe winter. But the farmers worked hard and developed the grasslands into highly productive farms. The farmers in Wisconsin found the climate of the state most suitable for dairying. Most of them became dairy farmers. However since the demand for fresh milk was limited they concentrated in making cheese and butter. I visited several dairy farms in southern Wisconsin and was fascinated to see how cheese was made. I had never eaten cheese before but became very fond of it during my stay in the US. In 1989 when I had to undergo coronary by-pass surgery I had to give it up because of its high cholesterol content.

Most of my classmates and other students at the University were very tall; the men were 180 cm tall or taller. Many female students were also taller than me. At 168 cm, I am not short by Indian standards. But seeing these men and women, I felt like a dwarf in the land of giants which has been so well described in Swift's classic *Gulliver's Travels.*

The Y Club

The city YMCA was located about one and a half kilometres from the Department of Geography and I could walk to it. There would be a dinner meeting of the Y club once a week where a group of young men would meet to discuss some topics of political or social importance. A fellow Indian resident at the YMCA and student at the University was P.L. Swaminathan son of Dr. Lokanathan, a well known economist who had just been appointed the first Secretary General of the ESCAP (Economic Commission for Asia and the Pacific.[2]) We had the privilege of listening to the discussion and having a free dinner in exchange for laying the table for the dinner and cleaning it afterwards.

One evening the group was very disturbed about the election as a senator of Mr. McCarthy a rabid anti-communist. They were wondering why the voters of Wisconsin who were so liberal and committed to the promotion of social causes had elected such a man. Their disturbance was justified because during his six year term as a Senator, Mr. McCarthy headed a Committee which started a witch hunt of a large number of officials of the American Government (particularly the Department of State). They were branded as communists and were forced to resign. Some of them were charged with having worked as spies for the Soviet Union and were imprisoned. A number of film stars in Hollywood were also accused of being communists and had to undergo long and painful questioning by the Committee. The world famous actor, Charlie Chaplin, was included among them. He left Hollywood for good and settled down in Switzerland in order to escape the humiliating questioning by the McCarthy Committee.

My daily routine was to leave for the University after a cold breakfast of milk and corn flakes in my room. It was followed by a steaming hot cup of coffee and a doughnut at one of the restaurants located near the YMCA. I would have lunch and dinner at the cafeteria in the University Union. I had to live within the $80 a month which was the monthly amount of the Fellowship. Of this amount, $ 31 went for room rent, $ 30 for food, leaving $ 20 for expenses on clothes, toiletries, etc. In order to supplement my income I worked for two hours every evening in the cafeteria stacking dishes or picking pins in the bowling alley located in the Union. Bowling is a popular American game. It consists of hitting a number of wooden pins located at the end of a long wooden slope with a large wooden ball. The aim is to hit all the 10 pins with a single throw of the ball down the wooden slope. The pin-boy's job is to restore the 10 pins to standing position after every throw of the ball. I would get 50 cents for two hours of work in the cafeteria or the bowling alley.

On Saturday afternoons I would work for about three hours thoroughly cleaning the house of a school teacher couple and get $3. These amounts appear ridiculously low today when a cup of coffee costs $ 1 or more in a small way-side restaurant and up to $ 4 in the coffee shop of a luxury hotel. But they were adequate then when a cup of coffee cost 5 cents in the Union and dinner in the cafeteria was 30-35 cents. A shirt which costs $30 or more today could be purchased in $ 3. Except for two shirts, I did not buy any clothes in Madison. But later in Maryland I bought three good woollen suits for $ 30 and $ 35 each. Today they would cost $ 300 – 400 or more.

The year at Wisconsin was one of the happiest in my life. I learnt concepts in Geography and techniques of research about which I had been quite ignorant before. In India a good student was one who could reproduce correctly in the examinations what had been written in the textbooks. In Wisconsin however, it was necessary to prepare a term paper for every course in which one had to consult the most important books and articles in journals on the subject of the paper and quote from them. Thus the students were trained to look for the literature and quote from it selectively in order to support what he or she had written in his paper. The professors constantly emphasized the need for asking. "Are the statements of the author of a book or a paper correct.? If so why, and if not why not". I greatly appreciated this training which was essential for being a good post-graduate student. One of the reasons why I did not do well in a course on China and Japan taught by Prof. Trewartha was that I chose a subject for my term paper on which I could find only one book and quoted extensively from it. Prof. Trewartha was not pleased. He had expected me to go to him, explain the paucity of literature on the subject and ask him to suggest another subject on which more literature was available. However I did well in the courses taught by other professors because I could find more literature on the subjects of my term papers. I was also happy that my health had improved rapidly. Within one year of my stay in Madison my weight went up by about 14 k.g; this was reflected in greater zeal for physical and academic work.

Immediately after the university closed for the summer, four of us Whitbeck fellow and an American classmate Allwyn Keinard, decided that we would take a sight seeing tour by car of the national parks, cities and most scenic areas of central and western United

States. The fellows were, Jacque Spelt from Holland, Ingmaar Persson from Sweden, Chou from China and myself. Keinard would furnish the car; the Whitbeck fellows would pay for petrol. Expenses on groceries would be shared by all. We would cook breakfast and dinner on a gas stove and buy sandwich lunches at restaurants wherever we were at lunch time. We would camp in the camping grounds maintained by the various cities and in national parks. So we equipped ourselves with a tent and sleeping bags acquired at throwaway prices from the Army Surplus Disposal store.

The tour which lasted five weeks, 1 June to 5 July, was so enjoyable that its memory is etched deep in my mind. Seeing ourselves as budding teachers of geography, which Allwyn, Ingmaar and Jacque did become—we have never heard from Chou—we discussed among ourselves, the physiography, climate, soild and vegetation of the areas and economy of the cities and villages that we passed through. However, what I remember most is the breath-taking beauty and splendour of what we saw in the national parks and smaller natural preserves in the western United States.

We spent more than ten days in California, going up and down its central valley. Its vineyards supply most of the grapes and table wines consumed in the U.S.A; its orchards and vegetable gardens similarly supply most of the fresh and canned fruit and nuts — oranges, peaches, apricots, olives, almonds, walnuts, etc. and vegetables to cities in central and eastern USA. Its two main cities, San Francisco and Los Angeles, are most interesting for their scenic beauty and their economic importance.

While we camped in a campig site in San Francisco, we pitched our tent on the lawns of the house of the parents of a class fellow, Mr. Peter Nash. Mrs. Nash took us on a tour of Los Angeles along the coast and the Nashes entertained us to dinner on the night before our departure. We camped at more than 12,000 ft. in the Rocky Mountains and were quite comfortable; but in Death Valley which is located 500 ft. below sea level, we could not get a wink of sleep. It was so hot.

Yellowstone National Park with its geysers, brown bears, enormous areas of forest and grasslands and large herds of bison—(the American buffalo) and wild horses and the Grand Canyon of the Colorado river in Arizona are the most unforgettable sights in western U.S.A. I have never seen such vast areas of forests or grasslands, untouched by man as in the Yellowstone; nor have I seen such an awesome piece of nature's architecture as the Grand Canyon.

In New Maxico, people of Mexican descent form the majority of the population and Spanish, not English, is the first language. This was a surprise to us. One night when we happened to be near a village in Utah and could not get a camping site, a Mormon farmer offered to put us up in the lawn of his houses. He was dead drunk because his wife had died that day leaving him two young children to look after. But he was kind enough to pick some vegetables for our dinner and gave us eggs for our breakfast. I have never seen before or later such kindness in an hour of extreme distress.

After the tour, Jacque Spelt left for Holland and married his girl friend. Allwyn Keinard got his Master's degree and resumed his senior teacher's position in a school near his home town. He remarried and was well settled; I saw him again when I was in Maryland. Ingmaar and I stayed for the summer in Wisconsin. He accompanied me to College Park in September. I had letters from him that he had become a school teacher, which he wanted to be.

V

SUMMER IN WISCONSIN

During summer in the University I attended a most interesting course in Medical Geography. The lecturer, Prof. Bowman, had served during Second World War as an officer in the American Navy in the Pacific. He described the high casualties in the armed forces from diseases which were unknown in the US and remedies for which were developed only after long research. One of them was a deadly strain of malaria which was caused by a mosquito that bred in the rivers of New Guinea and neighbouring islands. This was a revelation to doctors who had believed till then that malaria was carried by mosquitoes which bred in stagnant water.

After completing two semesters and the summer course, I

wanted to go on studying at the University for two years in order to get a Ph.D degree. I requested Prof Trewartha for an appointment as a Graduate Assistant in the Department, so that I could meet my expenses for the studies. Prof. Trewartha refused as I had not done well in the course taught by him. Furthermore, I had the bad habit of interrupting him frequently by asking questions during his lectures. This irritated him because he did not want any interruption while he was teaching. He would interrupt his lectures several times, to ask "any questions?" but did not want that there should be any. Other students understood this but I did not. I was not too disappointed because I had the offer of Prof. Baker for an assistantship in his department. So I telegraphed him to say that I would accept his offer. I knew that the Department in Maryland would not be as good as the one in Wisconsin.

The same afternoon, Prof. Trewartha told me that he would offer me an assistantship, because Dr. Finch, the former head of the Department and other professors were pleased with me because I had done well in their courses. I wish to this day that I had accepted Prof. Trewartha's offer. But this would have meant breaking my promise to Prof. Baker. So I declined the offer.

I shifted in September 1947 to College Park Maryland, a suburb of Washington D.C. where the University of Maryland is located. The travel by bus, the cheapest mode of travel in those days and even now involved passing through the industrial heartland of the US about which I had read so much. I was appalled to see the air and water pollution produced by coal mining and steel and heavy machine building industries. The pollution was worst in Pittsburgh, the largest steel producing city in the US. Even during the day the air was full of haze. Instead of bright sunshine one saw a dusty haze through which a pale glow came from the sun and most of the buildings in the city centre were black with coal dust. Since then highly effective measures have been taken to reduce the pollution of air and water in the city centre of Pittsburg. It is today a mass of gleaming towers of office buildings. My companion on this trip was Ingmaar Persson who was going back to Sweden to resume his job as a school teacher. I greatly enjoyed his company because we had become good friends.

VI

COLLEGE PARK, MARYLAND: SEPTEMBER 1947—AUGUST 1949

On reaching College Park, I telephoned Prof. Baker informing him of my arrival. Mrs. Baker answered the telephone and said, "Dr. Baker has gone to his farm in Virginia (about 100 km. from the University) but you come right over and stay with us until you find suitable accommodation". I was surprised by this generous offer, but gratefully accepted it. I moved to their house which was within walking distance of the place from where I had telephoned. Mrs. Baker gave me a room in their house. I stayed in the house for three days before I found a room in a house located a short distance from the campus.

During my stay with the Bakers, I was stuck by the simplicity of Mrs. Baker's lifestyle and the old fashioned way in which she ran the house. The two storeyed wooden frame house was located in a field of about three acres where the Bakers grew grass for the three cows that they had. They also had a small vegetable patch and a shed for raising poultry. Mrs. Baker looked after the cows, the poultry and the vegetables. Her day started with churning of milk for butter, collecting eggs and vegetables from the vegetable patch. She was also dressed like a farm housewife. The house was very sparsely furnished. But it had room for any student like me who did not find accommodation immediately on arrival. Besides the members of their own nuclear family, consisting of two daughters and a son, the Bakers had an old widowed cousin, 'Aunt Annie' living with them.

Prof. Baker was an equally simple man. He was always dressed, summer or winter, in a grey pin stripe suit, a white shirt and a polka dot bow tie which hung loosely from his neck and a slouching gray felt hat. He had invested all his savings from long years of service with the US Government in buying a farm located about 100 km from his house. He would visit it every week-end. He would supervise the operations and would also work as a labourer himself. He was worried that the farm was running at a loss. On week days, he would work on the pasture around his house.

Students joked about his ungainly appearance and simple dress and also about some of his views. For instance, he was much against family planning. He would say, "a child and an automobile are in competition for a family's savings; that American couples limited their families in order to have a car and expensive furniture and clothes." He was worried that a stationary or shrinking population, was a threat to the security of the U.S. But he had a generous heart and did his best to help any student who had a personal problem. I had a problem about taxation of my salary, the University administration started to deduct 30 per cent as tax on my meagre salary of $ 100 dollar per month. When I told him that I could barely live on the remaining $ 70, he immediately talked to a friend of his in the Department of Internal Revenue — the tax department of the US Government — and the tax was reduced to $ 6.25. He was also very hospitable. His weekly two hour long seminar on agricultural geography was held in the evenings at his house where Mrs. Baker served hot chocolate and biscuits to all the students. The Bakers never drank tea or coffee or any soft drinks.

After staying with the Bakers for three days, I shifted to the house of a bus driver where I stayed with Mr. Patil, a Government of India scholar in Poultry Science. He was a congenial roommate and we shared a room until he left in May 1949 after getting an M.S. in Poultry Science, I left in August 1949.

We stayed in this house for four months and left it when we found more suitable accommodation in Riverdale which was located about three km. from the campus. We were not happy in the driver's house, as the driver and his wife were constantly smoking, drinking and quarrelling. Thus there was tension in the house which we resented. I was also very worried about the fate of my family in India. The newspapers carried reports of mass migration of Hindus and Sikhs from West Punjab, North West Frontier Province and Sindh, which had been included in Pakistan, to India and of Moslems from East Punjab, Delhi, Western U.P. and parts of Northern Rajasthan to Pakistan; of mass murders of migrants by frenzied Moslem mobs in Pakistan and of Sikh and Hindu mobs in India. The total number of migrants is estimated at 12 million–5 million Hindus and Sikhs and 7 million Moslems. The number of people killed and of women abducted and forced to convert to the faith of their kidnapper husbands has been estimated at hundreds of thousands. I was sure that my family would have left Lahore which was included in Pakistan, but I did not know whether they had reached India safely.

It was only in October, two months after the formation of the Indian Union and Pakistan in August 1947, that I received a letter from *Bauji* saying that they had reached India safely and were living in Najafgarh, a village located about 25 km from Delhi and that they would move to Delhi after the riots in Delhi had ceased. They would rent a suitable house there. The letter relieved my anxiety. Thereafter I would get a letter from him every week. In one of his letters, he mentioned that they had moved to Karolbagh and that he had started his business in a small shop in Sadar Bazar, the principal market for the kind of goods in which *Bauji* was dealing.

The house in Riverdale was owned by a widow who rented a room to University students. I have two vivid memories of my stay there. First, I spent a lot of time learning German, passing an examination which was an essential requirement for getting a Ph.D degree. I passed the examination after intensive study for four months. Later, it took me only six weeks to pass a similar examination in French, the second foreign language that a candidate for the Ph.D. degree was required to know.

The second memory concerns the death of Mahatma Gandhi on 30 January 1948. I had spent two most painful hours at the Georgetown University Dental School, located in a suburb of Washington D.C. Two surgeons had spent two hours extracting the roots of two teeth. They had been extracted in Lahore but their roots were left in the gums. I have suffered from dental trouble throughout my life, and the presence of these two roots within the gums had been a constant irritant. I was lying in bed, bleeding and writhing in the pain caused by the extraction when the landlady came to me excitedly and said, "I have just heard on the radio[3] that India's great leader, Gandhi has been shot dead." I could not believe what she had said and asked her to lend me the radio which she kindly did. For the next two hours, the radio carried reports about the shooting and the arrangements for his funeral.

I learnt that Gandhiji had been shot dead by a Maharashtrian young man, Nathuram Godse, in Birla House in New Delhi where he was staying when he was going to address his daily afternoon prayer meeting at 5 p.m.

After the initial shock was over, I began to reflect about Gandhiji, how he led the struggle for Independence and the economic and social reforms that he had tried to introduce. Again and again, the thought came to me that it was an irony of fate that the apostle of peace and non-violence should meet a violent death. Then came also the thought that it was a mercy that the killer was a Hindu because if he was a Moslem, it would have caused Hindu-Moslem riots in which thousands would have died. Altogether, the winter of 1947 was a miserable one. I had dental trouble and had to visit the Georgetown University Dental School frequently for treatment. I went to the school because I could not afford to pay for treatment by a dentist. Their fees were so high. Furthermore, the two houses that Patil and I stayed in were not too comfortable.

During the next semester, Mr. Patil and I shifted to a room in the house of the late Prof. Jenkins. He had been a Professor in Psychology at the University who had been sent as a Counsellor to relieve the suffering of severely wounded soldiers in the Pacific during Second World War. The pain of seeing the suffering of severely wounded soldiers day after day, was more than he could endure and he shot himself dead soon after the war. His widow, was letting out three rooms in her house to earn money to supplement her pension from the American government. This was a neatly built brick house located in University Park, an extremely clean neighbourhood in which the streets were lined with trees and there were woods to the rear of most of the houses. The other houses in the neighbourhood belonged to other Professors. Also, it was much closer to the University campus than the other two houses. Patil and I stayed in this house until both of us left for India. The house was well heated in winter and Mrs. Jenkins kept it scrupulously clean. The other two rooms in the house were occupied by two congenial persons; one was an Assistant Professor at the University and the other was a fellow graduate student of Patil in Poultry

Science. Thus we were both very comfortable in this house.

It was here that I saw the problem that arises between American parents and their teenage children. Mrs. Jenkins had a fifteen year old son and a twelve year old daughter. Both were constantly quarrelling with their mother. On three occasions Mrs. Jenkins came frantically to the Assistant Professor, Bob Cornell, at about midnight and requested him to go out and bring back her son who had run away from the house. He had gone to his aunt's house near the Potomac River in Washington DC after quarrelling with her. She was afraid that the boy might commit suicide in a fit of anger. Bob obliged, brought the boy back and advised both mother and son to be more relaxed. All three of us knew that Mrs. Jenkins was an excitable woman and was mainly responsible for the boy's behaviour.

On Saturday evenings, three of us, Patil, Joshi another Government of India scholar in poultry science and I would have dinner together and then see a movie. I became very fond of seeing movies and saw a large number of them during my three year stay in the U.S.

Here I should mention an incident which illustrates the colour bar in Washington D.C. in those days. One evening the three of us went to see a movie at our favourite movie theatre. The girl at the ticket counter gave me a ticket and I went in. But Patil and Joshi arrived several minutes later, accompanied by a profusely apologising manager. After the movie when I asked Patil what was the reason for the unprecedented incident he said that the ticket girl had not issued them the tickets thinking that they were blacks who were not allowed to enter the whites only cinema hall. So she rushed to the manager for advice, who immediately recognized that they were not blacks but were Indians and instructed the sales girl to issue them the tickets. Messrs. Patil and Joshi were dark in complexion, while I had become so fair that I would often be mistaken for an Italian or a Spaniard and people would stop me on the street and begin to talk to me in Italian or Spanish. Since I could not understand them, I would politely explain that I was from India.

The blacks were the underclass in Washington D.C. and Maryland in those days. Most of them worked as janitors or as doormen in hotels and had other similar very low paying jobs. An educated black middle class, working in white collar jobs and the professions had not emerged yet. When I passed through their areas I used to wonder why the richest and most powerful nation on earth should allow an important part of its population to live in poverty and why there should be residential segregation in a country which called itself ' the land of the free'. The blacks lived in small brick row houses mostly in S.E. Washington just behind the Library of Congress and the Capitol, the imposing building which houses the Senate and the House of Representatives of the U.S. Congress. Many of their houses would have broken window panes and were otherwise dilapidated. They were not allowed to live in the areas in which the whites lived.

I remember also a visit to Washington which illustrates my forgetfulness and the kindness of a bank clerk in helping me out of an embarrassing situation. I used to go to Washington by a Greyhound bus and would buy a book of 10 tickets for my travel. One morning when I reached Washington, I discovered that I had forgotten my wallet at home and had also used up the last ticket in the book of bus tickets. Thus I would have to walk back 16 km. and could not do any work in Washington that day. In order to avoid this situation, I walked into a bank, explained my predicament to the clerk at the counter and requested him to give me $ 10, which would be debited to the account in my bank in College Park. When he refused, I walked into a second bank with the same request. Appreciating my predicament the bank clerk telephoned my bank, satisfied himself that there was enough money in my account and gave me the $ 10 that I needed. I was most grateful and vowed never to start from home without checking that I had my wallet and my passport in my pocket.

I have vivid memories of two visits to Washington in the springs of 1948 and 1949, in order to see in blossom the Japanese cherry trees planted along the Reflecting Pool located between the Lincoln and Jefferson memorials. Both of them are built of pure white marble. Another vivid memory concerns a visit in January 1949 to see the motorcade on the occasion of the inauguration of President

Truman. It was a delight to see the motorcade, but by the time I reached the city, his inaugural address was almost over. In the part of the address that I remembered, there was an announcement about providing technical assistance to the developing countries to assist their economic development. The U.S. had assisted in the rebuilding of Western European industries and cities which had suffered extensive damage during Second World War by providing large economic assistance to European countries under the Marshall Plan, named after one of the foreign ministers of President Truman. Technical assistance to developing countries was expected to provide similar assistance to these countries. It did not. The funds provided for it were meagre and most of them were utilized for paying the salaries of American experts posted in these countries and for the equipment and supplies bought in the U.S. The assistance was called Point 4 programme because it came at No. 4 in his address.

Writing a Dissertation

After completing my course work for the Ph.D degree, I had to choose a subject for my dissertation. Since I was going back to India after getting a degree, I felt that the subject should relate to India so that after some further work on it, it could be published as a book. Prof Baker agreed but Prof. Van Royan, the second senior professor in the Department did not. He argued that I could not do any field work on an Indian subject in Maryland and that they would not be able to evaluate my dissertation because no professor in the Department knew anything about India. Eventually, it was decided that I should make a study of production and marketing of milk for Washington D.C. The milk was produced in about 1600 dairy farms located within 100 km. of Washington D.C. All the farmers were members of a cooperative which had the monopoly of purchase and sale of milk in the Washington area. The cooperative also fixed the price at which milk was sold which was invariably somewhat higher than the price in Baltimore, 60 km. from Washington. The manager of the cooperative justified the high price on the ground that its member farms maintained very high standards of sanitation which had been prescribed by a U.S. law. This was just an excuse because maintenance of such high standards of sanitation on the farms was unnecessary because all the milk was pasteurized before it was sold. But since the consumers did not protest against the price differential, the cooperative got away with it.

For the field work, I selected a sample of 60 dairy farms located in Maryland and Virginia which supplied milk to Washington. Since I had no means of travel to the farms, I would request the County Agents of the various counties in which the farms were located, to allow me to accompany them on their visits to the farms. The County Agents are officials of the Departments of Agriculture of the various states with the responsibility of teaching the farmers improved methods of farming and animal husbandry to obtain higher yields from the crops and livestock and better farm management to reduce soil erosion and maintain productivity of the land. The County Agent system has been most effective in progressively improving productivity of American farms and making the US the largest producer in the world of wheat, maize, soybean and several other crops besides beef and pork.

The six County Agents whom I requested for such visits were most obliging. They would not only take me around the farms, but would often invite me over for lunch. Detailed discussions with them helped me greatly in understanding the economy of the farms. I completed the field work in about four months and spent another five months writing my dissertation. The stipulated period to complete it was nine months. During my field work I saw the very rapid physical expansion of the Washington metropolitan area. Farm after farm was being sold to developers who built housing colonies on the land. People were leaving the inner cities to live in houses where they could have a small yard where their children could play. I did not know then that it was a country-wide phenomenon, and would result in most American cities having a medium-sized core and a series of suburbs. The second is concerned with finishing the dissertation in time for presentation. I had completed the hand written draft about three weeks before the due date. But the typists I engaged to type it proved unreliable. One left after typing about half the draft, and the other finished the remainder only the day before the last date for submission of the draft. As a result, Harbhajan Singh, a Government of India scholar in poultry science, Marilyn Hubert, a fellow graduate student in the Department and I sat until midnight assembling the typed pages and making charts to go with the typed draft to prepare the six copies of the dissertation of which four were presented to the University and two were retained by me. I cannot to this day forget the assistance of Singh and Marilyn in helping me out of a near crisis situation.

The final examination, in which the Ph.D. candidate defends the dissertation before a panel of professors was held a few days later. I passed it with distinction. After the examination, my adviser, Prof. Baker remarked that he was impressed by both the content and the language of the dissertation as he could detect hardly any mistake of language in it. Since the dissertation related to production and sale of milk, the Department of Dairy Science of the University promised to publish it. I spent another two months revising the dissertation for publication. Prof. Baker gave me a summer fellowship of $ 200 a month to cover my living expenses during this period. Besides revising my dissertation I did some work for the Agricultural Atlas. I submitted the finished draft to the Dairy Science Department for publication, but to my regret the Department never published it. In retrospect, I feel that my original idea of working on an Indian subject was correct, because after return from the U.S. I could have done further work on it and got it published in India.

Return Home

I had made two promises to my parents before I left for the U.S.A First, that I would return home and not settle in the U.S. Second, that I would marry an Indian in India and not bring an American wife. The migration of my family after Partition, confirmed my resolve. I considered it my duty to return home to help in the rehabilitation of the family. Second, I could not marry an American girl because I knew that with the high standard of living to which she was accustomed she could not live as a member of a refugee joint family. So, I never had a girl friend. Among the girls that I knew, I liked Marilyn Hubert, a very sweet tempered and attractive French-Canadian girl. If I had decided to stay in the U.S. I might have married her.

Since I would need a job immediately on return, I applied to the Universities of Delhi and Baroda which had advertised jobs of Readers (Associate Professors) for their newly opened departments of Geography. I applied also for a job as a Lecturer in Geography at the University of Ceylon (now called Sri Lanka) in Colombo. I had come across the advertisement for this job almost by accident. A fellow graduate student in the Department saw an advertisement for it in the monthly bulletin, *Jobs in Geography,* published by the Association of American Geographers and suggested that I apply for it. I did. However, I did not get any reply to my application until I left for India.

For my return to India, I got a seat in a Liberty ship which would take me from New York to Southampton, England, from where I would have to get another seat in a ship going to India. I recall to this day my final meeting with Prof. Baker before leaving. Dressed in shirt sleeves he was digging a part of the yard around his house to improve it for production of grass for his cows. He wished me well. This is the last I saw of him because he died a few months after my return. However he had been so satisfied with my performance that he gave me a certificate in which he mentioned that I was the best student he had come across in his whole life.

The four day voyage across the Atlantic on the Liberty ship was quite uncomfortable. The ship, which was no more than a steel tub, would rock and roll so violently in the storms that very often the crockery would come down crashing and be reduced to pieces even before we had sat down for our meals. There were about 80 passengers of which four—Mitra an official of the West Bengal Government, Gaur who was going to work as a forest officer in the Himalayan part of Punjab, Chopra, another Government of India scholar and I were Indians. Because of the small number of passengers there was a spirit of camaraderie among the passengers and between them and the head of the crew. The captain would often sit with us during our meals.

VIII

THREE WEEKS IN LONDON

On reaching London I found myself stranded along with about ninety Government of India scholars because we could not get a boat to India. Every day we would gather at India House, the office of the Indian High Commissioner and ask the Education Officer if there was a boat available for our return. The answer would invariably be 'No'. I would also go daily to the office of the Peninsular and Oriental (P&O), the principal shipping company, whose ships plied between Britain and India, Myanmar, Australia, Singapore and Hong Kong. I was very happy when the clerk at the office told me one morning that a seat was available on the S.S. Carthage, which would leave Southampton for Bombay and Hong Kong on 20 September. I booked my seat immediately by paying a fare of £ 60.

During the three weeks in London I stayed in one of the small and dingy rooming houses in the Russell Square area which was close to India House. Bed and breakfast was provided by the landladies for ten shillings (half a pound). For lunch we would all gather at India House, which had a cafeteria in its basement which served a very good Indian lunch at a very low price. Having nothing else to do, we would spend our time seeing the sights of central London, including particularly the British Museum. Most of the students were men but there were a few women too. Among them I remember a very attractive young woman, Miss Kapila Malik who was returning home after taking her M.A. degree in English literature from one of the prestigious women's colleges in the U.S. I see her many times in Delhi and continue to meet her as she has become an authority on India's cultural history. She has received several Indian and international awards for her writings on the subject. She was elected in 1998 the first woman Director of the India International Centre, the principal centre in Delhi for holding seminars and lectures by Indian and visiting foreign scholars, hosting plays in various European languages and performances of Indian and western classical music and dance.

I was impressed by the British Museum. It has one of the

biggest libraries in the world. Its Egyptian and Indian sections were particularly impressive. The British who had explored the valley of the Nile had brought home giant statues of the Pharaohs and their queens. In the Indian section there were paintings of the different campaigns that the British had fought and won, of Nawabs and Maharajahs and rare objets d'art, including idols of Hindu gods and jewel studded robes, which British administrators had collected from the princes and more manuscripts.

Central London had suffered severe damage during Second World War and there was feverish construction activity to rebuild it. Furthermore, rationing of food, introduced during the war, was still in force. Essential food—bread, meat, milk, eggs, sugar, tea and coffee were all rationed. For breakfast we would get two slices of buttered toast, powdered eggs, and a cup of tea or coffee. Occasionally, we would be served baked beans and kippers, a highly salted fish. Since I was a vegetarian, I would not eat the fish and would remain quite hungry. Then I would go to one of the numerous cafes and have another helping of coffee and buttered toast to complete my breakfast. In the Russell Square area and adjoining Bloomsbury had lived some of the outstanding men and women of English literature including John Ruskin, the philosopher and Virginia Woolf the writer. Their names were displayed in brass plaques outside the grimy brick buildings in which they had lived. When we were growing up in the 1930s and 1940s we had thought of Britain as a great and beautiful country from where our British rulers had come. However seeing London was a disappointment after seeing New York and Washington. It appeared to be a large, dirty overgrown city. Even the best suburbs of London compared poorly with suburbs like University Park in which I had lived.

Oxford Street and its adjoining streets which were the principal shopping centres were a pale shadow of New York's Fifth Avenue or the shopping areas of Washington D.C.

One day I visited Oxford to see the buildings of its famous colleges. I was impressed by the green countryside and the buildings of the colleges, built in the Gothic style of architecture like the Government College, Lahore. There were few cars. Everyone rode a bicycle. On seeing Oxford, I realised that the beauty of England was in its countryside and London gave a false impression of England.

London was dirty and crowded and Londoners were rude and inefficient. For getting a shirt washed one had to pay a pound, compared to 40 cents in College Park. Instead of a crisply washed shirt one would get one which appeared to be dirtier than when it was given. One had to queue everywhere. I remember that when an American tourist complained about the slow service in a bank the clerk shot back: "We, and not you Americans, have won the war after suffering the raids of German bombers and enduring shortages of food and clothing for years".

On the ship I saw for the first time the colour bar between the British and the Indians. It appeared immediately after the ship crossed the Suez canal. Several Britishers who used to talk to us between London and Port Said in Egypt stopped talking to us after the ship entered the Red Sea after crossing the canal. My only company on the ship was a South Indian young man who shared the cabin with me. The few other Indians included a South Indian doctor who told me that I had a slight hearing defect in my left ear but that I should live with it as the surgery that would remove it was not free from danger. The British passengers were mostly officials of the Governments of Hong Kong, Singapore or of British companies, there. They were returning to their places of duty with their families after their "home leave". There were also a few Australians who were returning home after seeing the "mother country".

The journey from London to Mumbai took two weeks. We had to go through some stormy days between London and Port Said, but thereafter it was calm. The Red Sea, was so calm that one could see its bottom. As the ship approached Mumbai I was full of apprehension because I was returning home after three years absence with a Ph.D. degree but no job. Also, my parents had become refugees and had lost most of what they had during their migration from Lahore to Delhi. These fears vanished however when I met my old friend Dharam Prakash immediately on landing. I had written to him from London about my arrival. He told me that there was a telegram from *Baujee* that the University of Ceylon had offered me a job as Lecturer in Geography and that I should accept it and go to Colombo after a few days stay with them in Delhi. The university would also pay the cost of my travel from Delhi to Colombo by air and rail.

What relief! I would not be unemployed after all!

Dharam had a large room in the city YMCA behind the Gateway of India. After depositing my baggage in his room and having dinner, Dharam and I sat along the beach talking late into the night. In this conversation, he told me the details of my family's migration from Lahore to Delhi, about Savitri's marriage and about his own coming from Lahore to Mumbai soon after Partition. He was working as a reporter on the stock exchange and commodity markets for three weekly papers. The earning, from his writing was enough to pay for his living expenses and also gave him a small saving to invest in stocks. Before that, he had worked as a research scholar for three years in Lahore after passing his M.A. examination in 1944. I stayed with him in Mumbai for three days during which I met Krishan Khandpur who was working as a Deputy Director in the Films Division of the Government of India after returning from the U.S. Dharam took me to the stock exchange where I saw the mad crowd of brokers who bought and sold stocks and shares. Almost all the traders and brokers were Gujaratis. He explained to me that all the transactions were verbal — today they are computerised — and that any trader or broker who did not keep his word, was debarred from further trading in the stock exchange.

Dharam took me also to meet a most interesting man, Mr. Sachin Chowdhury, editor of a newly started weekly economic journal, called *Economic Weekly,* which was one of the journals for which he wrote a weekly column.

Sachin was a frail looking, middle aged Bengali who had started his journal with some money borrowed from his younger brother. His ambition was to make his journal the Indian counterpart of the London *Economist*. He worked long hours with the help of a small staff in order to ensure that the weekly was published regularly. Sachin liked me and asked me to write for his journal as soon as I had settled down in Ceylon. He gave me his visiting card, at the back of which he scribbled a few words introducing me to his friend, Dr. Ram Verma, Secretary of the Finance Commission which had been appointed by the Government of India in order to decide the allocation of taxes collected by the Central Government between itself and the state governments.

The appointment of such a Commission once every five years has been made a statutory obligation of the Central Government under the Constitution of India which was being drafted by the Constituent Assembly at the time. This introduction whose significance I did not know at the time eventually helped me get a job in the Planning Commission. Dharam also told me that Krishan Khandpur would be an excellent match for my sister Amrit and would be happy to see her during one of his numerous visits to Delhi. I liked the proposal and hoped that it would materialise. When I reached Delhi I found my family living in a set of two rooms, kitchen and a bathroom located at the back of a house on Original Road (now Desh Bandhu Gupta Marg) in Karolbagh.

Sachin died in 1965. But before his death he had made the *Economic Weekly,* the best economic journal in India. It was read eagerly by senior officers and members of the Planning Commission and by senior officers in the economic ministries. The views expressed by him on various economic policy issues were discussed at great length. I did not write much for the *Economic Weekly* until Sachin's death, but have published many papers in the *Weekly's* successor *Economic and Political Weekly,* which is being edited since Sachin's death, by Mr. Krishna Raj, an economist from Kerala. Because of his ability and hard work, the *Economic and Political Weekly* remains the most respected economic journal in India, even today.

NOTES

1. Wattumul was a Sindhi who had gone to Honolulu in Hawaii early in this century and set up a clothing store there. He became quite wealthy and established a Foundation for promoting closer relations between India and the USA. The scholarships were being awarded by his American widow; he himself had died many years earlier.
2. It was called at that time ECAFE (Economic Commission for Asia and the Far East)
3. There were very few television receivers in those days.

4

Colombo, Sri Lanka 1949-1950

In Delhi, I met Sir Maurice Gwyer, Vice Chancellor of Delhi University to enquire about my application for the post of Reader in Geography at the University. I had two hour long conversations with him. Sir Maurice told me that I would be suitable for the job but regretted that he could not appoint me. The Home Minister, Sardar Patel, had issued an order that there would be no further recruitment in the Government and all vacant posts in the Government and even in Delhi University which were financed by the Government would remain vacant.

Bauji and I were greatly disappointed. Both of us were very keen that I should get a job in Delhi so that. I could stay with them. He had started his business of selling buttons by building a small wooden structure as a shop in Sadar Bazaar, the principal market for them in Delhi.

Delhi was full of refugees from West Pakistan. Some of them were living in small houses vacated by the Moslems or as tenants in houses owned by the Hindus. Many had crowded into old monuments like the Old Fort. Others had sublet one or two rooms in houses allotted by the Government to its junior officials. Since most of the refugees had been traders, they had built thousands of wooden structures which they used as shops in the principal commercial areas, like Karol Bagh, Chandni Chowk and Sadar Bazar, in old Delhi, in Connaught Circus and along Janpath (then called Queensway) in New Delhi. The Central Government had established a Ministry of Relief and Rehabilitation which had started construction at a feverish pace of one or two room flats in various parts of Delhi. The transport system was chaotic. A bus service started by a private company operated a few rickety old buses which ran fitfully and were terribly overcrowded. Thus the horse drawn tongas and bicycles were the principal means of transport for the middle and lower income residents.

After two weeks in Delhi, I flew to Madras (now renamed Chennai), and from there took a train to Dhanushkodi, the last point from which a steamer took passengers to Talaimannar in Ceylon, for the onward overnight journey by train to Colombo. The plane travel, my first, was in a Dakota (DC-3) which had been acquired by one of the newly started airlines. The Dakotas had been built in thousands during World War II to carry American soldiers to various theatres of war. Like the Liberty ships, they had minimum amenities. During the four hour journey from Delhi to Madras, the plane flew at an altitude of 8000 feet which gave me a good opportunity to see the Indian peninsula. It was so dry and brown. I stayed in Madras for a few hours before boarding a train which took more than 24 hours to reach Dhanushkodi. Despite being India's third largest city, Madras appeared to be like an overgrown town with many beggars. The Madras Secretariat, the University, the buildings of the Legislature, banks, insurance companies, and of big business houses, owned formerly by the British, were all located along its principal street Mount Road which ran parallel to its beautiful beach. But immediately behind Mount Road, there were unending slums and small houses owned by its middle income residents.

At the restaurant where I took lunch and at the railway station, several educated young men approached me with letters in English asking for alms. I had never seen so many beggars in my life! Another first experience was to see that few people wore shoes. At the main stations, I would see apparently affluent ladies wearing expensive sarees, and men wearing gold braided turbans walking without shoes or wearing thin *chappals*. It was hot and most people carried umbrellas as protection from the sun. But I wondered why they did not wear any footwear to save their feet from being burnt and to avoid catching diseases like hookworm which came from walking barefoot.

The entry permit system had been introduced a few months earlier to regulate the entry of Indians into Ceylon. Most of the passengers were labourers who worked on tea estates in Ceylon and were returning to their jobs after availing themselves of their home leave. Others were traders in Colombo. One of them told me that much of the wholesale and retail trade in Colombo was in the hands of Indians who were concentrated in Pettah, the principal market of Colombo.

The 40 km long Palk Straits which separates Ceylon from India is so shallow that I could see the bottom of the sea. The steamer arrived in Talaimannar late in the evening and after completing the entrance formalities I boarded the night train to Colombo. I was struck by the contrast between Indians and Ceylonese. The Ceylonese clerk was courteous and prompt. The train was very clean, with spotlessly clean linen on the beds.

In Colombo, I stayed in the City YMCA where I got a room immediately. Thereafter I saw Mr. Chand, a trader in sports goods. Hailing from Sialkot in West Punjab, he had gone to Ceylon to open his shop about 30 years earlier. One of *Bauji's* friends, had given me a letter of introduction for him. Mr. Chand told me that so long as I was in Colombo I could think of his home as mine and that I was welcome to ask him for any assistance that I needed.

When I went to the University, I found that there was only one assistant lecturer, Mrs. Corea in the Department. Prof. Lebon, a British national who had been the Professor of Geography had left about three months earlier, after he had found a suitable permanent post in a British university. Dr Parameshwar Dayal, who had succeeded him as lecturer and Head of the Department, was also due to leave in two weeks because he had been appointed a Reader in Geography in Patna University in Bihar, his home state. Mr. K. Kularatnam the other assistant lecturer was away in London on study leave to get his M.A. degree and would return only in March 1950. Meanwhile, there were three students who had been preparing to appear for the B.A. examination of London University in April 1950, but were stranded because there was no one to help them prepare for the examination.

The University itself had been upgraded from the University College of Ceylon which prepared students in various subjects for getting their degrees from the University of London. This was the system in all the larger British colonies in which one or more colleges prepared students for getting their degrees from London or another British University to which they were affiliated.

The faculty of the University of Ceylon was headed by the Vice Chancellor, Sir Ivor Jennings, a British expert in constitutional law. He had been invited by the Government to draft the Constitution of Ceylon and later became Vice Chancellor of the University.

I took it as my personal responsibility to ensure that the three students did pass their B.A. examination and devoted a lot of time, preparing them for it. I am glad that all three passed the examination. Two of them, both Sinhalese, joined the Ceylon Civil Service, while the third, a Tamil, Mr. Thambayapillai joined the department as junior lecturer and steadily rose to be its Head and the best known geographer of Ceylon.

I stayed in the City YMCA throughout my stay in Ceylon. Like the City YMCA in Madison, it was the place where budding politicians, civil servants, journalists and other intellectuals met every evening for discussions on the political and economic problems of Ceylon. I enjoyed listening to them and was to find that some of them became leaders of various political parties. They included Mr. Peter Kunnemann leader of the Communist party of Ceylon for almost 20 years in the 1950s and 1960s.

After staying six weeks in Colombo I returned to Delhi to spend my 6-week long Christmas vacation. This time I flew from Colombo to Trichy (Tiruchirapalli) a large city in Tamil Nadu (then Madras Presidency) which is famous for its two temples, one of them, located on a small hill, is called the Rockfort temple and the other, Srirangam temple, is situated in the centre of the city.

During my three month stay in Colombo, between the end of the Christmas vacation and closure of the University for the summer I organised a week-long field visit for the three students who were preparing for the B.A. degree. During this visit, we saw the tea, rubber and coconut plantations that provided the principal exports of Ceylon. In the countryside it was green everywhere and the villages and small towns looked like islands in a sea of green. I was charmed by the beauty of the countryside and the sparkle of the beaches south of Colombo. I decided that if I did not return to Ceylon after the summer vacation, I would visit it as a tourist. I did with my wife in December 1982. The economy of Ceylon was booming. Several new hotels had come up and shops were full of imported goods.

The tea estates located at a height of 6,000-8,000 ft. were particularly fascinating. Most of them had been owned by the British before Ceylon became independent, but had been purchased by wealthy Ceylonese when the British left. The labourers were almost all Tamils. They had come in the late nineteenth century to work on the plantations as the Sinhalese, mostly small subsistence farmers were not willing to work for long hours.

Including the estate workers about one third of the population was Tamil in 1950; most of the remaining were Sinhalese. The Tamils, who had steadily migrated from Tamil Nadu over the centuries lived in the northern and north-eastern parts of the island; the Sinhalese lived in the southern and central parts. Most of the Tamils were Hindus while most of the Sinhalese were Buddhists. Out of a total population of about five million, nearly 600,000, both Tamil and Sinhalese were Christians. The Sinhalese regarded themselves as racially superior to the Tamils. They also considered themselves as the real people of Ceylon which they always called 'Sri Lanka Matha' (Sri Lanka, our mother) and regarded the Tamils as intruders. There was an active and successful movement to reconvert Christian Sinhalese to Buddhism, but there was no such movement among the Tamils. Almost 10 per cent of the population was Moslem; they were descendants of Arab traders who had married Sinhalese women over the centuries. Most of them lived in the eastern province and were small farmers or fishermen.

Since the Tamils had taken to English education earlier than the Sinhalese, they dominated the Civil Service and the professions. This was resented by the growing class of educated Sinhalese. Thus there was growing tension between the Sinhalese and the Tamils. It was to increase during the following decades and was to culminate in the late 1980s into a demand by the Tamils for division of the island into two. Since this demand was not acceptable to the Sinhalese, there was armed conflict between the two communities. The conflict lasted for several years. Occasional battles between the Sir Lankan army and the guerrillas of the LTTE still rock the peace of the island.

In January 1950, the Government of India announced the formation of the Planning Commission to prepare five year plans for the economic and social development of the country. The idea of preparing long-term plans for India's development had gained increasing popularity during the closing years of World War II. Several plans were prepared of which two, one prepared by a group of Bombay industrialists in 1945 and the other by the Government of India itself in 1946, were the most important. The formation of the Planning Commission was due to the initiative of the Prime Minister, Pandit Nehru, who had been a devotee of planning since his visit to the Soviet Union during the 1930s.

Since I was keen to get a job in Delhi. I saw in the formation of the Commission an opportunity to get a job. Therefore, I prepared a paper accompanied by a large map on the Planning Regions of India and sent it to the Secretary of the Commission.

Mr. Kularatnam, returned from London in March 1950 after getting his M.A. degree and since he was very keen to get the post of Lecturer that I was holding, he would tell me every day that there was no future for me in Ceylon and that I should get a job in India as soon as possible.

When I was returning to Delhi to spend the summer vacation, I went to the Vice Chancellor to inform him about my plan and seek his formal approval for it. In this meeting, he told me, "I don't think you will return to the University". His words were prophetic because I did not return, But I don't know what prompted him to say them.

Ceylon had become independent in February 1948 and the Government celebrated its Independence Day with great enthusiasm. I was invited to attend the second Independence Day celebration in February 1950. It was a memorable experience. I was fascinated by the masked dancers from Kandy in central

Ceylon.I consider my short stay in Ceylon as a very happy period. I liked my work, and it gave me a lot of leisure to devote to personal reading and writing.

The Prime Ministers of Ceylon and India discussed the issue of the number of estate labourers who were to be given Ceylonese citizenship in the 1950s. The number who got the citizenship after several discussions between the Prime Ministers of the two countries was much lower than the actual number of estate workers so that large numbers had to return to their ancestral home in Tamil Nadu and Kerala and make a fresh start in earning their livelihood.

One night I had to share my room with Mr. Alfred Edward, a young and friendly Tamil member of the Ceylon Civil Service. We had a long discussion on relations between India and Ceylon and the growing tension between the Tamils and the Sinhalese. I was to meet him later in Sierra Leone because by then he had left the Ceylon Civil Service to join permanent service with the United Nations Development Programme. He was the UNDP Resident Representative and was quite friendly with me during my first few months in Sierra Leone.

It is interesting to note that during its entire 50 years of independence, Ceylon has had as its Prime Ministers, members of the small class of Sinhalese aristocracy who purchased the tea and rubber estates from the British. The first Prime Minister, Sir Don Steven Senanayake belonged to it as have all his successors. The Bandaranayake family in particular has dominated the political life of the island. Mrs. Sirimavo Bandaranayake, widow of the principal opponent of Sir Don, who was assassinated by a militant Sinhalese, was the Prime Minister for more than a decade. The present Prime Minister Mrs. Kumaratunge who has held this office for over six years is her daughter.

These aristocrats have managed to stay in power by continuing the welfare programmes, including a public distribution system through which rice is distributed to the public at a highly subsidised price which have made the Sri Lankan people the best fed, the most educated and the longest living people in South Asia. But they have not paid too much attention to industrial development perhaps because it could lead to the emergence of a group of industrial entrepreneurs, several of whom could be hard working and enterprising Tamils who may challenge their position of dominance of the political life of the country.

Relations between India and Ceylon (or Sri Lanka) have fluctuated over the decades between friendship and cool neutrality. They would be enormously better if successive governments in New Delhi appreciated the fact that the ethnic and cultural roots of the Sri Lankans, both Sinhalese and Tamils, are in India and that because of its location Sri Lanka's friendship is of vital importance for the defence of India. The Sinhalese are proud to be descendents of people who went from Bengal with the son and daughter of Emperor Ashok in the third century B.C. and converted the people to Buddhism. The Tamils have been migrating to Ceylon from Tamil Nadu over the centuries. Living in Colombo, I felt that I was in a part of South India. The climate, the landscape, the dress of men and women and their behaviour patterns are in many ways so much like those of the people of Kerala. However, the Sinhalese are less officious, more courteous and much keener to maintain cleanliness in their person and their immediate living environment than the people of Tamil Nadu. I received nothing but smiles from my students and the few Sinhalese whom I met during my brief stay.

5

Planning Commission 1950-1953

In December 1952 at the signing of the final plan document Gulzarilal Nanda timorously asked Pandit Nehru, "Panditji, the staff of the Commission are quite worried about their future. They are afraid that since the Plan has been prepared, the Planning Commission would be wound up, like other Commissions appointed by the Central Government which are wound up after they have submitted their report." Panditji replied almost angrily "What nonsense ! Planning is a continuous process. The first plan will be followed by a Second Plan, which will be followed by a Third Plan, a Fourth Plan and so on and you can assure the staff that they should have no fears about their career prospects".

Despite the differences in their background and views on different economic and social issues, personal relations between the members were cordial and expressions of strong differences in views by one member with another were made and received in good humour. In one meeting on land reforms, an issue on which V.T. Krishnamachari and R.K. Patil had strong differences of views, VTK remarked, "Patil you want to bring about revolution with *pan, supari* (betel nut, which is chewed by a large proportion of India's population) and rose water". The implication was that a revolutionary change like radical land reforms could not be made peacefully. The remark was made in good humour and received without offence.

Similarly in their discussions with the ministers and top officials of the state governments, the members would express their reservations about advisability or otherwise of particular projects or programmes strongly but then leave the state governments to take their own decisions. In one meeting VTK and C.D. Deshmukh expressed strong reservations about some aspects of the Hirakud Project – a large irrigation-cum-power-cum flood control project being constructed in Orissa — to the Chief Secretary of the state and asked him to convey them to the Orissa Cabinet. But they did not urge him to ask the Cabinet to change its decisions in the light of their criticism! VTK and Deshmukh were right and the programmes on which they had expressed their reservations failed.

Because of the importance that Pandit Nehru attached to the views of the Planning Commission, no project or programme could be implemented by any Ministry without the approval of the Planning Commission. If the Commission wanted any changes in any part of a project or programme, they would have to be made before the project or programme was approved by his Cabinet.

This influence of the Planning Commission was expressed succinctly in a humorous remark which was popular among senior officials of the ministries. "There are three policy making and deliberative bodies within the Government of India – the *Lok Sabha* (the Lower House of Parliament), the *Rajya Sabha* (the Upper House of Parliament) and "the Planning Commission".

On reaching Delhi for my summer vacation, I sought an inter view with Sardar Tarlok Singh I.C.S., Deputy Secretary and officer-in-charge of the Planning Commission. He had read my paper on Planning Regions of India with interest and readily granted me an interview. After two hour-long meetings, he offered me the post of a Research Officer in the Economic Division of the Commission. I joined the post on 1, May 1950. I was the second officer to join the Commission, the first being Dr. K.N. Raj, an economist who had served as Secretary to C.D. Deshmukh who had joined the Commission as Member (Finance) after retiring from his post as the first Indian Governor of the Reserve Bank of India.

The Commission had five members, besides Pandit Nehru who was its Chairman. The Deputy Chairman was Gulzari Lal Nanda, a highly successful labour leader of Ahmedabad. C.D. Deshmukh was the member-in-charge of Finance and Economic Affairs. Another member was V.T. Krishnanachari who had headed the

Finance Commission, after retiring from a long tenure of service as the Dewan (Prime Minister) of two princely states - Baroda and Jaipur. He had been put in charge of development of natural resources, which included development of irrigation, power and mineral resources. Another member was G.L. Mehta, who had been given the portfolio of industries. He had retired as a top executive of the Scindia Steam Navigation Co. which operated ships between various Indian ports. The fifth member, who had responsibility for development of agriculture was R.K. Patil. He had resigned his post as a member of the ICS in 1943 during the Quit India Movement and had become an ardent Congressman.

Sardar Tarlok Singh offered me a salary of Rs. 450 per month. Since I had been getting a salary of Rs. 500 per month in Ceylon I told him that I must be given the same salary. He was hesitant in offering me this salary, and was also hesitant in offering K.N. Raj the salary of Rs.800 p.m to which he was entitled as Assistant Chief of the Economic Division. On hearing about this from K.N. Raj, C.D. Deshmukh told T.S. "You give these boys the salaries that they want; otherwise I shall take my full salary of Rs. 2250 as Member and pay them their salaries myself." He had taken a token salary of Re. 1 per month on joining the Commission. Sardar Tarlok Singh could not disobey C.D. Deshmukh.

Sardar Tarlok Singh arranged my interview with C.D. Deshmukh, two weeks after I joined the Commission. I was expecting him to be a middle aged man wearing a gold laced red turban and a jacket which was favoured by Maharashtrians. Instead, I found a handsome youngish looking man dressed in western clothes. I thought that he was probably his secretary, but when he started talking about his experience as a young ICS officer in Central Provinces (presently Madhya Pradesh), I realised that he was C.D. Deshmukh himself. I talked very little in the hour long interview, but apparently I had impressed him enough to make him intervene on my behalf in case of fixation of my salary.

My parents, particularly *Bauji,* were extremely pleased with my appointment in the Planning Commission. When I joined the Planning Commission it was located in a few rooms in a wing of the Rashtrapati Bhawan. I would cycle every day, a distance of about seven km. from our house in Karolbagh to my office. It would be extremely hot in the summer, with the *loo* (hot dusty wind from Rajasthan) blowing, and extremely cold in winter. But there was no choice as there was no bus service and I could not afford to keep a car.

After 18 months of commuting on a bicycle, I was allotted government accommodation, in G-Block. This was one of the numerous barracks constructed hastily during Second World War for housing officers of the armed forces. The accommodation had two large rooms, a kitchenette, and a small bathroom, a little room with a tap under which one took a bath. The 50 odd families living in G-Block used eight common toilets which were however kept fairly clean. We were all very happy when I got this accommodation, Since it was located about 2 km. from my office, it meant an end to cycling several kilometers in the searing heat and biting cold of Delhi's summer and winter. *Bauji* and I greatly enjoyed our morning walks on the lawns of India Gate and along the roads around G-Block.[1] Our neighbours in G-Block were all middle-level government officials. Among them, I remember Sardar Pritam Singh, a young irrigation engineer who was working on design of the Bhakra Dam in Punjab. It was one of the large irrigation and power projects started immediately after Independence. He rose to be the Chairman of the Central Water Commission before retiring from service. Owing to his outstanding ability he is still consulted frequently when there is any problem in construction or operation of large irrigation dams. He lives with his family in Vasant Vihar close to our house and our two families meet quite often.

Work on formulation of the First Five Year Plan 1951-56, started in right earnest only after J.J. Anjaria, an economist who had been working as a Professor in Economics in Bombay joined as Head of the Economic Division. He was a very able economist and also one of the finest men that I have worked under. Since I was a Geographer in an Economic Division he did not quite know what to do with me. Therefore, he left me to do the studies that I wanted to do. In about 18 months that I worked under him, I wrote two papers, one of which "On Land Utilisation in India" was published in a journal of the Soil Conservation Society of India, which had been started by a soil scientist, Dr. M.L. Dewan. He had started work as a soil scientist in the Damodar Valley Project, another large irrigation, power and flood control project located in Bihar. He got the job after getting a Ph.D. in Soil Science from Cornell University in the U.S. The journal and the society were closed after Dr. Dewan left in 1952 to join the Food and Agricultural Organisation (FAO) of the United Nations.

In December 1981, after working in the Economic Division for 18 months I was appointed as technical secretary to V.T. Krishnamachari. My principal work in this post was to read and comment on technical papers prepared by the Central Water and Power Commission, the apex body for formulating and overseeing implementation of large irrigation and power projects. The Commission was headed by A.N. Khosla, who was one of the best Indian irrigation engineers. He was also a great visionary. I met him a few times and was greatly impressed by the vision that he had for optimum utilization of the waters of India's major rivers for irrigation, generation of power and control of floods during and after the monsoons. One of his dreams was construction of a canal linking the rivers of the Gangetic plain with those of the plains along the east coast.

Krishnamachari was a remarkable man. I have never seen another individual who could read a technical paper and comment on it as fast as he could. At the same time, he was a meticulous draftsman, and would ensure that any paper written by him was flawless in content and language. He was also a kind boss and was quite willing to overlook small short-comings of his subordinates. I got an inkling of his ability when I submitted to him my paper on "Land Utilization in India" on writing which I had spent two months for comments. The 30-page paper was returned within half an hour. On looking through it, I found that he had read it very carefully and indicated the points on which he did not agree.

While I was working with Krishnamachari, the Central Public Works Department constructed a block of 48 flats quite near G-Block. I requested him to get one flat alloted to me by speaking about the allotment to the officer-in-charge. He readily agreed and I was allotted a flat in which we were to live for six years, until I left the Planning Commission to join the IAS and the family moved to our own house in Lajpat Nagar.

In contrast, to most south Indian bosses, who had only south Indians on their personal staff, Krishnanachari had no such predilection. Whenever meetings of the Planning Commission were held middle level officials like me were allowed to sit in the back row and listen to the discussion. One such meeting was with C. Rajagopalachari (popularly known as CR), who was then Chief Minister of Madras. He had taken this post, after working for two years as the first Indian Governor General of India.

After this meeting, Krishnamachari (we used to call him 'Sir V.T.' after his initials and the fact that he had been knighted by the British Government for his outstanding work as the Prime Minister of Baroda and Jaipur, but had renounced it when India became independent), introduced me to C.R. He said, "This is my private secretary, Nath". The instant question of C.R. was "who is he; Swaminathan or Jagannathan", Sir V.T. said "No he is a north Indian". On hearing this, C.R. lost all interest in me and I was left with the impression that a man, who had been the most outstanding Congressman from south India and had occupied the highest office in the land, was a narrow casteist at heart and that South Indian Brahmins like himself were the only persons who were fit for his personal staff.

The draft of the First Five Year Plan was prepared in December 1951, after 18 months of work in the Commission. Pandit Nehru used to attend most of the important meetings of the Commission. Thus when a paper outlining the economic projections for 1951-56 and for the next 20 years (up to 1975) was prepared by the Economic Division, Pt. Nehru came and spent an hour reading it in pin-drop silence. After that, he raised a number of questions which were answered to his satisfaction, by Anjaria and Deshmukh. I was greatly impressed with Pandit Nehru's strong interest in planning. Although he knew little economics, he had considered it his duty to understand the future of the economy, as outlined in the paper.

The Plan was generally received favourably by the press. It was considered realistic because of its emphasis on agriculture and rural development and because the modest investment envisaged in it could be mobilized easily. However, the irrepressible cartoonist, Shankar Pillai, had on the cover of his weekly journal, a cartoon which showed a famished Indian groaning under the weight of two thick volumes of the Plan document. Incidentally, Shankar was a personal friend, an admirer and a critic of Pandit Nehru.

After a year of working with Sir V.T., R.A. Gopalaswamy I.C.S., Census Commissioner and Registrar General of India, who had the responsibility for conducting the Population Census of 1951, and writing the report on it, requested Sir V.T. that I should be deputed to his office to assist him in preparing the Report on the Census. I had sent him two papers in which I had suggested that the population figures should be presented not only by states, as had been done in earlier censuses but also by natural regions based on variations in topography, climate, soils, development of agriculture and industry because density of population in different regions of India depended on variation in these. Gopalaswamy had liked this idea and had suggested that I should work with him in refining the scheme of natural regions and divisions so that he could present the Census figures by them. Sir V.T. agreed and I was deputed to work with him for four months, from December 1952 to March 1953.

During this period, I assisted Gopalaswamy to finalise the scheme of natural regions and divisions. Then he asked me to make an analysis of the growth of cultivated and irrigated areas and of population in 60 districts of India, the boundaries of which had not changed during the past 60 years i.e. from 1891-1951. This analysis revealed that growth of population had kept pace with increase in cultivated and irrigated areas during 1891- 1921, but had outstripped the latter during 1921-51. In the earlier 30-year period net growth of population was quite slow because millions died during the epidemics of bubonic plague in the first decade of the twentieth century and of influenza during 1918-19. Furthermore endemic diseases—malaria, respiratory diseases like asthma and tuberculosis and stomach diseases like diarrhoea and dysentery —took a heavy toll of life every year. At the same time, the cultivated and irrigated areas were steadily increasing because of extension of cultivation into cultivable wastelands by the farmers and the irrigated area was increasing rapidly as a result of construction of irrigation canals on the major rivers, particularly in Punjab and U.P. and the Madras Presidency (present Andhra Pradesh and Tamil Nadu) by the Government. During the period 1921- 51, however, increase in cultivated and irrigated areas had slowed down, because most of the uncultivated wastelands had already been brought under cultivation. Extension of irrigated area was also slow because only one major irrigation project had been undertaken in Punjab. Meanwhile, operation of Malthusian checks–famine and disease-had weakened with better control over epidemic and endemic diseases and improvement in sanitation. Thus, during the 30 year period, 1921–1951 growth of population was faster than growth of cultivated and irrigated areas and India became a net importer of foodgrains; about 2 million tons of rice began to be imported annually from Myanmar during the 1930s to meet the deficit in foodgrain production within the country. Cessation of the imports during World War II due to the occupation of Myanmar by the Japanese, was followed by the Bengal Famine of 1943 in which about 2 million people died.[2]

On the basis of this analysis, Gopalaswamy forecast that with increasing use of improved seed, chemical fertilizers, and pesticides and improved farm management practices, agricultural production would continue to increase to keep pace with growth of population up to 1969-70 after which Malthusian checks, particularly widespread famines would begin to operate unless growth of population which had been 13.3 per cent during 1941-1951 was reduced to 5 per cent a decade. To achieve this reduction, he advocated a vigorous and effective programme of family planning.

Although I greatly respected Gopalaswamy — he was one of the finest officers under whom I have worked — I would strongly express my disagreement with his gloomy forecast. I would argue that in a predominantly rural country in which most of the population was illiterate, adoption of family planning by the people would be slow, despite the best efforts of official and non-official agencies to propagate it. But there would be no famines because agricultural production would increase much faster than he had estimated because humankind has such a strong instinct for survival.

The rapid increase in agricultural production would be due to more intensive and effective agricultural research and through vigorous extension programmes to ensure that the more efficient production methods were rapidly adopted by the farmers. In contrast to most senior officials and Ministers of today, who cannot tolerate a different view by officials who work under them, Gopalaswamy did not mind the disagreement. On the contrary, he would keep senior officers working under him waiting, while he was having a discussion with me.

In retrospect, we were both right and wrong.Growth of agricultural output kept pace with the growth of population until the early 1960s, although the latter, about 20 per cent during 1951-61 was much higher than Gopalaswamy's estimate of a about 12 percent for the decade. During the mid-1960s, however famines could be averted only by import for two years, 1962-64, of about 10 million tons a year of wheat from the US under the PL-480 programme. Cessation of these imports from 1964-65 by orders of President Johnson, because the accumulated surplus stock of U.S. wheat had been exhausted coincided with rapid adoption from 1965-66 of new, very high yielding varieties of wheat seed developed by Dr. Norman Borlaugh in Mexico. These varieties were modified by Indian agricultural researchers to adapt them to suit the climate and soils of irrigated areas of Punjab, Haryana and Western U.P. in which wheat was the main food crop. Since the varieties yielded 2-3 times more than the old varieties under conditions of assured water supply, intensive use of organic manures, chemical fertilizers and pesticides and better farm management their use spread like wild fire. Consequently production of wheat increased so rapidly that India became self sufficient in cereals by the end of the 1960s. With further steady improvements in wheat production and similar rapid increase in production of rice, by using new high yielding varieties of rice in the 1970s and 1980s, agricultural production has continued to increase steadily.

Production of cereals has increased steadily from about 60 million tonnes in the mid 1950s to almost 200 m.t. by the end of the 1990s.

Improved varieties of rice were first developed at the International Rice Research Institute in the Philippines, and were then modified by Indian scientists to adapt them to the great variety of conditions of climate and soils under which rice is grown in different parts of India. The country produces enough foodgrains to meet the entire food needs of the population. The fact that an estimated one third of the population gets less foodgrains than it needs for living a healthy life is due primarily to defects in distribution of the available supplies.

After completion of work with the Census office, I returned to the Planning Commission to work as Deputy Director of the Programme Evaluation Organisation. The organisation had been established within the Commission to undertake concurrent and independent evaluation of the Community Development Programme, which had been launched by the Government of India in October 1952. The programme was a massive effort for integrated rural development. It aimed at: (i) increasing agricultural production through intensive and effective agricultural extension and increase in irrigated area through construction and improvement of minor irrigation works such as tanks and irrigation wells; (ii) breaking the isolation of villages through construction of approach roads to them, (iii) providing villages with other essential service facilities like primary and secondary schools, and primary health centres to provide them with medical care in case of sickness and educating them in prevention of diseases through improvement of sanitation; and (iv) ensuring that every village had access to adequate and clean drinking water.

The programme was started in a limited number of carefully selected areas in different states but was expanded rapidly during the 1950s to cover the whole country by 1961. A separate organisation headed by Mr. S.K. Dey as its head was established by the central government to (i) provide to the state governments a part of the funds needed for implementation of the programme and (ii) to oversee implementation of the programme according to the guidelines provided by the community development administration. The state governments were requested to establish separate departments, headed by the most senior and dynamic civil servants to implement the programme. The Prime Minister took personal interest in the programme. He launched it by wielding a shovel and carrying a basket of earth on his head, like a labourer for construction of a drinking water well in a village near Delhi. He also exhorted the Chief Ministers of the states in his fortnightly letters to take personal interest in efficient implementation of the programme so that the rural population which formed 80 per cent of the total population of the country would feel that the Government was taking special interest in their welfare in its efforts for economic development of the country.

The Planning Commission established a separate organisation called the Programme Evaluation Organisation to evaluate the success or failure of different components of the programme and suggest measures for increasing its efficiency. Funds for establishing the organisation and its working for the first three years were provided by the Ford Foundation, an American Foundation, funded by the Ford family, which had established an office to provide economic and technical assistance in India's economic and social development. Prof. D.G. Karve, a Maharashtrian economist was appointed as its head. I joined him as his deputy on return from my deputation with the Census office.

A vivid memory of the Planning Commission in those days relates to the courtship and marriage of C.D. Deshmukh and Durgabai. They met each other during discussions on formulation of the Second Five Year Plan in the mid-1950s, when Deshmukh was the member in-charge of finance and Finance Minister and Durgabai had been appointed member-in-charge of social welfare programmes. Deshmukh was a widower; his wife had died a few years earlier. He had lived like a bachelor throughout his life because his English wife preferred to live in England to coming to India to live with him. Thus he was an intensely lonely man.

Durgabai was a child widow, who had worked very hard and with great success for the welfare of women and children in her home state of Andhra Pradesh. Their liking for each other grew during a year of their meetings and culminated in their marriage in 1956.

Both Deshmukh and Durgabai were great achievers. While working as Finance Minister, Deshmukh nationalised the life and general insurance sectors of the Indian economy. He resigned his post in 1958 because of a difference of opinion with the Prime Minister on the status of Mumbai. He wanted it to be included in his home state of Maharashtra whereas the States Reorganisation Commission, appointed by the Government of India, had recommended that it should be administered directly by the central government. Deshmukh was right. The Maharashtrians were so furious with the recommendation of the Commission that the central government had to agree to the inclusion of the city in Maharashtra. It has been the capital of the state since then.

After his resignation as the Finance Minister, he was appointed by Pt. Nehru, as the first Chairman of the Universty Grants Commission. He built it up as a body which provides a large share of the funds needed by the Universities for their functioning and exercises a major influence on their maintaining high standards in teaching in their various departments and affiliated colleges.

Durgabai founded the Central Social Welfare Board and built it up as the principal organisation for financing programmes of welfare of women and children.

The legacy of Gandhiji's emphasis on simple living was still strong in the 1950s. I remember that one morning, while I was working as technical secretary to V.T.K., a short, slim man, dressed in spotless white khadi (home spun cotton) came to me and said, "I am U.N. Dhebar. Please tell Krishnamachari that I want to see him." I did and he went in immediately! Dhebar was the Chief Minister of the state of Saurashtra which had been formed in 1948 by merger of about 400 small princely states of the Gujarat peninsula. But despite his high status, he did not have a phalanx of security guards around him.

The Chief Ministers of large states like West Bengal and Uttar Pradesh would often come to see members of the Planning Commission. They would be accompanied by their Private Secretaries and a maximum of one or two security guards. They were not insecure about their live as the ministers of today are! Pandit Nehru, although he lived in the palace like Teen Murti house, had one armed motor cyclist ahead of his Hindustan car (the only car manufactured in India at the time) and one car full of security guards following him when he travelled between his office in South

Block of the Central Secretariat and his house. His habit of jumping into a crowd to ask it to get back and restore the cordon made by volunteers of the Congress Party in pre-Independence days and by the police when he was Prime minister is well known. In contrast, one Prime Minister in the early 1990s had a fleet of about 40 cars preceding or following his car when he travelled between New Delhi and his farm in Haryana.

The number of cars forming part of the Prime Minister's motorcade has been greatly reduced since then. But the need for personal security of the VVIPs (very very important persons) and VIPs is so great, that a large part of Delhi's police force is employed in providing security to them.

NOTES

1. Built of light brown and rust sandstone, on the model of the Arc de Triomphe in Paris, India Gate is a memorial to the officers and men of the Indian Army who died in World War I. Their names are inscribed on it. But whereas the Arc is at one end of Champs Elysee, the most fashionable shopping street of Paris, India Gate faces across a 2 km. long vista of green, the buildings of the Central Secretariat and Rashtrapati Bhawan. Since it has an oil lamp burning in it 24 hours a day, in memory of the brave, it is now called *Amar Jyoti* (Eternal Light)
2. It would not be correct to link the Bengal Famine to cessation of rice import because many independent observers reported that people were dying on the streets of Calcutta when there were enough stocks of rice to feed them in the state and that the scarcity of rice was caused primarily by the activity of a few large stockists who hoarded the available stocks and made millions by selling them at inflated prices.

6

The P.E.O. 1953-1958

I

Prof. D.G. Karve selected me as a Deputy Director because I had helped him in the location of 23 Evaluation Centres each of which was located in one of the first 60 community development projects in which the C.D. programme was started.

I would periodically visit various evaluation centres to see the working of the programme in them and get to know the background of the periodic reports sent by the evaluation officers. I greatly enjoyed the travel because it gave me an opportunity to see and appreciate the great differences in climate, soils, systems of agriculture, ethnic composition and economic and social conditions of people of different regions. The mental picture of different regions provided by the travels is deeply engraved in my mind and helps me to this day to understand the background of events in different parts of the country. I learnt from the travels that it was not appropriate for the central Community Development Administration to prescribe one pattern of development for the whole country. I felt that the Administration should indicate the broad outlines of the CD programme and allow the governments of various states and union territories to work out the details to conform to the physical, economic and social conditions in their area. This lesson was brought home to me most dramatically in Kerala which I visited in June 1954 and again in January 1958.

One important component of the CD programme was pavement of streets in villages in order to improve sanitation within them.

Two other components were to provide financial assistance for construction/ improvement of drinking water wells or other sources of water supply and opening of primary and secondary schools. None of the three components had much meaning in Kerala. There were few villages in the state; most of the families lived in individual houses, each located within a compound which had its own drinking water well and a small green patch which had a few coconut trees and a small vegetable garden. Furthermore, most of the population was literate because of the existence of a large number of primary and secondary schools established by the churches, voluntary organisations of Hindus and Moslems, and the government. Travelling through Kerala, one saw an unending procession of children going to school in the morning and returning home in the afternoon. The funds earmarked for these three components of the progamme could have been better utilized by concentrating on extension programmes aimed at improvement of yields of the principal crops of the state, — rice, coconut, tapioca, cashew nut, and pepper and improvement of the extensive network of inland canals (locally called backwaters) which along with roads are the principal means of communication.

Unfortunately, the existence of the immense variety in physical, economic and social conditions within the country and the need to vary development programmes in the light of these has never been appreciated adequately by the technical officers of the central government who formulate various development programmes and oversee their implementation by the state governments. All rural development programmes would be more successful if the central government indicated only their objectives and principal components and left it to the state governments to formulate details to suit conditions within them.

The five years that I spent working in the P.E.O. were very happy. Prof. Karve was a kind and understanding boss; he treated me with such affection that I felt more as a pupil or a nephew than as a subordinate. I do not recall any occasion when he did not agree with the details of any programme worked out by me within the guidelines provided by him. Although he dressed very simply in a long jacket, trousers and a scarlet gold laced turban, he was immaculately clean and punctual. He would arrive at his office at 5 minutes to 10 a.m. and leave at 5 p.m. I could set my watch after watching his movements. When he attended any meeting or conference, he would never speak until asked by the Chairman to do so. He was greatly respected by all for these qualities. I wish I had learnt them from him. I would have been happier and more successful in my service career if I had.

Prof. Karve left the P.E.O. after two years because he wanted to devote the rest of the few remaining years of his working life to development of cooperative societies which had been his first love.

On Prof. Karve's recommendation, I was appointed the Director of the Organisation, and held this post for three years 1955-58 when I left the P.E.O. to join the Indian Administrative Service. I had independent charge of the organisation for one year, 1955-56. Thereafter a Programme Evaluation Board was constituted with Prof. V.K. R.V. Rao, founder-Director of the Delhi School of Economics, as the Chairman and I had to work under him. Prof. Rao left after eight months of his appointment to become the Vice Chancellor of Delhi University. His place was taken by Prof. D. Ghosh, an economist, who had just retired from the United Nations in New York after working for several years with it. I worked under him for a year, 1957-58.

During the year that I held independent charge of the P.E.O. and had the responsibility for writing the annual evaluation report, there was some doubt in the minds of both Sardar Tarlok Singh and Dr. Ensminger, Head of the Ford Foundation in India, whether I would be equal to the task and whether the annual evaluation report written by me would be as good as the two reports written by Prof. Karve. These doubts were set at rest, however, when the report came out. It was read with great interest and was greatly appreciated by all concerned — the Administrator and other top officials of the Community Development Administration and the Development Commissioners of the state governments. The Prime Minister wrote to the Chief Ministers of all states to take suitable measures to overcome the shortcomings in implementation of the programme pointed out by it and implement its recommendations.

Soon after the publication of the report, S.K. Dey, who had been Administrator of the community development programme since its inception in October 1952, was appointed Minister of State for Community Development in the Ministry of Agriculture and Rural Development. His appointment did not please S. Tarlok Singh and V.T. Krishnamachari *et al*. They felt that Dey had cleverly used the findings of the report relating to the success of the CD programme to impress upon the Prime Minister the great work that he and his officers had done. So they wanted that the deficiencies of the programme should be highlighted in the next report and the best person to do it was Prof. V.K.R.V. Rao, who had a reputation for being a convincing critic.

When Prof. Rao joined as Chairman of the Programme Evaluation Board in December 1956, he was very critical of the work of the PEO and was personally rude to me. I was so distressed by his harsh criticism that one afternoon, I broke into tears in the house after listening to an hour long hectoring by him. I was distressed because I had done good work and had been rewarded by having to listen to such harsh criticism. However, during the next three months Prof Rao slowly began to appreciate my competence and hard work and began to treat me with great consideration. He was also very kind to Kamla who had been a student in the Delhi School of Economics for one year.

During April 1957, when I was writing various chapters of the Evaluation Report, Prof. Rao would often call me to his house late in the evening for discussing its various drafts. We would generally spend two to four hours, during which we would have dinner together. On these evenings he would telephone Kamla himself and say that she should not mind my not coming home for dinner. I found his house to be thoroughly disorganised. He was a widower — his wife had died of cancer a year earlier — and the house was being managed to the best of her ability by the elder of his two teen-age daughters. He had a son who was in college but was not a brilliant student as he himself had been. He would often scold him quite harshly for not working hard enough to do well in his examinations. When I saw his treatment of his son I realised that harsh criticism of students and those who worked under him was one of his habits and I should not have been so distressed by his outbursts of anger during the first two months of our working together. One evening, he confessed to me that although he was often harsh in criticism of his junior colleagues and subordinates, he never did them any harm and would ensure that they got all the chances of promotion in their careers that were due to them. I noticed also that he had a deep sense of remorse for not caring enough for his wife during her long sickness, because he was too busy with his efforts to establish the Delhi School of Economics.

The new building of the school was constructed in 1952; the school itself had been established in 1948. Owing to Prof. Rao's untiring efforts to recruit brilliant young economists for its staff, it became an outstanding institution for teaching and research in economics. Several outstanding economists, including the Nobel prize winning economist A.K. Sen, Jagdish Bhagwati and late Sukhumoy Chakravarti worked in it during the 1950s and the 1960s when Prof. Rao and his successor, Dr. K.N. Raj, were its Directors.

The Fourth Evaluation Report was published in April 1957 in time for discussion at the Development Commissioners' Conference held in May in Mussooree. Prof. Rao made no major change in the Report written by me, but added an Introduction in which he focussed on the shortcomings in implementation of the community development programme.

S.K. Dey had persuaded Pt. Nehru to be the chairman of the conference; earlier conferences had all been chaired by V.T. Krishnamachari. Pandit Nehru was a very efficient and considerate chairman. He would ensure that the Development Commissioners and others attending the conference had adequate opportunity to express their views. He ensured particularly that every Development Commissioner had an opportunity to explain in some detail the difficulties in successful implementation of the programme in his state. Prof. Rao would request the chairman to allow him to speak for a few minutes once in every hour. Pt. Nehru did not mind the interruption and would allow him to speak.

In the lunch interval between the morning and the afternoon sessions of the conference, and at the end of the afternoon session, Prof. Rao would ask me whether his interventions had made a significant contribution to the deliberations of the conference. I would invariably say that they had; but his asking the question made me feel that he was seeking my approval. One evening, after the conclusion of the conference, I saw Pandit Nehru riding a pony with his two grandsons, Rajiv and Sanjay, on separate ponies. I had read about his love of animals and that the lawns of Teen Murti house in which he lived had a number of deer and other exotic animals and birds sent by the Prime Ministers or Presidents of the countries that he had visited. Pandit Nehru enjoyed playing with some of them and personally ensured that they were looked after well. Delhi did not have a zoo at that time; thus the Teen Murti house was a miniature zoo.

Prof Rao was a brilliant economist and a great builder of academic institutions. He had already built the Delhi School of Economics. During the eight months that we worked together, I found him drafting a proposal for establishment of an Institute of Economic Growth in Delhi University. He wanted the Institute to be the premier institution of economic research in India. The Institute was established in the late 1950s when he was Vice Chancellor of Delhi University. But like many other brilliant people he was an insecure man.

The Institute did not come up to Prof Rao's expectations however, because he was not successful in getting for it the staff of outstanding caliber that he could get for the Delhi School of Economics.

During his Chairmanship of the P.E.O., I was asked by Balwant Rai Mehta, Chairman of the Estimates Committee of Parliament, who had been appointed Chairman of a Committee to evaluate the performance of the community development programme, to be its Secretary. During the year that I was Director of the P.E.O. he had discussed with me the working of the organisation for an entire day. The discussion with deeply probing questions had exhausted me. But apparently I had impressed him enough for him to ask for my services. Prof. Rao refused on the ground that if I joined the Committee, there would be no one to look after the P.E.O. I am sorry that he did because if he had allowed me to join the Committee for the nine months of its tenure and allowed one of my deputies to hold temporary charge of the P.E.O. I would have participated in writing a report whose recommendations on establishment of

Panchayati Raj institution have been of historic importance. The institutions were established by all state governments during the 1960s but were abolished by most of them by the early 1970s, because their functioning did not come up to the expectations of the state governments. They began to be revived in the 1980s, with larger grants from the state governments and more precise definition of duties and responsibilities. Whereas the Balwant Rai Committee had envisaged that the institutions would be non-political and would concentrate on rural development, the new institutions were recognised to be political bodies and in reviving them the parties in power in various state governments ensure that they would become the rural counterparts of the party.

Establishment of these institutions for implementation of rural development programmes has been made mandatory on the state governments through the 73rd Amendment to the Indian Constitution, enacted by Parliament in 1993.

The Development Commissioners' Conferences also enabled me to meet some outstanding men, all members of the Indian Civil Service, who were working as Development Commissioners in different states. I would mention three in particular — M.S. Randhawa in Punjab (I had an opportunity of working with him in the Planning Commission during the 1960s), K.S.V. Raman in Bihar and A.N. Jha in Uttar Pradesh.

Randhawa was a man of few words but plenty of action and a born leader of men. During the years that he was Development Commissioner he ensured that most of the villages in Punjab had approach roads, adequate and safe drinking water, primary schools and paved streets to improve sanitation within them. He greatly encouraged the farmers — he was himself the son of one — to increase agricultural output by use of improved seeds, chemical fertilizers, pesticides and improved implements and better farm management. And as increased supplies of electricity began to be available with completion of the Nangal Dam part of the Bhakra Nangal project, he encouraged the farmers to fit electric motors on their irrigation wells to obtain larger and more dependable supplies of irrigation water. The extension of essential service facilities to all villages and the agricultural extension work done during his tenure as Development Commissioner prepared the ground for the Green Revolution in the Punjab in the late 1960s which made Punjab the largest producer of cereals in India—the bread basket of India and the state with the highest per capita income. His subordinates followed his orders without question. Since he used to carry a small stick on his inspection tours, the officials working in community development projects, used to say, " Randhawa's *danda* (short stick) accomplishes every thing".

Raman was Development Commissioner in Bihar, which was then as it is today, the poorest and most backward state in the country. However, despite the difficult conditions under which he worked, he did succeed in providing approach roads and other service facilities to most of the villages included in the community development projects in the state. A.N. Jha was Development Commissioner of Uttar Pradesh, India's largest and most populous (but a backward) state. He was a scholar administrator. Coming from a family of erudite scholars of Sanskrit, he himself was a scholar and would punctuate his conversation with reciting verses in Sanskrit. He too assembled a large team of devoted deputies who did useful work as officials in charge of the community development projects in his state. I was to meet him and know him better during 1959-60 when I was working as Vice Principal of the Central Institute of Community Development in Mussoorie and he was the Principal of the National Academy of Administration which trains officers of the Indian Administrative Service and some other all India Services.

At the annual session of the Congress party held in Nagpur in January 1955, a resolution was passed at the instance of Pt. Nehru that cooperative farming should be the future pattern of agricultural development in India. Panditji had been greatly impressed by the cooperative farms that he had seen in the Soviet Union during his visit to it during the 1930s and again in the 1950s. He did not, however, know that while 99 per cent of the cropped area of the country was under cooperative and state farms, almost one third of total agricultural output came from the small plots comprising 1 per cent of the total cropped area which the peasants had been allowed to retain for their families' needs for cereals, meat, eggs. fruit, vegetables etc. He felt that the tiny land holdings of Indian peasants were too small for efficient adoption of improved methods of agricultural production, and that larger cultivation units formed by the peasants pooling their land holdings into cooperative farms would permit efficient use of improved agricultural practices. This resolution came as manna from heaven to S. Tarlok Singh because in his book, *Poverty and Social Change,* which he had written in the late 1930s while working in Punjab, he had said, that 'cooperative village management' should be the future pattern of economic development in rural India.

He asked me to ask all Project Evaluation Officers to study the working of cooperative farms in their project areas and send their reports within six to eight weeks. I did provide the guidelines for the study. The Evaluation Officers carried out the studies and sent reports on working of 23 'cooperative farms'. The reports indicated that there were two kinds of cooperative farms in their areas. The first were formed by landless agricultural labourers belonging usually to the scheduled castes, in order to get allotment of cultivable fallow lands from the state governments. After allotment the members of the 'cooperative' would divide the land among themselves and cultivate it as individual farms. The other kind were 'family farms'. In their case large, land owners had formed 'cooperative societies' consisting of members of their own families and were farming their land as one unit. These 'cooperative farms' had been formed primarily to escape the operation of the act on the ceiling on size of farms. The large land owners would have lost part of their holding which was above the ceiling, if they had not formed the cooperative. I edited the reports, adding a brief introduction in which I summarised the findings of the study.

The introduction did not please S. Tarlok Singh at all because it indicated that there were no real cooperative farms in the Project Evaluation Centres. He therefore wrote an Introduction which stated that cooperative farming could succeed in India. On seeing this Introduction, I mentioned that with the Introduction written by him, the study should be published as a document of the Planning Commission, and not as a document of the P.E.O. This made him furious, but he did not show his anger. After a few days he asked me to publish the study with my Introduction as a P.E.O. document, which I did. A few months later, when he met Prof. Karve at a meeting, he told him : "Prof. Karve you have left the P.E.O. but you have left your conscience behind". In retrospect, I am sorry that I had alienated S. Tarlok Singh on a trivial matter without realising it at the time.

II

TRAVEL : MAY-JUNE 1954

Kamla accompanied me to the Development Commissioners' Conference at Ooty. After the Conference we travelled for three weeks in the three southern states of Kerala, Tamil Nadu and Mysore. Both of us regard this travel as our honeymoon travel which we enjoyed greatly and during which we got to know each other well. We had been married in 1953 in Hoshiarpur, where her father, Dr. M.L. Gulati, was posted as head of the medical service in the district. But we had not had a honeymoon because the day after she came to live with us in Delhi, I left on one of my tours. Kamla greatly resented this but had not complained about it. We visited Kerala first and spent almost a week travelling through its central part. Arrangements for our travel and stay at various places were made by Mr. K.T. Varkey, the Evaluation Officer in-charge of the Project Evaluation Centre, located in Chalakudy, a small town located a few miles north of Kochi. Our travel included visits to the temple at Kaladi, the birth place of Shankara, (or Adi Shankaracharya) who formulated the doctrine of Vedanta. Shankara was a genius; during his short life of 32 years in the eighth century A.D., he travelled all over India, and made a pioneering and successful effort for the revival of Hinduism and decline of Buddhism in India. The decline was due also to the fact that many corrupt practices had crept in among the Buddhists. Shankara established four *Maths,* located respectively at Kedar Nath in the Western Himalayas in U.P.; Dwarka along the sea coast in Gujarat, Jagannath Puri in Orissa and Sringeri in the South. These *Maths* in the four corners of India are among the most important places of pilgrimage for devout Hindus and remain to this day, great centres of learning Hindu scriptures.

We visited also the small church believed to have been located at the spot on which a church had been built in the fist century AD by St. Thomas, who is believed to have brought Christianity to India. St. Thomas was one of the twelve apostles who were present at the last supper taken by Jesus Christ before his crucifixion in Jerusalem.

Kamla and I both fell in love with Kerala. It was so green, with fields of rice, groves of cashew nuts, arecanuts, pepper and other spices, and of coffee in the uplands. Both men and women wear white and are the cleanest people that I have seen in rural India. However, we saw also great poverty among the women workers who stand in waist deep water in the marshes to make coir by beating the husks of coconut. Our greatest pleasure was travelling in boats in the backwaters of the state.

Coconut oil is the principal cooking medium in the State. Every dish, except boiled rice is made with coconut oil or coconut milk as a principal ingredient. The food is highly spiced. I remember that while large tiffin boxes containing rice, curd and a variety of curries were brought for our meals at the guest houses in which we stayed, I would take only rice and curd because I could not stomach the highly spiced dishes, but Kamla who did not mind eating spicy food had a full meal.

After a week of travel in Kerala, we spent a few days travelling through Tamil Nadu. Our principal stops in this travel were Coimbatore, Erode and Madras. We stayed for two days in Coimbatore, where the Czech owner of Praga Button Factory, which was the principal supplier of buttons to *Bauji,* had arranged for our stay in the guest house of the Coimbatore Club of which he was a member. He also put at our disposal a car which took us round this principal textile industry centre in the South. We greatly enjoyed our stay. Kamla and I liked particularly the colourful jacaranda trees whose deep orange flowers covered the entire compound of the guest house. The stay in Erode, where there was a project evaluation centre was rather uninteresting. The Tamil countryside was dry, because the rains had not yet arrived and except for the areas irrigated by wells, many of which had electric motors to lift water, the land was lying fallow. Jayachandran, the Project Evaluation Officer was very critical of the working of the CD programme. He mentioned that 'public participation' in the construction of public works, such as approach roads to villages and buildings of primary and secondary schools was a fraud. He explained that the presidents of the village panchayats so arranged the accounts that the works were constructed mainly out of the grants given by the Community Development Administration and the taxes collected by the Panchayats, and no additional funds were collected by them for construction of these works.

We stayed in Madras for two days. I took Kamla round the city which I had seen earlier during my travels to Colombo. It had not changed much during the intervening five years. We took most of our meals at the Woodlands Hotel , which formed part of a chain of restaurants throughout Tamil Nadu. I appreciated its spice-free food. When I admired the cleanliness in the restaurant, the manager was so flattered that he took us to the kitchen and shared us how spotlessly clean it was. Madras and all the stations at which our train stopped during its journey through Tamil Nadu, were full of beggars. They had been conspicuous by their absence in Kerala. Another difference was that while tea was served in all road side villages in Kerala, in Tamil Nadu only coffee was served at railway stations.

From Madras we travelled to Bangalore, Mysore city and Mandya, where there was an evaluation centre. The area between Bangalore and Mysore city is irrigated by a canal on the Kaveri river, and is the most prosperous part of the state. Among the sights of the state we enjoyed most the palace of the Maharajah, set amid vast lawns in the heart of Mysore city and the Vrindavan Garden, laid out by Sir Mirza Ismail the town planner—Prime Minister of Mysore State during the 1930s. The gardens which are a few miles outside Mysore city follow the pattern of gardens like Shalimar in Kashmir and Lahore, laid out by the Mughal Emperor Shah Jahan. We saw it after sunset, when the fountains splashing water in the shallow canals, in the background of multi- coloured electric lights created the atmosphere of a fairy land. Because of its location at an altitude of 3000-4000 feet the area between Bangalore and Mysore is cool even in the summer. Mandya, where the Project Evaluation Office was located was in those days a medium-sized town with a population of about 60000. It was the centre of the sugarcane producing area of the state and had two sugar mills.

In contrast to Jayachandran in Erode, the evaluation officer, Moorthy, greatly appreciated the work being done by the community development project, both in providing essential service facilities to the villages and improving yields of the principal crops — rice and sugarcane, through its agriculture extension programme. Mysore is the principal raw silk producing state in India and Mysore city has a large silk mill. Kamla bought three silk sarees which she wore for years.

Bangalore, which had been built by the British early in the nineteenth century as a cantonment for stationing their troops for the defence of Mysore state, has steadily grown to be the largest city in Karnataka. It had a population of about 500,000 in the early 1950s and had extensive lawns and gardens within it. It was not crowded or heavily polluted then, as it is now. The only factory, located a few miles out of the city was that of Hindustan Aircraft, which had been established during Second World War primarily for repair of aircraft. The principal means of public transport besides buses were scooters. I cannot forget the bumpy rides in them. In contrast to the drivers of the 3-wheeler scooters in Delhi today, who are generally rude and past masters in the art of overcharging, the drivers in Bangalore were courteous and scrupulously honest. From Bangalore, we returned to Madras to catch the train for Delhi. The travel back took two days. We were stuck by the transformation in the countryside in central India which had taken place during the three week interval between our departure and return. The monsoon rains had started and the hills and plains, which had been brown earlier, were so green.

III

THE FAMILY 1953-58

While I was enjoying my work in the P.E.O. the situation at home was not free from tension. After our marriage, Kamla and I began to live with *Bauji, Beji* and my younger brother, Narendra as members of a joint family. My younger sister, Amrit, had been married to a young man who held a degree in pharmacy and was working in a small drug manufacturing firm. *Beji* and *Bauji* liked Kamla very much. However, as was her habit, *Beji* would often throw a tantrum on some small matter. One reason for the tension was that while Kamla had been used to living in a home with several servants, *Beji* would never keep a full-time servant or even a part time maid for such tasks as cleaning the house and utensils, or washing clothes. She was afraid of them. She thought that most of the servants or maids were rude and were petty thieves. Besides they would take leave and not be available when you needed them most. Kamla showed remarkable capacity in adapting to living in a servant-less household.

Thus *Beji* and Kamla had the primary responsibility for looking after a household several members. Our two sons, Virendra and Arvind were born in 1955 and 1957 respectively. *Beji* was mighty pleased. She had a deep desire to have grandsons and Kamla had fulfilled it. She would bestow all her love on helping Kamla raise them and would get very disturbed when they suffered some minor ailment. Virendra was particularly prone to having them. *Beji* would get worried and would often try traditional treatment on him, which would make him worse. One afternoon in his excitement on seeing the dog of a neighbour he fell down from the verandah of our first floor flat on the lawn of the ground floor flat. Fortunately, although he had fallen about 12 feet on a cemented floor, he did not sustain any injury. But Kamla got a tongue lashing for not looking after him well.

In 1956, Narendra, who had graduated as an Electric and Mechanical Engineer from Delhi Polytechnic, left the house to join the Indian Army as an officer in the Corps of Electrical and Mechanical Engineers. *Beji* and *Bauji* were very happy that he had got a well paid job in the army.

When our second son, Arvind, was born the pressure on Kamla's time increased greatly. She had to raise two young children, besides participating in household work without any assistance.

Despite tensions, our six years in Meena Bagh were a happy period. We had a comfortable flat located near my office and had good neighbours. They included Subhash Dhar, a colleague in the Planning Commission. His wife, Neelanjana, daughter of G.L. Mehta, was particularly friendly to Kamla.

During the first year of our marriage, Kamla and I would often go to see English movies despite *Beji's* objection. On Sunday afternoons, we would go to the small canals in the long green between the buildings of the Central Secretariat and the India Gate which had been built to commemorate the memory of the officers and men of the Indian army who had died during World War I. I would hire a tiny boat and pedal down the lake, singing 'Cruising down the river on a Sunday afternoon'. This was a very popular song during the years that I was in the U.S.A. Kamla would love these afternoons. Our other pleasure was to see the annual flower show held in March quite near our house.

When I became Director of the P.E.O. I was senior enough to be invited with Kamla to the reception given by the President in the Moghul Gardens which formed part of the Rashtrapati Bhawan complex, on an afternoon immediately before Republic Day on 26 January. The garden laid out on the pattern of the Shalimar Garden has shallow canals with fountains playing in them amid its lawns. The flowers in the innumerable flower beds were in full bloom at the time. It was a delight to attend this reception.

Watching the parade, and the folk dances in the evening of the Republic Day and two evenings after it was another pleasure. Kamla and I would often be invited by Dr. Ensminger to attend receptions hosted by him in honour of some visiting dignitary of the Ford Foundation. We would enjoy attending these receptions. Once we were invited for dinner by the American Ambassador who was greatly interested in the progress of the community development programme.

7

Joining the I.A.S. 1958-59

In 1956, the Union Public Service Commission announced that in order to overcome the shortage in the number of IAS officers in the central and state governments, about 250 officers would be recruited; 150 through promotion of officers of the administrative services of the states and 100 by direct recruitment. I was one of the nearly 23,000 persons who applied for joining the service through direct recruitment and was selected.

On the morning when the list of successful candidates was going to be announced, Kamla told me that I would be selected and would have the 23rd position in the order of merit of the persons selected. We wonder to this day how her forecast came true because I did get the 23rd position among the 100 successful candidates. The candidates were to join the service in August 1958 for a six month training course organized for them in Simla, before going to the states to which they would be posted.

Meanwhile I availed myself of a five week assignment with the Food and Agricultural Organization (FAO) of the United Nations, located in Rome, in order to advise its Nutrition Division on evaluation of its programme of assistance to various developing countries. During this period, Mr. S.K. Dey I.C.S., whom I had known as Development Commissioner of West Bengal and who had been appointed Special Assistant to Mr. B.R. Sen, the new Director General of the FAO, told me one day that the D.G. planned to establish an Evaluation Division within the FAO and asked me if I would like to join the organization to establish it. The appointment would be permanent and my salary etc., would be fixed taking into consideration my age and experience of service in the Government of India. This offer threw me in a dilemma; on the one hand there was an opportunity of a permanent appointment in an international organization; on the other hand, there was the offer of joining the highest administrative service in India.

After thinking about Mr. Dey's offer for a day, I politely declined it. This was one of the big mistakes that I have made in my life. I had made two friends in the FAO and should have consulted them before taking a decision. One of them was Mr. Rao, Deputy Director of the Nutrition Division; the other was Dr. Erich Jacoby, who had known me when he came to India as member of an FAO Team to evaluate India's land reform programme. Both of them would have advised me to accept the offer. One fact which influenced my decision was that many senior FAO officers were flirting with good looking secretaries and many had extra marital relations with them. It did not strike me that their life style was no concern of mine and that I could continue to live a perfectly normal family life as most Indian experts were doing. I never got such an offer again although I longed for it throughout my service career. The English saying 'Fortune never smiles on a man twice' proved to be true in my case.

Shimla

Within a few weeks of stay in Simla I came to the conclusion that I had made a serious mistake in joining the IAS. The officers were expected to do a variety of jobs and the principal criterion for judging an efficient officer was that he or she should be able to do them reasonably well. Second, since my salary was higher than what I would get under the rules framed by the Home Ministry for fixation of salaries of officers of different seniority, I would continue to get my existing salary and would not get any increments for several years.

I had opted for an assignment Rajasthan in preference to Punjab, for three reasons. First, it was near Delhi, so that I could come to Delhi easily in case of need. Second, it was free from the recurring agitations of Akali Sikhs which made the job of officers like Deputy Commissioners of districts extremely difficult. Third, the then Chief Minister of Punjab was an overbearing man and one had to obey his order to the letter breaking rules if necessary.

The staff of the training programme consisted of a Principal and lecturers in economics, political science and law. The Principal was Mr. Jacob, a senior and kind officer from Kerala. His bearing was so much like that of a priest that we used to call him Papa Jacob.

Mr. Pathak, a lecturer in law was most interesting. He would insist that we memorized every word of the relevant sections of the Indian Penal code, the Criminal Procedure Code and the Law of Evidence which an IAS officer needed to know for being a successful District Magistrate and understood their precise implications. His insistence cast such a spell on us that we spent an enormous amount of time in trying to satisfy him.

The training was organized in Grand Hotel, an old hotel, which was owned and managed by a Department of the Central Government. Because of the limited number of rooms in it, two trainees had to share a room. My room-mate was Mr. Laldenga, from Mizoram, a small state with a strategic location on the border of India, Myanmar and East Pakistan (now Bangladesh). He was a nice fellow and we got along very well. He was a devout Christian and told me that all the tribes of the North East had been converted to Christianity by missionaries who had educated them and done welfare work among them without disturbing their traditional tribal organization.

One day when he received a letter from home that bamboo trees had flowered, he told me that there would be famine and great political trouble in his home region. The flowering of bamboo trees is followed by a rapid increase in the number of field rats who eat not only the bamboo flowers but also most of the rice crop, which is the principal food of his people. His word proved prophetic because there was a great scarcity of food despite the central government's efforts to supply rice to the area by air, which did not have good road connections. The insurgency which followed lasted for several years and was controlled with great difficulty by the Army. It ended finally when the separate state of Mizoram was constituted in the late 1960s.

Besides the rooms in which the trainees lived, the hotel had a small number of cottages in which families could live. Kamla and the children came to stay in one of them for a month during October-November. Both of us enjoyed this visit.

On joining the IAS and leaving New Delhi, I had to vacate my flat in Meena Bagh. The Estate Officer allowed me to retain it till January 1959, when the family moved to the small two-bedroom annexe of our house in Lajpat Nagar. *Bauji* had been allotted the building lot of 800 sq. yds in 1954. He started construction in August 1958 when he knew that we would have to vacate the Meena Bagh flat. The annexe consisting of two garages, one of which *Bauji* used as a bedroom and two bedrooms on the first floor had been completed by January 1959; the main house was constructed during 1959-60.

Two of my classmates, when I was studying for my M.A. degree, who belonged to Simla, had opened a book shop. They had an excellent collection of old books written by British officers describing Simla and its environment in the late 1840s when it was made the summer capital of British India. They had also a good collection of Tibetan wall paintings (locally called *Tankas*) which depicted various events in the life of Lord Buddha and his disciples. They persuaded me to buy some of them. I regret not buying them as the prices of *tankas* have gone up steeply.

Our six months in Simla included two months of winter. Occasionally the town would be under a blanket of snow. On these days we would stay in our rooms for much of the day and would come out only in the afternoon when it was comparatively warm. During the winter, the Principal organized two visits to places outside Simla. One was to Kufri and Narkanda, located about 15 and 20 kms. respectively north west of Simla which had been built by the British for winter sports like skiing. The ski slopes in them are still widely used by Indian tourists. In Kufri there was a small cottage with a telescope through which one could have a magnificent view of Annapoorna and other snowbound peaks of the western Himalayas. Narkanda is a small village which was famous for a hotel called Wildflower Hall because planted in its compound were the best looking wild flowers found in its environs. The hotel, which was built of wood was burnt some years ago and has unfortunately not been rebuilt by the Government of Himachal Pradesh or the Tourism Development Corporation of India. I wish it had been rebuilt because it would be very popular with the tourists, Indian and foreign. Furthermore if its garden was replanted, it would have great educational value for the tourists and students in Himachal Pradesh.

The second trip was to a small town situated about 60 km below Simla. On this trip I saw for the first time the effect of drinking on my fellow trainees. Some of them would burst into laughter after the first drink; others would become quarrelsome while still others would slump to sleep after a couple of drinks. I did not drink. The drinking was in a way a stress reliever. Most of the trainees were in their early or late thirties, who had not done any study for years after leaving college. Thus, they found the need to pass the law examination quite strenuous.

Jodhpur

After completing the training course in Simla, four of us, who had selected Rajasthan as their state of posting went to Jodhpur for our training in the field. The group included besides me, Mr. B. Hooja, a journalist-cum-broadcaster who had worked for a couple of years in the India section of the BBC, besides years of work in Delhi; Mr. R.C. Sood, who had a business background and (the late) Mr. Mukerjee who had worked as a lawyer for a company in Calcutta. The training included three months of stay in villages and small towns which formed part of community development blocks in Jodhpur and its adjoining Nagaur district, both of which formed part of the desert of western Rajasthan.

We began our training with a three week stay in Nagaur. During this stay our duty was to learn to survey croplands for settling the revenue payable by the farmers to the State government. Nagaur was a small town, with a population of about 15,000. From its brown, mud-brick houses , narrow winding streets, and turrets and numerous mosques, it looked like a Middle Eastern town.

A large proportion of its population is Moslem. The town is famous for its cattle fair, held every year in March in which bullocks, buffaloes, horses, camels, sheep and goats are bought and sold.

For training in land records we had to live for three weeks in the small government rest house in one of the large villages. Mr. Sood had wisely brought with him a servant who used to cook our meals. After a day spent in surveying the fields we would spend about three hours eating our dinner. Mr. Sood had brought also a supply of beer and would burst into laughter with the first sip which would continue until dinner was served.

Our next stop for three weeks was in a small town, Phalodi, located at the edge of the Rajasthan desert. Here we saw the effect of scarcity of drinking water on the lives of villagers. Men living in villages or hamlets which did not have their own drinking water wells would ride their camels for 8-10 km. from their homes every day to fetch water from a well which had sweet water. The water was carried in large leather buckets strapped on both sides of the animals.

Most of the men are Bishnois, followers of a faith started by Jamboji, who they revere as a prophet. The 29 tenets of their faith include rules of conduct which they follow scrupulously. Men and women are tall and well built; the women are quite good looking. They are strict vegetarians and do not allow killing of deer, peacocks or other wild animals or cutting of trees in the areas inhabited by them. Thus the tenets of their faith are well adapted for preserving the flora and fauna of their region.

While staying in Phalodi, we visited one day a small town called Kheenchan. Its population of about 6000, consists mainly of old men, women and children of Marwari merchants who work as traders in Mumbai, Pune and small towns of Maharashtra. They have built large brown sandstone houses called *havelis* for their families whom they visit for a few weeks every year or on occasions like marriages and funerals. The older Marwaris were strict vegetarians, teetotallers and lived very simply, despite their wealth. They married invariably within their caste.

In Western Rajasthan, most of the rainfall is received in a few showers during July and August. In some villages, the houses of the more affluent villagers have small tanks just below the roof in which rain water is stored for drinking through the year. There are few deep wells, but there is a large number of *bawaris,* (shallow step wells) into which the women have to walk to fill their earthern or metal pitchers with drinking water. The women of merchants and Brahmins invariably tie a muslin covering at the mouth of the pitcher. This covering, filters the water against ingress of an insect's eggs, which if it enters the body breeds in it and comes out as long worms. Extraction of the worm is very painful. Often the limb has to be chopped off by a surgeon in order to protect the patient from death because of gangrene. I saw many sufferers from this disease during my work as Collector in Sawai Madhopur.

After completing three months of training in the field we were posted as Assistant Magistrates in Jodhpur. The job consisted of trying cases of petty crime like small theft and quarrels between individuals which resulted in non-serious injuries. The training is not too relevant because Rajasthan has a separate judicial service. The only use of the training is that it forces the young trainee officers to get to see the conditions under which the farmers live and work.

Kamla and the children joined me in Jodhpur. We had some difficulty in finding a suitable house. The first house we rented was a newly built house in a new, well planned neighbourhood. But there were snakes and scorpions in it. Arvind, who was only two year old barely escaped being killed by the bite of a black scorpion whose bite can be fatal. Therefore, we moved to a house in an older neighbourhood. This house, although well built and spacious, was near a waste water pond, with the result that the children occasionally fell sick. Virendra, who was four at the time, joined his first school, St. Patrick's Convent, which was within walking distance from the house. Kamla or I would accompany him to or from the house. One morning Kamla noticed that Arvind was walking by himself and asked me to go and bring him back. When I reached him, I found him mumbling, *Moo bhai ke school ja raha hoon* (I am going to the school of my brother, Vinoo). Thereafter we were careful that he did not stir out of the house unescorted in order to escape being hurt by a speeding cyclist or by a motor driver.

Jodhpur was at that time a medium sized city with a population of about 150,000. It was built below and around the fort, perched on a small hill. The fort used to be the residence of the ruler until the early 1930s, when a new residence, Umaid Palace, was built by Maharaja Umaid Singh, the grandfather of the then Maharaja, during the 1930s.

Umaid Palace is a magnificent structure, built of yellow sandstone and located about 3 km. outside the city. It was vacant at the time because the then Maharaja who was only 12 years old was studying in England. His father, an adventurous young man had died a few years earlier, when the small plane that he was flying crashed by hitting an electric cable. We got a good tour of the palace, courtesy of the caretaker, a retired I.A.S. officer from U.P. The palace is now being run as a deluxe hotel by the Taj Group of hotels of Mumbai and is popular with the tourists. It has beautiful frescos on its walls and ceilings and rich tapestries.

Most of the people of Jodhpur are Hindus or Jains. The men are tall and well built and wear beautiful saffron colored turbans above their shirts (jackets or waistcoats in winter) and *dhotis* or narrow trousers called 'Jodhpurs'. The women wear a long scarf to cover their head, a blouse and a sari or long skirt. The scarf and the skirt are made of cloth which is printed in a tie and dye (or *bandhani*) design for which Jodhpur is famous. The design, consists of printing small white dots within a colored fabric. It is popular in Delhi and abroad.

Because of its proximity to Pakistan, Jodhpur has a large cantonment for the residence of a contingent of the army. Besides, it has a school for training of pilots of the Indian Air Force. Thus it is a city of considerable strategic importance.

After completing our nine-month training, we were expecting to be posted as junior officers in various departments of the Rajasthan Secretariat in Jaipur. While the other three got these postings, I did not, because Mr. S.K. Dey, Minister of Community Development persuaded the then Chief Secretary, Mr. B. Mehta, to release me to be posted as the Vice Principal and Director of Research at the Central Institute of Community Development at Mussoorie.

The Institute had been opened in early 1959, as the apex institution for training of senior officials such as Collectors, Deputy Development Commissioners, and Presidents of *Zilla Parishads,* the district-level institution in the Panchayati Raj programme. The central concept of the programme, recommended by the Balwant Rai Mehta Committee, was that rural development should be overseen by elected institutions of the rural people, established at the village (or multi-village level in case of very small villages) community development block and district levels.

The village level institution was to be called the *Panchayat,* the block level institution was to be called the *Panchayat Samiti,* while the district level institution was to be called the *Zilla Parishad.* The officials of the community development organization, as well as those of some technical departments of the state governments would work under the administrative control of these institutions, while taking technical direction from their superiors in the technical departments. Thus, the village level worker, the multi-purpose extension worker posted in a group of five or more villages, and primary school teachers would work under the *Panchayat.* The Block Development Officer (BDO) and his team of technical officers in agriculture, animal husbandry, education, primary health care etc., would work under the directions of the *Panchayat Samiti,* while taking technical directions from their superiors in their respective departments.

The BDO was to be the Secretary of the *Panchayat Samiti.* The position was different at the district level. The District Development Officer appointed to coordinate rural development programmes in the district became the Secretary of the *Zilla Parishad* which was responsible for coordination of the development programmes in the district. However, the district level officers of the technical departments would be advisers to the *Zilla Parishad;* their administrative control and technical direction remained with their respective departments. The Collector was expected to be the 'friend, philosopher and guide' of the institutions and would periodically report to the state government on their working. Rajasthan was the first state to introduce Panchayati Raj in October 1959; most other states introduced it in the early 1960s.

Mr. Dey was keen on my appointment in the Institute because he had had difficulty in finding suitable staff for it. Two Development Commissioners and a Joint Secretary in his Ministry had served as Acting Principals of the three courses organized by the Institute during the summer of 1959. The Vice Principal, an IAS officer from Bihar, who had been appointed for three years, had to leave within a few months of his appointment because there were some adverse reports about his personal conduct.

Mr. Dey had been impressed by my work as Director of the P.E.O. and felt that I had both the technical expertise and administrative capacity to get along with the Principal, Mr. S. Chakravarti ICS and to establish the Institute on a sound footing.

I was not too keen to join the Institute for three reasons. First, I knew that Mr. Dey had become an overbearing boss, since his appointment as a Minister. He liked to have yes men under him Second, I felt that since I had joined the IAS, I should work as an administrative officer for two to three years before being drafted as a technical officer. Third, I did not believe that Panchayati Raj in which Mr. Dey believed passionately, would achieve its stated goal of accelerating rural development programmes. I felt that these institutions being political bodies would be preoccupied with the struggle for dominance between rival groups and individuals. In the prevailing social situation in rural India, the institutions would be dominated by people of high castes or the dominant cultivating castes and the programmes for welfare of the Scheduled Castes and other poor rural people would suffer.

However, since Mr. Dey and Mr. Mehta, the Chief Secretary were good friends, the latter agreed to my release for the Institute.

8

Mussoorie, 1959-60

I joined the Institute in October 1959. It was located in the summer palace of the former Nawab of Rampur, a small princely state in U.P. It had several buildings which included a large building for holding lectures and seminars and rooms for the Principal, and other staff. It had a magnificent view of the Doon Valley. The Principal's residence was a spacious bungalow, was in another hill with a good view of Mussoorie town. The Vice Principal's residence which we occupied was a 3-bedroom bungalow located just below the Principal's residence. It had a nice view of the valley to the east of Mussoorie town, where the National Academy of Administration is located.

Other buildings included houses for lecturers, the Manager of the estate and clerks and messengers. Kamla and the children joined me soon after I joined the Institute. We stayed in Mussoorie till the last week of December, when the Institute closed for the winter to reopen in March. During this period, Mr. Chakravarti, the Principal and I visited a number of centres for training block development officers and other workers of the community development programme. I remember, particularly, our visit to Nalanda in Bihar to see the ruins of the large residential University for training Buddhist monks and nuns who went out to different parts of India and neighbouring countries of South East Asia to spread the tenets of Buddhism and convert the people to Buddhism. It was due to the work of missionaries trained at Nalanda and similar other universities that people of most countries of South East Asia from Myanmar and Sri Lanka to Thailand and Vietnam and of Central and West Asia from Tibet, Afghanistan, and Mongolia to China, Korea and Japan were converted to Buddhism.

In West Bengal, we visited Viswabharati, the University founded by the great Bengali poet, Rabindranath Tagore, because a training centre for community development workers was located within its large campus. In Shantiniketan, where the university is located we saw besides the residence of the poet located under sprawling trees, a small art gallery which housed his paintings and those of other Bengali artists. Besides being a great poet, Tagore was a painter, a writer of novels and short stories and a pioneer in rural development. He and the staff and students of Vishwabharati spent much time in working for development of the villages located near it. Vishwabharati with its large open spaces was an oasis of peace, located next to Bolpur, a bustling, crowded and dirty small town.

Another vivid memory of the tour is of our visit to the Administrative Staff College located in Hyderabad which trained high ranking officials of companies and public sector industrial units in the essentials of good management. After seeing its beautiful campus, Mr. Chakravarti decided that he would strongly recommend to the Minister that the Institute should be shifted to the environs of Hyderabad.

Hyderabad is the capital of Mr. Chakravarti's home state Andhra Pradesh. He successfully persuaded Mr Dey to shift the Institute to Hyderabad. The Institute, now called the National Institute of Rural Development, is located in its large campus a few miles out of Hyderabad city. I was invited to deliver a series of lectures in it in 1991.

The institute conducted two training courses during the three months October-December before it closed for the winter. Among the trainees I remember particularly Mr. Srichand Chhabra, who was then the Deputy Commissioner of Jullandhar in Punjab. He was a lover of beauty and told me that if he became the President of the New Delhi Municipal Committee he would fill the round-abouts in New Delhi with fountains. His wish was fulfilled, and during the two years that he was the president of the NDMC, he did build a large number of fountains.

Kamla and the children joined me in March when the Institute reopened after the winter break.

Our only friends in Mussoorie were the Sens, a Bengali couple. Mr. Sen was an officer of the Audit and Accounts Service, and was the head of the small local office of the Accountant General of Uttar Pradesh. We would spend a couple of hours together every evening, walking up and down the Mall and having tea at our house or theirs. Mr. Sen had a deep and resonant voice and was very fond of singing songs composed by Tagore.

By the time I left the Institute in October, it had besides the Principal and Vice Principal, three other professors. Two of them were Americans recruited and paid for by the Ford Foundation. The third was an Indian.

The Institute conducted a number of 6- week courses on community development and Panchayati Raj programmes. The courses were attended by Collectors, Presidents of *Zilla Parishads,* Deputy Development Commissioners and division-level officers of the technical departments. Each course consisted of lectures by the staff of the Institute or by distinguished visitors, and discussions by groups of trainees from different states. The discussions showed that although Panchayati Raj had been introduced in several states it had not contributed to acceleration of rural development programmes. On the contrary, in several states the working of the Panchayati Raj institutions had been marked by inter-personal squabbles between various influential members which had caused a setback to progress of rural development programmes.

The distinguished visitors to the Institute included, Jaiprakash Narayan, the well known leader of the Socialist Party. He spoke for about three hours in a faltering voice in which he outlined his concept of rural development and the rural development work that he and some of his assistants were doing in the centre for rural development that he had established in his home state of Bihar. Despite being a poor speaker, he apparently had such charisma that it made him the successful leader of the revolt against political corruption, suppression of civil liberties and persecution of her political opponents by Mrs. Indira Gandhi, during the three years (1974-77) of Emergency rule by her. The revolt was successful, Mrs. Gandhi had to resign and a Government, initially headed by Morarji Desai remained in office for three years (1977-80) when it lost the election and Mrs. Gandhi returned to power.

I cannot understand what contributes to political charisma, because both Gandhiji and Jaiprakash who were so unimpressive to look at, had such charisma that they could mobilize the Indian people and political leaders to follow them.

Mr. Dey visited the Institute to see its working in August 1960. He had a 3-hour long meeting with the staff, in which I could not help explaining the difficulties in the working of the Panchayati Raj institutions as expressed by the presidents of the *Zilla Parishads* and officials of the state governments who had attended the various courses conducted by the Institute. This explanation did not please him at all.

I had heard also that in response to an offer of a 3-month consultancy appointment by the FAO, he had written that I would not be available, because I was doing important work at the Institute. After the meeting, I mentioned to him that while I had no objection to his refusing to release me, he should have informed me about the offer. This infuriated him and he said, "You do not deserve to be an I.A.S. officer". I kept quiet after this outburst but resolved that I would leave the Institute at the end of my 1-year appointment.

After Mr. Dey had left, Mr. Chakravarti told me that I should not have insulted the Minister by explaining the difficulties in the working of the Panchayati Raj programme and by mentioning the consultancy offer.

This episode brought home to me the mistake that I had made in declining the offer of a permanent appointment with the FAO and joining the IAS. I had declined a permanent appointment in the FAO and had now annoyed the Minister over a short term consultancy.

After Mr. Dey left, I telephoned Mr. Thapar, the Appointments Secretary in Rajasthan whom I knew slightly that I wished to return to Rajasthan and work as a Collector in a district near Jaipur. He replied that the State government would agree to my return. I wanted to work as a Collector because I wanted to see first hand, the working of rural development programmes and the economic and social conditions of villages, about which I had been writing since 1953.

We left the Institute in October 1960 and stayed in Delhi for two weeks with *Bauji* and *Beji* before I received the order of my appointment as Collector of Sawai Madhopur, a district located about 125 km. east of Jaipur. Furthermore, Sawai Madhopur town was on the Delhi Bombay railway line so that one could reach Delhi from it in about six hours. The formal agreement of the Ministry of Community Development to my release did not present any problems.

9

Sawai Madhopur and Pali, 1960-62

I was Collector[1] of Sawai Madhopur district for 20 months from November 1960 to June 1962 and of Pali district of Rajasthan for 4 months from June 1962 to October 1962. Kamla and I thoroughly enjoyed our stay in Sawai Madhopur and learnt a lot about the social structure, level of living and values of the rural people of the area. The rural studies that we did there were never published, but doing them gave us a lot of satisfaction. The posting in Pali, a district in western Rajasthan, having semi arid conditions, was a punishment posting as is explained later.

We arrived in Sawai Madhopur to live in a large 3-bedroom house, with a large lawn and a vegetable and fruit garden in which there were innumerable trees of the most delicious papayas besides other fruit. The house was located in Man Nagar, a township which had been planned and built in the early 1940s to house the offices and residences of the Collector, the Superintendent of Police and other district and sub-divisional level officers who were posted in Sawai Madhopur. It was called Man Nagar after Sawai Man Singh the former Maharajah (lit. ruler) of Jaipur; Sawai Madhopur was a district of the former Jaipur state. Man Town was connected with Sawai Madhopur town, a small town with a population of about 15,000; by a metalled road.

Sawai Madhopur railway station is the junction station where the Delhi-Bombay railway line and Sawai Madhopur-Jaipur railway line meet. It is about 125 km from Jaipur. There are two roads linking Sawai Madhopur with Jaipur. One of them could be used throughout the year, but the other could be used only for eight months of the dry season. It could not be used during the rainy season because the water in the river Banas about 30 km. north of Sawai Madhopur was too deep for crossing by jeep.

Located near Man Nagar was the largest cement factory in India. The power house in the factory supplied electricity to the houses in both Man Nagar and Sawai Madhopur town. However the smoke from the factory which passed over Man Nagar when the wind blew in the wrong direction. was a health hazard.

II

VISIT OF QUEEN ELIZABETH II OF BRITAIN AND HER HUSBAND, AND THE DUKE OF EDINBURGH, IN JANUARY 1961

As soon as I arrived in Sawai Madhopur I learnt that I had two important assignments ahead of me. The first was to provide security for the royal couple who were coming to Sawai Madhopur for two days in January 1961 at the invitation of the ex-Maharajah of Jaipur for a tiger shoot in the jungles of Sawai Madhopur. The visit was private and all arrangements for the stay of the royal couple and the tiger shoot would be made by the ex-Maharajah. My duty was only to ensure their personal safety with the help of the police. The second assignment was to conduct elections to the Panchayats in February 1961.

A New Market

In order to make foolproof arrangements for the safety of the royal couple, the Superintendent (Head) of Police and I decided that about 40 shops located in temporary wooden structures next to the junction of Jaipur-Sawai Madhopur and the Delhi-Bombay railway lines should be moved to another location in Man Nagar. The shops had been built in 1948 by Sindhi shopkeepers who had come to Sawai Madhopur from Sindh soon after the partition of British India, in August 1947.

The shops though illegally located on government land were allowed to remain there because they supplied the day-to-day shopping needs of residents of Man Nagar and the neighbouring villages.

After we had decided on the relocation, the Sub Divisional Officer of the Public Works Department was asked to ascertain the precise number of shops and mark out a plot of suitable size in Man Nagar for their relocation of all the shops. After the site had been demarcated, I called a meeting of the shopkeepers and told them about the need for and the proposed relocation of the shops. In this meeting I explained to them that their present location on government land was illegal and that they could be evicted at any time, but the new sites allotted by me free of cost would be permanent and no one would evict them.

They agreed to the relocation, but the next day they went back on their agreement. Investigating the reasons for this *volte face*, the SDO found that they had been instigated by a liquor vendor whose main business was to send bottles of whisky and other hard liquor to Mumbai (where there was prohibition) during the 30-minute stop of the Delhi-Mumbai train; the profits of the transaction were shared equally between him and the manager of the dining car attached to the train. Location away from the railway station would put a stop to this lucrative business. On learning this, I called the liquor vendor and threatened him with arrest for engaging in smuggling. This made him agree to the shift, and the process of relocation was completed a few days before the visit of the royal couple. This little market of 40 shops had grown over the years to house about 200 shops when we revisited Sawai Madhopur in 1977. The plots were being allotted by the Sawai Madhopur Panchayat Samiti, at a price which provided a handsome income to it.

A few days before the Queen's visit, a group of Jains of Delhi went to Dr. Rajendra Prasad, the then President of India, requesting him to order stopping the killing of buffalo calves which were used as bait for the tigers, at the spots where the tigers came in the evening or night to drink water. This age-old practice had developed because the hunters erected *machaans* on top of which there were seats for two or three hunters at the spots where the tigers came most frequently. At one or two of these spots the hunters sat on the *machaan* and shot the tigers from them. The President assured them that the killing would be stopped and this assurance was duly conveyed to me by the Chief Secretary of Rajasthan. When he telephoned me about this, I told him, "Sir, as an officer with long experience you know that the practice cannot be stopped". He laughed and said, "I know, you let the killing go on and just keep quiet about it." I heard no more.

A few days before the visit of the royal couple, Sawai Man Singh II,[2] the ex-Maharajah of Jaipur, came to Sawai Madhopur to see for himself the arrangements that had been made for the tiger shoot. He was a tall, dark, handsome man in his late 40s. Sawai Madhopur was his home district; he was the younger son of a small *Jagirdar*[3] of Sawai Madhopur. He became the Maharajah of Jaipur because the previous Maharajah, Sawai Madho Singh was childless and had chosen him as his successor. He can be regarded as the man behind the building of new Jaipur, the city located outside the boundary wall of the old city which had been built in the eighteenth century by the then Maharajah, Sawai Man Singh I.

Sawai Man Singh I was a genius. Besides being a great commander, he was a great scholar of Sanskrit, a town planner and an astronomer. Old Jaipur that he built had wide shopping streets and residential streets feeding into them. It was planned according to the principles of town planning laid down in ancient texts. Old Jaipur is called the Pink City because all the buildings facing the *bazaars* are made of pink sandstone.

Soon after he became the ruler in the early 1940s Sawai Man Singh II invited Sir Mirza Ismail the town-planner Prime Minister of Mysore, to become the Prime Minister and lay out a plan for building the city outside the city walls, in order to house its growing population and to provide modern commercial, cultural and recreational facilities like a large public garden, a museum and a zoo. Sir Mirza laid out the plan of a city with these facilities and wide motorable roads linking different neighbourhoods. On Sir Mirza's retirement in the mid-1940s, he invited Sir V.T. Krishnamachari to be the Prime Minister of the state. His major contribution was to modernize the land records of the state and bring them in line with those in British ruled provinces like Punjab.

Although I was not required to do so, I called on the ex-Maharajah, as a mark of respect for his past status. He had such respect for Sir V.T. Krishnamachari that when I mentioned to him that I had worked as his private secretary, he took an instant liking for me and asked me to accompany him on his inspection of the various sites which had been chosen for shooting the tiger. I gladly accepted his invitation. During this tour of about three hours he identified 11 places with pug marks of tigers. On the basis of this inspection he identified two places for erecting *machaans* for the tiger shoot. His judgment based on long experience as a hunter proved flawless because these were the two places from which a tiger and a tigress were shot.

During the tour we passed through several villages. I was stuck by the affection, respect, and reverence for him in the eyes of the men and women, who came out of their homes to see him. The look in their eyes seemed to say, "You are and will always remain our real Maharajah, although you have ceased to be one after the accession of Jaipur state to the Indian Union." I was amazed by this response of the people on seeing him, because I had read a great deal about the misdeeds of the princes and that the people of their states suffered them only because they had the protection of British troops and the people could not remove them.

I remember him also sitting for a few minutes at the base of the Ranthambhore fort, holding the cast iron cannon balls which were used in battles in earlier centuries, with nostalgia. The distant look in his eyes seemed to say "All this was once mine. But it had to go and I have no regrets that it is gone".

He was a keen businessman who had invested the money that he had got from his land and urban property in Jaipur city so well that he was considered to be one of the richest men in India. It was stated that he was one of the few *shikaris* (lit. hunters) who could shoot a tiger riding an elephant. This is a very risky operation because a wounded tiger can jump on the slow moving elephant killing or severely wounding both the beast and the rider.

Later, during the visit of the royal couple, I saw also his youngest and favourite wife Maharani Gayatri Devi, who was considered to be one of the most beautiful women in India and was much written about in women's magazines in the 1950s and the 1960s.

The Visit of the Royal Couple

The royal couple arrived by a special train from Jaipur on a cold January morning. I received them at the railway station which had been especially decorated for the occasion with a red carpet covering the entire platform. My impression of the Queen was of a cold person, with a look in her eyes which reminded me of the cold hills and brooks of Scotland. She did not smile while shaking hands with me or the other officers who received them. The Duke seemed, however, a much warmer person. I saw the Queen smile only after a successful shoot in which the Duke shot a tiger and his secretary shot a tigress. They stayed in the Maharajah's shooting lodge which was located at the edge of the forest about 2 km. from our house.

The arrangements for shooting the tiger are such that the poor beast cannot escape being killed. When it is known that there is a tiger in a particular part of the jungle, 200 to 300 men assemble on three sides of the jungle shouting and beating drums. In order to escape from them the tiger runs to the fourth side, where there is a *machaan* with the hunters sitting on it. As soon as the tiger appears, the hunters shoot, killing or severely wounding the beast. The severely wounded tiger is very dangerous because it is bound to jump at and kill human beings or cattle. Therefore the hunters must locate it with the help of the villagers and ensure that it is killed.

When I heard that a tiger had been spotted in a part of the jungle and a *haaka* (shouting and beating of drums by villagers) had been organised, I rushed to the spot. I had just arrived when I saw a large tiger jump and fall dead from a bullet from the Duke's gun. The next day the Duke's secretary shot a tigress. The royal couple and party left by a special train for Jaipur where they stayed two days before leaving for home.

About 200 journalists, Indian and foreign, wanted to come to Sawai Madhopur to file a report on the visit of the royal couple. When I explained to the Chief Secretary that there were no facilities for their stay the Government prohibited their going there. Thus, they had to base their report on the visit by the briefing given by the secretary of the Maharajah.

On hearing about the tiger shoot from my driver, Tufail Ahmed, and the other servants my sons were keen to see a tiger. We had gone about 4 km. into the forest when the driver suddenly stopped the jeep and asked us to be absolutely quiet. After a minute we saw a small tiger cub going to a rivulet to drink water about 200 metres ahead of us. We were all thrilled. From his long experience of driving in this forest, Tufail had sensed the coming of the tiger. He explained to us later that when a tiger is passing all the birds and animals in the forest become absolutely quiet. The animals become quiet in order not to attract his attention to escape being killed. Incidentally, throughout our 20-month stay in Sawai Madhopur we saw a tiger again only once, although we would often go to the forest.

Driving into the forest was one of the favourite pastimes of the family. On Sundays, we often had our lunch in the forest sitting by the side of a brook. I have always loved to watch the flow of water. It reminds me of the flow of days and nights in our lives. We would see herds of *sambhar* (a large brown horned deer), *cheetal* (the beautiful, golden spotted deer which is one of the fastest animals in the jungle) black buck, wild boar and several multi coloured wild birds.

Another favourite pastime was to spend a night in a rest house located along one of the numerous irrigation tanks which are full immediately after the rains. At this time there are hundreds of birds, ducks and others, swimming in the tanks or resting along their banks and feeding on the vegetation, and on the small fish. On these visits, Bijay Singh, the office messenger who invariably accompanied me in all my travels, would pack our food, water and bedding into the jeep. Early morning was the best time to see the birds. Kamla and I would enjoy seeing them by getting up early and walking along the banks of the tank. The boys would go with Bijay Singh.

When we arrived in Sawai Madhopur, we found that there were 11 persons working in the house. All of them were messengers in the offices of the Collector, the Sub Divisional Officers and the *Tehsildars*. The previous Collector, Mr. Mool Singh, was an officer of the Rajasthan Administrative Service, promoted to the IAS. He needed them because I was told that 30 to 40 persons were fed by him every day. Most of them were members of his extended family; others were visitors from his home town. We sent several servants back to their designated jobs and retained only four persons for our limited needs. They included a cook, Bijay Singh, the driver and an elderly Moslem (we called him *mian*) whose duty was to shop for our food. One of his duties was to stand at an interval of two to three days at the railway station and obtain a loaf of bread from the dining car of the Frontier Mail, the only train which had a dining car. Bijay Singh and Tufail Ahmed were among the best personal staff that I have seen in my life.

III

SAVING A PART OF THE SAWAI MADHOPUR FOREST

A few days after I arrived in Sawai Madhopur, I got a file on my table which said that the previous Collector had approved cutting down of a part of the forest in which the tiger shoot took place and the contractors who were to do the cutting were outside my office, waiting for my signature. Being a firm believer in conservation of the natural habitat, I was in no hurry to give the final order. Therefore, I wrote on the file that I would look into the case only after the panchayat elections, when I would have the time to study the file and ascertain the views of the concerned technical officers - the District Forest Officer (DFO) and the District Agricultural Officer (DAO). This greatly angered the contractors who had made all arrangements for cutting the trees. They used to supply free firewood for the previous Collector's kitchen. Their anger and dissatisfaction was conveyed to me by the local MLA, who, had been instrumental in obtaining the permission of the previous Collector. The argument used to justify cutting of the forest was that it would make available cultivable land which could be allotted to landless farmers, mostly of the Berwa *chamaar* (lit. leather worker) scheduled caste.

After the elections, when I studied the file, I found two interesting facts: (i) the DFO and the DAO had both strongly opposed the cutting of the forest, and (ii) the Board of Revenue of Rajasthan had pending for decision before it a case in which the Berwa *Chamaars* had petitioned for cutting the forest to obtain land for cultivation, while the *Gujjars* (lit. herdsmen) who grazed their cattle in the forest had strongly opposed it. The Collector had no authority to order the cutting of trees until this case was decided.

If he ordered the cutting, he would be guilty of contempt of the Board of Revenue and liable to such punishment as the Board may recommend to the state government. I duly conveyed this fact to the MLA as well as to the representative of the chamaars, who used to meet me in my ofice from time to time. The case was not decided until I left Rajasthan and apparently the decision of the Board of Revenue and the Rajasthan government must have been against cutting of trees, because the forest still stands and is part of the Ranthambore Game Sanctuary.

It is named Ranthambhore because the historic Ranthambhore fort which was the seat of a small Rajput kingdom in the thirteenth and fourteenth centuries is located in it. There is a historic legend associated with the fort. It is said that Padmini — the queen of the Rajah (lit. ruler) of Ranthambhore was an extremely beautiful woman and that Ala-ud-din Khilji, the Pathan ruler of Delhi wanted to marry her. Since her husband was in no mood to oblige him, Khilji laid siege to the fort. The siege lasted several months, and when the Rajah saw that defeat was imminent, he and his soldiers came out of the fort to battle with the pathans dressed in saffron clothes, the traditional suicide robe of Rajput warriors. They were all killed, while their women including Queen Padmini committed suicide by burning themselves in the fort. Thus, Alla-ud-din captured the fort and became the ruler of the territory of the Rajah but he could not obtain even a glimpse of Padmini.

Kamla and I would visit the fort often and see the spot where the mass suicide was stated to have been committed. I was impressed by the large area, within the ramparts of the fort, the several tanks and a large area of cultivable land besides palaces and places of residence of the officers of court and of the soldiers defending the fort. Thus it contained besides the royal couple, a community of soldiers and other functionaries within its ramparts. As a result, the Rajah, his ministers and a select force of soldiers could live in it for months while resisting an invader.

The Ranthambhore game sanctuary has now become one of the main tourist attractions of Rajasthan. It is visited by thousands of tourists in the winter and spring. The sanctuary has herds of wild animals mainly *sambhar,* black bucks, *neel gai* (blue bull) besides a few tigers and thousands of birds. The Maharajah's shooting lodge has become a hotel.

The representative of the Berwa chamaars who would see me often with the request for cutting down the forest, thought that I might grant the permission, if I got some bribe. One afternoon, when I was away from the house for village studies and Kamla was alone, two women came to the house and asked the constables guarding the house that they wanted to see her because being poor rural women they wanted to explain to her their problems which would help her in our village studies. On getting the permission, they saw Kamla, talked about their condition for some minutes, and then threw a bundle of notes containing Rs. 800 at her and ran away. Kamla was nonplussed. I had established a reputation for personal honesty and ensuring that corruption among the staff of my office was reduced to the minimum. But here was a bribe of Rs. 800 which would sully my reputation if she kept it.. Therefore, she immediately called the Additional District Magistrate, explained the episode and handed over the money to him. The ADM deposited the money in the sub-treasury located within the Collector's office and arrested the representative of the *chamaars,* the next day. When I returned home, I admired her for her presence of mind. The *chamaar's* representative was kept in the 2-room lock-up for two days and then released after an apology because there was no documentary evidence against him.

The practice of keeping a 24-hour guard of armed policemen at the gates of the residences of the Collector and the Superintendent of Police, in order to prevent entry into their houses of any intruders and to guard them and their family members from attack by any person(s) whom they had alienated by their decisions, was introduced by the British. It was abolished in some states but it continued in Rajasthan. The house was so large that it had a small room in one corner of the yard where the policemen cooked his food and slept during the night. Our elder son, Virendra, was so fascinated by the stay of the policemen and their practice of saluting the Collector whenever he entered or left the house, that he insisted that he should have a uniform exactly like theirs.

IV

PANCHAYAT ELECTION, JANUARY 1961 AND GENERAL ELECTION MARCH 1962

During my 20-month stay in Sawai Madhopur, I had the responsibility for conducting these two elections. Elections to single or multi village panchayats (the bodies responsible for rural development in the villages) under the Panchayati Raj system, offered me an opportunity to visit all parts of the district which extended over an area of about 2500 sq. km. I found great interest among the people in voting for members of these bodies. Groups of men and women, dressed in their colorful best, would go singing and dancing to the various polling booths to exercise their vote. There was no comparable interest in the General election through which members of the Rajasthan assembly and members of Parliament were elected, and large numbers of people did not vote. Reflecting on the contrast, I concluded that the rural people realised that the decisions of the MLAs and the MPs would not affect their lives as much as those of the president of village panchayats and other members of the panchayati raj institutions.

The arrangements for conducting the panchayat election were finalised in consultation with the 4 sub Divisional officers and 11 *tehsildars* of the district. It was decided that there should be about 500 polling booths in which the people would go to exercise their vote. These would be located in buildings of primary or secondary schools, offices of panchayats or other vacant buildings which were large enough for establishing the polling booths and the residence of the officials who were conducting the poll.

The arrangement for stay of the polling parties were made by the *patwaris*. The *patwaris* were under the direct control of the Collector through the *tehsildars* and the sub-divisional officers. Seeing this role of the *patwaris* I felt that orderly governance of a state depended upon the *patwari* obeying the orders of the Collector in letter and spirit. The day this stopped, orderly governance would end and I cannot visualise the state of governance thereafter.

The General Election of March 1972

The arrangements made for the panchayat election were followed also for the General Election. Sawai Madhpur had 8 constituencies for election of 8 members of the state legislature and formed part of 2 constituencies for election of members of Parliament. One of the two constituencies was reserved for a member of the scheduled castes or scheduled tribes.

The general election taught me two things. First, that the polling process was an agent of social change. The Rajput ex- *Jagirdar* who would not have allowed a person of the scheduled caste to enter his house before Independence was going to their hamlets to seek their votes for himself.

Second, that the electoral process led to monetary corruption. Each of the two constituencies for election to the Parliament had a population of about 1 million and about 400,000 voters. The candidate for the post of a member of Parliament, had to incur large expenditure in the form of arranging vehicles for election tours etc. Furthermore most of the workers canvassing for him had to be fed and paid small amounts in order to compensate them for their loss of earnings during the time that they were working for him. Only a wealthy person could become a candidate for an M.P.

The constituencies for election of member of the state legislature were much smaller but large enough for the election expenses to be afforded only by a person with relatively high income. If he did not have it, he would have to borrow the money from his friends and relatives. He too had ample opportunities to be corrupt if he was elected, because a recommendation by him on behalf of a wealthy contractor or businessman could swing the government's decision in the latter's favour. But if he lost the election, he would be in debt for the rest of his life. The newspapers are today full of allegations of massive corruption by MLAs, MPs and Ministers including a former Prime Minister. Without going into the veracity of these charges, I would say that there is need for radical reform in financing of election expenses in order to reduce corruption.

Expenses by a candidate on fighting the elections to the state legislature or Parliament are enormously larger now than in the early 1960s. One reason for this is that serving food and liquor to the 'volunteers' canvassing for a candidate has become common. Serving of liquor started in the late 1960s and has progressively increased. And the opportunities for corruption are much greater now because contracts are much larger in value.

Before 1969, leading business houses made large contributions for elections to the Parliament and state legislatures. They were duly recorded by the treasurers of various political parties and were permitted by the Election Commission. However this practice was disallowed thereafter, with the result that the parties and the candidates have to get money from various sources — business houses, other wealthy men including smugglers and not report it.

V

VILLAGE STUDIES

My routine work as a Collector was not very heavy and left me a lot of time which I used for village studies.

The economic and social conditions of the people of different castes, their social customs and the child rearing and home making practices of the women of Meena farmers were so interesting that Kamla and I interviewed a large number of men and women and wrote about them. The Collector and his wife going to the villages and talking to the *sarpanch* and the leaders of different communities was a novel experience for the villagers. However, after the initial reserve was broken, leaders of different castes were quite fourthcoming about their economic condition, customs, the impact of land reforms, the working of village level institutions and changes in inter-caste economic and soical relations. With the abolition of *jagirdari* in the early 1950s, the Meena, Mali and Gujar farmers had got full and heritable rights to the land that they had been cultivating. The Rajput former *jagirdars* had reconciled themselves to their changed status as non-cultivating owners of the lands that had been left to them for self cultivation.

The Berwa Chamaars, who were the largest group of scheduled caste sharecroppers and agricultural labourers and had certain obligations in the houses of the former *jagirdars* were adjusting themselves to their changed status. Land reforms had led to abolition of their traditional obligations. They had become peasant proprietors by getting for themselves cultivable wastelands. They were congregating in areas in which such lands were available. They had stopped flaying hides and skins of dead animals and eating meat and drinking and were adopting the customs of the Meenas so that they could be recognised as a clean caste. Wherever they could not get enough land for cultivation, they supplemented their income by working as share-croppers for Rajput, Mahajan or Brahmin landowners or as unskilled workers on roads at the railway station and in the cement factory.

We studied the impact on the economic conditions and life style of the villagers of the community development and other rural development programmes that had been undertaken for their welfare for about ten years. We also studied the working of the *panchayati raj* institutions that had been established two years earlier.

The papers based on our findings that we prepared in 1961 were never published. But when Kamla and a social scientist revisited the same villages in January, 2001, forty years later, the changes that they observed were so great that we now proposed to publish our observations

Earlier, these people were poor, illiterate and stricken with disease. Now, most of them have risen to middle income status and are literate and well informed. In 1961, the Meenas, Malis, Gujars and Chamaars thanked their stars if they could enough cereals to eat and avoid hunger during the lean season (August - October) before the summer crop of sorghum or millet was harvested. Now, they have enough cereals to eat and milk, vegetables and fruit form a regular part of their diet. They have enough foodgrains and cash crops to sell and buy cloth, clothes, shoes and other consumer goods and building materials for rebuilding their homes. Their health is much better and mortality among women and children has fallen so much that a large percentage of couples practise family palnning. In 1961, they could not bear to hear about it. In 2001, a large number of women and many men had undergone 'operations' so that they would not have more than two or three children. However, one son was a must for couples of all castes.

Agricultural output has doubled or more owing to the use of tractors for cultivation of land, irrigation by pump sets, powered by diesel oil, and the use of dwarf high yield varieties of wheat along with chemical fertilizers and pesticides as recommended by the agricultural extension officers. Sorghum and millets remain the principal cereals in the summer monsson season, wheat and gram are eaten in winter. Mustard grown at the same time as wheat is the principal cash crop.

There has been a major increase in facilities for education and health care. In 1961, there was a middle school for boys and girls in one of the large villages and a middle school and a primary school for girls and another large village. Now, there are five schools each in both the large village. In 1961, there were 175 boys and 5 girls in the school in the large village; now there are 400 boys and 350 girls in the school in the same village. There had been similar increase in the number of schools and students in the other large village. The primary school in the hamlet of the Chamaars has become a middle school. In 1961, it was housed in a temple, now it has its own building.

Education of girls was considered useless by the farmers and the scheduled castes. Girls were *paraya dhan* (husband's property). Now, it is appreciated that educated women make better mothers and housewives. They learn something about sanitation, nutrition and health care. Their homes are cleaner, their health and that of their men folk and children is better. Acceptance of the value of education of girls is apparently state-wide. Female literacy has doubled in Rajasthan between 1991 and 2001. In 1961, the villages had virtually no access to medical facilities. The small hospital in Sawai Madhopur town was 15 km. away. Now, there is a hospital run by a non-governmental organisation in one village and a district hospital run by the government within 8 km. of both villages.

VI

WORKER'S STRIKE IN THE CEMENT FACTORY: BUILDING OF AN OFFICERS' CLUB IN SAWAI MADHOPUR

Sometime in the January of 1962, there was a workers' strike in the cement factory. The principal issue in the strike was the workers' demand for payment to them of a bonus of 8 per cent of their wages. They argued that the factory was running to full capacity because of shortage of cement in the country and was making large profits and they were entitled to a share of it as bonus. The management argued that since the price of cement was controlled by the government, the factory was not making large profits. The books kept by the accountant of the factory showed a nominal profit of Rs. 80,000 on an investment of Rs. 6 crores (60 million).

Before the strike began, I called the representatives of the workers and the management to see if a settlement could be reached among them and the strike averted. At this meeting, the workers' leader, a fiery speaker presented the workers' case and told me that since a general election was impending the Chief Minister and the Revenue Minister who belonged to Sawai Madhopur district would intervene on their behalf. I replied that they should be under no such illusion because Sawai Madhopur was not important enough for a visit by any minister.

I told them further that I sympathized with them and would help them if I was consulted by the management. But the workers had to fulfill two conditions to win my support. First, the strike should be entirely peaceful, because it was my responsibility to ensure that there was no breakdown of law and order. Second, I insisted that the supply of electricity to Sawai Madhopur town and the Man Nagar officers' colony was maintained. This was essential because both the town and the colony obtained electricity from the generators in the factory. He feared that workers going to the power house would be used by the management to break their strike. I mentioned that the Superintendent of Police would issue special passes to these workers so that they alone could enter the factory. They agreed and the strike began. It lasted 15 days and was completely peaceful. As I had mentioned to the workers, no Minister came to help them. Even the local MLA said not a word on their behalf.

After about 10 days, a Mr. Jain, who was the secretary of the Sahu Jain group of companies which owned the factory came from Delhi to Sawai Madhopur to see if the strike could be ended. The closure of the factory was causing a huge loss to the management. When he met me, I explained to him that the workers' demand was justified and since they were making good profit they should share some of it with their workers, by granting them bonus. The negotiations between Mr. Jain and the workers' representative continued over the next five days and when an agreement was imminent, Mr. Jain asked me if he could do anything for me. I told him that I did not want anything for myself but would be very happy if the factory management would build a club for Man Nagar. He agreed and a building costing about Rs. 10,000 was built on the plot of land which had been earmarked for it. I hope that the building is well maintained and is being used by families of officers posted in Sawai Madhopur for recreation.

VII

THE VISIT OF MAHARAJKUMAR OF KARAULI

Before the accession of princely states to the Indian Union, Karauli had been a small princely state located in the central part of the district. Its area now formed part of one of the four sub-divisions of the district.

One day, I received a telegram from the Maharajkumar of Karauli that he would arrive in Sawai Madhopur from Mumbai by the Frontier Mail at 1 p.m. and would leave for his home by an evening train, after taking lunch with me. We were surprised by the telegram because although I had heard about him, I had never met him. However, he was met at the station by one of my senior officers and came home for the very simple lunch that we used to have ourselves.

After lunch, he told us that the telegram was meant for my predecessor, Mr. Mool Singh who was a good friend of his and that he was sorry to have imposed himself on us, but he was thankful for our spontaneous hospitality. He invited us to visit Karauli during the Holi festival which was celebrated with great enthusiasm there. We visited Karauli during the Holi festival and stayed for two nights. We stayed in the guest house constructed by the rulers of Karauli for stay of their European guests and other distinguished visitors to the state.

On the first night the Maharajkumar invited us for dinner. He and his beautiful wife who was the daughter of a small prince of western Gujarat were gracious hosts and we thoroughly enjoyed the sumptuous dinner that had been prepared for us. It was a new experience for us to see the large round revolving dining table in which there were 36 small dishes each containing a different curry or a condiment.

After the dinner, the Maharajkumar and his wife came out to bid us goodbye. We thanked them profusely for their hospitality and told them that we would love to have them over for lunch whenever they passed through Sawai Madhopur. After they left, our driver, Tufail Ahmed who belonged to Karauli told us that he was very surprised that the Maharajkumar's wife had come out of the palace to see us off, because she observed very strict *purdah.*

The next morning the Maharaj Kumar came to the guest house and spread before us skins of a large tiger and a bear as gifts for us. We were surprised by his generosity, thanked him and accepted the gifts. The tiger skin remained the principal wall decoration in our houses for more than three decades.

VIII

MEETING OF THREE COLLECTORS AT KHANDAR

Mr. Sher Singh, the Collector of the neighbouring district of Bharatpur was a frequent visitor to our house on his way to Khandar, where he had a farm and a large house for the stay of his family and those of two or three guests.

On one of these visits he told us that he had obtained a licence from the District Forest Officer to shoot a tiger during the *Durga Pooja* holidays in September 1961. I told him that although he had obtained the license from the DFO, I would not allow him to shoot a tiger, because I was the Collector, unless he promised to give me its skin. He agreed and invited us to be his guests during the *Pooja* holidays. He had also invited Mr. A.P. Dewan, Collector of Jaipur, who was our common friend, for stay at the farm house during the holidays. I had known Mr Dewan since we had met in Ootacamund in 1954 and had become good friends. Thus the three families spent a very enjoyable three days at Mr. Sher Singh's farm house. He shot a tigress and gave me the skin, which I got properly dressed for preservation by a Dutch company located in Mysore which had the reputation of being the best taxidermists in India. This skin also remained the favourite wall hanging of our drawing rooms until quite recently.

This visit allowed the three families to know one another.

One memory of this trip is of Mr. Sher Singh personally killing a goat kid in the course of the ceremonial worship of the goddess Durga on the Durga Ashtami day. He told us that all Rajputs—he was one—were devotees of the goddess.

IX

DEPARTURE FROM AND REVISIT TO SAWAI MADHOPUR

We left Sawai Madhopur in June 1962 to join my post as Collector, Pali. The *Sarpanch* of the village that I used to visit most often was in tears when I visited it the last time. I was moved to see this. The workers in the Cement Factory gave me a farewell party in which they thanked me for my assistance in their strike and helping them get the bonus from the management.

Jyotsna, our daughter, who was born in 1963 and I visited Sawai Madhopur again in 1976 when I had come to India on leave from my UN post in Sierra Leone. I was surprised to see how little the place had changed during the nearly 15 years since we had left it. The major changes were the following:

(i) All the 4 villages that we had studied had been electrified. Most of the irrigation wells had electric motors fitted on them. However only the more affluent households had electricity in their homes. Agricultural production had increased somewhat but the villages had changed very little and most people in them had remained as poor and backward as during our stay. I was greatly disappointed to see this.

(ii) The population of both Sawai Madhopur and Man Town had increased greatly, and the 10 km stretch connecting the two was getting dotted with houses and farms producing fruit and vegetables for the markets of Sawai Madhopur, Man Town and neighbouring villages. A motorable over-bridge had been constructed over the meeting place of the railway line and the road connecting Sawai Madhopur and Man Town. The bridge removed a time consuming bottleneck for travel between the two towns.

(iii) The cement factory was running at a loss because of poor management and could close down any day. It was closed a few years later throwing temporarily almost 8000 people out of employment.

(iv) The shooting lodge of the Maharajah of Jaipur situated at the edge of the Sawai Madhopur Game Sanctuary had been converted into a de-luxe hotel run by one of the companies which manages a large number of hotels in India. There was a small 4-bed room guest house run by the Rajasthan Tourist Development Corporation in the middle of the game sanctuary. Both had full occupancy during the busy tourist season of October to April.

(v) Mr. Fateh Singh, the game warden in 1961, was running a profitable agency showing tourists around the game sanctuary and making arrangements for their stay at the hotel or the guest house.

X

COLLECTOR, PALI, JULY-NOVEMBER 1962

Because of my good work in Sawai Madhopur, the Chief Secretary wanted to post me as Collector, Jaipur, to succeed Mr. Dewan who was going on a UN assignment to Sudan. Collector, Jaipur was a prize posting in his view. But it was not without problems. The collector had to keep in good humour all the ministers, senior officials and influential MLAs. Furthermore, he had to contend constantly with some agitation or other launched by a political party or religious group to air its 'grievances'. While Mr. Dewan had handled these with great aplomb, I felt that I lacked the capacity to do this. Therefore, I told him that while I greatly appreciated his offer, I could not accept it and would prefer to be posted in the Secretariat in Jaipur or sent to the central government in Delhi, whenever there was an opportunity for such a deputation. This did not please him at all and he posted me as Collector Pali, a district in western Rajasthan bordering Jodhpur. This was clearly a punishment posting.

I must confess that I have a weakness for annoying my superiors after having done good work. I had annoyed S. Tarlok Singh and Mr. S.K. Dey and now I had annoyed the Chief Secretary who had a great regard for me. I feel also that I should have accepted his offer and if I was not successful as Collector, Jaipur—most likely I would have been—he would have posted me in the Secretariat or deputed me to the central government.

Pali was a medium sized town with a population of about 50,000 in the early 1960s. Its only claim to distinction was that it had a mill manufacturing coarse cotton cloth, established by a Marwari merchant of Calcutta in his home town.

In contrast to our house in Sawai Madhopur with extensive lawns and an orchard, the house was small; the yard was stony where hardly a blade of grass grew. Furthermore it had several snakes, including the highly poisonous cobras, whose bite can instantly kill. The servants warned us to avoid going near one cobra which had been living under a stone for 13 years. Putting it in their picturesque language they said that, "It is the king of the house and all the residents of the house are its tenants."

There was a big problem of water supply. There was no well in the house and we had to fulfill all our needs of water for drinking, washing etc. from a truckload of water supplied by the Municipal Committee. Scarcity of drinking water is a serious problem in western Rajasthan. However, the domestic servants, most of whom had been there for several years were very efficient, and we did not have to change any of them as we had to in Sawai Madhopur. The office staff similarly was quite efficient.

My office work was much heavier than in Sawai Madhopur and I did not have the time for village studies that I had in Sawai Madhopur. One of my principal tasks was to decide about 300 complaints about corruption and arbitrary conduct by presidents of village panchayats or influential members of *Panchayat Samitis*. On examining them with the help of a very efficient Deputy Development Officer, I found that most of them were made by defeated candidates for the office out of frustration on being defeated. We dismissed most of them. However, where we felt that the complaint had some basis, we called both parties, and decided the case. If we felt that the charge of corruption or misconduct was genuine we sent the case for trial to the judicial magistrate.

During my brief stay, I visited all parts of the district and found that its southern part was much more productive than the northern part in which Pali was located. It received more rainfall, and there was a large number of small tanks built on the numerous streams. The hard working farmers produced large crops of grains and fodder. The area had a number of enterprising ex-Jagirdars who bred race horses which they sold in Mumbai.

The largest reservoir in the south is the Jawai Dam which had been completed in the late 1950s at the cost of several crores borne by the central and Rajasthan governments. However when I visited it in October, at the end of the monsoon when it should have been full, I found that it was only one-third full. This was my first experience of the several uneconomic irrigation projects started under the First Year Plan.

Kamla accompanied me on these tours, and she and the boys greatly enjoyed the travels. One of the most vivid memories of our travel is of a visit to the Jain Temple at Ranakpur. It is a huge temple built of off-white marble, every inch of which is beautifully carved. It is full of idols of the 24 *Tirthankaras* (saints) of the Jain religion, the last of which was Mahaveer, the founder of the religion in the fifth century B.C. Although little known outside, it is visited by thousands of devotees from southern Rajasthan and northern Gujarat and has excellent arrangements for their stay, cooking food etc., in its vast complex. Excepting the Taj Mahal and the great cathedrals of Europe it is the most beautiful building that I have seen and would recommend a visit to it to any friend who wants to visit Udaipur as a tourist. Ranakpur is located about 160 km. from Udaipur and is connected to it by a good motorable road.

XI

THE INDIA-CHINA BORDER CONFLICT

In October 1962, when I was in Pali, there was a conflict between the Indian and Chinese forces on the eastern and western borders of India and Tibet. The conflict which lasted three weeks ended in a humiliating defeat of the Indian forces. As a result of the conflict, the Chinese occupied all the territory that they wanted in the eastern and western sectors and then withdrew. Much has been written about the background of the conflict and the reasons for the defeat of the Indian forces[7]. What concerned us in Pali was to collect funds to pay a part of the cost of the conflict, in response to an appeal by Prime Minister Pandit Nehru.

Mr. Sukhadia, the Chief Minister of Rajasthan had indicated to Pandit Nehru that the Government of Rajasthan would collect enough gold to weigh Pandit Nehru in gold, besides a large amount of cash. The government fulfilled the promise.

The Chief Secretary fixed a target of Rs.100,000 and as much gold as would be contributed by the people of Pali. When the Chief Secretary told me about this target, I called a meeting of the officers, assisting the Collector. They told me that the largest contribution would be made by the merchants in the textile market and that the best person to arrange the contributions from them was the manager of the textile mill. The merchants were indebted to him for supply of the cloth manufactured by the mill, which they sold at a handsome profit. The manager promised to do his best in getting the contributions from the merchants.

Two days after my first meeting with him, he came to me in the morning with the request that I should accompany him that afternoon to a meeting of the textile merchants in their *panchayat ghar* (community centre) where all the textile merchants would assemble and announce their contributions. I did and cannot forget the experience because it gave me an insight into the working of the traditional organisation of Indian businessmen. All the textile merchants were present in the meeting. Eleven of the biggest merchants announced contributions of 1000 each. Smaller merchants announced contributions of between Rs. 500 and Rs.1000. If a merchant announced a contribution smaller than what his peers thought that he should make, they would argue with him and make him agree to the contribution that they felt he should make. All of them kept their promises; their total contribution was Rs.50,000. There was not a case of going back on his promise because any one who did, ran the risk of being ostracized by the others in his business. Since most of them were related to one another, the renegade ran the risk also of having great difficulty in finding suitable matches for marriages of his sons and daughters.

We had much greater difficulty in getting contributions from the Moslem manufacturers of plastic bangles. They were quite wealthy because the bangles were very popular with the women of Pali and neighbouring districts. We fixed a modest target of Rs.5000 for them, but had much difficulty in getting the contribution. They argued that they could not afford to make such a 'large' contribution. The officers did succeed however in getting them to agree to make the contribution. At the risk of being called a communalist, I could not help thinking that in contrast to the textile merchants, they did not regard the India-China conflict as their 'cause'.[4]

Another memorable experience of this campaign relates to the offer of contributing all her jewellery by a Rajput widow. She came to my office one afternoon and put before me all her jewellery as her contribution to the 'national' cause. The office staff who knew her advised me to politely decline the contribution, because if I accepted her jewellery, which was all she had, she would become a pauper. I had great difficulty in persuading her to take her jewellery back. The target of a contribution of Rs.100,000 was met. The people of the district also contributed a large quantity of gold.

In October 1962, Mr. Mehta visited Pali and asked Kamla and me how we were doing. We told him that we were quite happy. But he was perceptive enough to conclude that we were not and decided that a four month stay in Pali was punishment enough for defying his wishes and that he would transfer me to Delhi at the first opportunity. The order of my transfer as Deputy Secretary to the Planning Commission came a month later. We were happy to bid farewell to Pali although we had enjoyed our brief stay there.

NOTES

1. The Collector is the officer responsible for maintenance of peace and security, collection of land revenue and performance of a host of other duties.
2. Sawai (lit. one and a quarter) is a title conferred on the rulers of Jaipur by the Mughal Emperor, Akbar, to indicate the superiority of the rulers of Jaipur over the other Rajput rulers. The ruler of Jaipur was the first Rajput ruler to ally himself with the Emperor in the 16th century. He gave his sister in marriage to the Emperor and accepted service as a commander in his armies. The rulers of other large state like Udaipur and Jodhpur which did not capitulate to the Emperor until much later, regarded the rulers of Jaipur as traitors to the Rajput cause.
3. *Jagirdars* were people with responsibility for collection of land revenue and maintenance of peace and security in the few villages forming part of their *jagirs*.

4. For a biased account written in defence of his failure to lead the Indian forces to victory, see B.M. Kaul's, *The Untold Story*. Lt. General Kaul was the commander of the Indian forces in the eastern sector. When he saw that defeat was imminent, he fled to Delhi on grounds of being sick.

10

Planning Commission, 1962-1966

It was a meeting of the Planning Commission's National Development Council held in October 1965, called to provide guidelines for preparation of the Fourth Five Year Plan. Besides the members and top level advisers of the Planning Commission, Chief Ministers of state governments and some senior ministers of the Central Government were present. Mr. Lal Bahadur Shastri, who had become the Prime Minister and Chairman of the Commission, after the death of Pandit Nehru in May 1964, was presiding.

Opening the meeting Mr. Shastri said, "as you might know war has broken out between India and Pakistan. Our forces have crossed the border in Punjab and are within six miles of Lahore. Now I would request the Chief Ministers to assemble at my house for a more detailed briefing". Not a word more was said and the meeting was adjourned. I was impressed with the directness and brevity of Mr. Shastri's remarks. He did not make a speech as Pandit Nehru might have done in a similar situation.

The war lasted for three weeks. A cease fire was brokered by the Secretary General of the United Nations, Mr. U. Thant, and an agreement to end hostilities was brokered by the Russians in Tashkent, four months later in January 1966. Mr. Shastri died of a massive heart attack on the night after signing the agreement.

Mr. Shastri was a man of short stature , which made him look very unimpressive. But behind the unimpressive appearance there was steely determination and a clear vision of what he wanted to achieve. Furthermore, he was honest and maintained a frugal life style. As soon as he took over, he initiated policies which have been described later in this chapter. If he had lived longer, there would have been major changes in policies, and some of the mistakes that gave a major setback to India's development and economic growth could have been avoided.

The Rajasthan Government had been pressing the Central government for some time that the number of its IAS officers working in Delhi was too small and should be greatly increased. The government was so anxious that the Chief Secretary had placed before the Establishment Board almost the entire list of IAS officers to select any officer whom a Ministry or Department would accept for work in it. Since I had already worked in it, my name was accepted by the Planning Commission to work in it as a Deputy Secretary.

We arrived in Delhi in November 1962 and started living with my parents in our Lajpatnagar house until March 1964 when we moved to a government allotted flat in Bharati Nagar which was much closer to my office than the house in Lajpatnagar.

My parents and we were very happy with our stay together. We were with them after a lapse of four years. They were alone and lonely because my younger brother, Narendra, was away with his family at his place of posting in the Army. The boys were admitted after some hassle to the Frank Anthony Public School, which was quite close to the house.

But I was not happy with my work in the Commission. I had expected to join the Agriculture Division of the Commission because I considered myself to be well qualified for it on account of my experience in the PEO, supplemented by field experience in two districts of Rajasthan. The head of the Agriculture Division was also keen to have me; I knew him very well because he was Deputy Development Commissioner in U.P. when I was in the PEO and we had met several times. However S. Tarlok Singh decided otherwise and at his insistence, I was posted as Deputy Secretary in the newly established Natural Resources Division, headed by Mr. M.S. Randhawa ICS.

Mr. Randhawa and I worked together for about three years and I developed excellent working relations with him. He was one of the most remarkable men that I have met. Trained as an agricultural scientist before joining the Indian Civil Service, he was a good scientist, an excellent administrator, and a well known art critic. He was the Deputy Commissioner of Delhi during the Hindu-Moslem riots in late 1947 and early 1948 and but for his administrative ability, the death toll would have been much higher than the actual several thousand. He used to tell me about his meetings every evening with Sardar Patel, the then Home Minister of India to brief him about the situation in Delhi; how simply Sardar lived, and how precise he was in his instructions. He was also an outstanding art critic, who had written several books on Himalayan paintings of the seventeenth and eighteenth centuries. He was also writing a book on Indian art in collaboration with the American Ambassador to India, Mr. John K. Galbraith.

However, workwise we were both wasted. I helped him write short monographs on India's principal crops. They were discussed with the research scientists and economists working on the crops, but little action was taken on their recommendations. The whole effort was a waste of time and money.

Later Mr. Randhawa was transferred as Agricultural Commissioner in the Ministry of Food and Agriculture. His main duty in this job was to ensure that supplies of improved seed of India's main food, fibre and other important crops, chemical fertilizers and pesticides needed to increase production reached the farmers in time. Being the person that he was, he enjoyed the job thoroughly and did it very well. The system developed by him for timely distribution of the essentials of increasing agricultural output and appropriate extension education for their use made a major contribution to rapid increases in output of cereals in the late 1960s, when new very high yielding dwarf varieties of wheat, developed by Dr. Norman Borlaugh in Mexico and modified by Indian agricultural research scientists to suit Indian conditions, began to be used by farmers in Punjab, Haryana, some districts of western Uttar Pradesh and two districts of western Rajasthan in which a large area was irrigated. Their use spread like wild fire because under conditions of adequate and controlled water supply and with use of chemical fertilizers and pesticides and improved methods of cultivation, the use of these seed varieties increased yields of wheat by two to three times. As a result, the country which had to import 9-10 million tonnes of wheat from the U.S.A. during 1962-64 became self-sufficient in cereals by the end of the 1960s.

II

PLANNING FOR CALCUTTA

Mr Randhawa's departure was also the signal for me to be shifted to more interesting and useful work. Prof. M.S.Thacker, the member-in-charge of the Natural Resources Division, had been appointed by the Central government as its liaison officer with the Government of West Bengal to ensure speedy formulation of a long-term plan for the development of Calcutta, India's second largest city, and capital of British India until 1911, when the capital was shifted to Delhi.

Keeping in view the numerous problems of the city ranging from widespread unemployment among educated Bengali youth, a severe shortage of housing, extremely inedequate supply of safe, pollution-free drinking water, poor sanitation and a chaotic transport system which were causing great dissatisfaction among its residents, a special allocation of Rs. 100 million had been made in the Third Five Year Plan (1961-66) for programmes aimed at alleviating these problems. The West Bengal Government had created a new organisation, the Calcutta Metropolitan Planning Organisation (CMPO), to prepare a comprehensive long- term development plan for the city and its surrounding towns. The Ford Foundation had fielded a large team of about 20 experts—physical planners, economists, geographers, sociologists, experts in finance, housing, water supply, drainage and transport to assist the CMPO.

However relations between the West Bengal officials and the Ford Foundation experts were so bad that stories began to appear in local newspapers that the Ford Foundation experts, mostly Americans, were spies appointed to keep watch and report to the American government on the political situation in the highly sensitive Eastern India against the background of the defeat of Indian forces by the Chinese in 1962, and the Cold War between the U.S.A. and the Soviet Union and China. These stories created an ugly situation for the Government of West Bengal, the Central Government and the Ford Foundation. All of them decided that if a comprehensive long term development plan for Calcutta was prepared soon, the stories would disappear because it would be demonstrated that the CMPO officials and the Ford Foundation experts had done the job for which they had been appointed.

Prof. Thacker's responsibility was to ensure that the plan was prepared as quickly as possible. He had been selected for the job because he knew Calcutta well. Trained as an engineer in Britain, he had worked for several years in the 1930s as Chairman of the Calcutta Electric Supply Co. Furthermore, he had a great capacity to bring different parties together to sort out their differences and reach an agreement. Both the West Bengal Government and the Ford Foundation changed the leaders of their teams. The Government appointed a senior IAS officer with instructions to work in close cooperation with the Ford Foundation experts. The Foundation brought in Mr Jack Robin, who had established a reputation as an able negotiator because of his work in helping formulate an interstate agreement for utilization of waters of some rivers in the eastern United States.

Prof. Thacker selected me as his deputy because of my interest in regional and urban development. I worked with Prof. Thacker for just one year, May 1965—May 1966, before I left the Planning Commission to go as a Professor of Planning at the Kuwait Institute of Economic and Social Planning in the Middle East established by a division of the United Nations. But in that year, a long-term comprehensive development plan was prepared for the Calcutta Metropolitan District which included besides Calcutta and Howrah about 45 small towns. Some of the projects included in the Plan such as a second rail-cum-road bridge over the river Hooghly, along which Calcutta is situated, and an underground railway in central Calcutta were implemented only during the 1980s; others were implemented during the 1970s.

When we first visited Calcutta and held discussions with the West Bengal officials and Ford Foundation experts, we found that an enormous amount of work had been done already on the study of Calcutta's problems and projects and programmes to alleviate them had been prepared by the joint efforts of the senior officials of the CMPO and the Ford Foundation experts, and all that was needed was to make a careful selection of these and prepare the Plan. Our job was to expedite the process and get the two parties to prepare a suitable draft plan within a year. We visited Calcutta several times, to review the progress of plan preparation, select the projects and programmes in order of priority and which could be implemented within the available funds.

Some of the meetings were presided over by the Chief Minister of West Bengal who assured us that his government would take all steps needed to get over any political problems that might arise and would provide its share of the funds needed to finance the projects: the rest would be provided by the Central government and through foreign aid. The World Bank had indicated its interest in contributing to finance implementation of projects for improvement of water supply and sanitation and to consider favourably assistance to the programme for improvement of *bustees* (slums) in which lived most of the city's poor population. The World Health Organisation (WHO) had indicated its willingness to provide technical assistance for preparing programmes for drainage of waste water in order to improve sanitation in the city.

After agreements had been reached on its basic elements viz. the projects and programmes to be included in it and the finances for their implementation, a draft plan was quickly prepared through the efforts of a very able young IAS officer, (late) Mr. Kutty. Excepting for the Transport projects, the others were implemented during the 1970s and contributed greatly to improving living conditions in the city.

The year of work with Prof. Thacker was one of the most productive and pleasant years in my professional career. Prof. Thacker respected me, and I had the satisfaction of doing interesting work. After seeing the problems of Calcutta, Prof. Thacker got so interested in urban development that we visited Mumbai, Chennai and his home city of Ahmedabad to see what work had been done by the planning and development organisations in these cities. All of them had done the basic studies on the problems of these rapidly expanding cities and prepared projects and programmes for alleviating them.

The most interesting project related to building of a new city – New Mumbai – on the mainland opposite the existing city which is located on Bombay island, as an urban and industrial city and linking the two cities by a number of road-cum-rail bridges across the creek that separates Mumbai from the mainland. The plan also envisaged building of another harbour at Uran, to relieve the congestion in Mumbai port. The new harbour would serve the foreign trade needs of the country and would also be used for handling bulk products such as crude oil and petroleum products. New Mumbai and the port of Uran and one eight lane road bridge across the creek have been built. A large number of industries have come up in the new city, which had a population of about 1 million in 1991. The new port has also been built and is being used for handling imports of crude oil, petroleum products, cement and food grains. But the projects have not contributed to decongestion of Mumbai or its port. On the contrary because of rapid growth of its population, Mumbai has become the largest and most congested city in India.

We visited Ahmedabad twice where Prof. Thacker had a large number of friends. A long-term development plan had been prepared by a competent team of architects and town planners to meet the needs of the rapidly increasing population of the city. In one of these visits, I accompanied him to the home of the late Mr. Ambalal Sarabhai because his son, Vikram, a physicist and a pioneer in space research, was his friend. Mr. Ambalal was one of the richest men in India in the 1930s–he was the principal financier of Gandhiji. I was stuck by the utter simplicity of the style of living of the family. Much of the household work was done by the ladies of the family themselves despite the presence of several servants.

During the nearly two years that we were in Bharati Nagar, Kamla began her professional career by starting to teach economics for a few months at the Lady Irwin College for Home Economics and later for a year at the newly opened Kamala Nehru College for Women. She published also in the *Economic and Political Weekly* a number of articles on Indian women's participation in economic activities particularly in agriculture and household and small scale industries. The articles so interested Mrs. Ester Boserup, a Danish economist who was writing her book *Women and Economic Development* which remained for a long time the standard work on the subject, that she included their results in her book . During the course of her tour of developing countries to collect material for the book, she visited Kuwait to discuss the articles with Kamla.

By late 1965, I was getting worried that my salary was barely enough to meet our day to day living expenses and that there would be no money to meet the expense of any emergency like a serious sickness. A UN agency job appeared to be the only solution to the problem. Moreover, a number of senior officers of the Planning Commission were being sent to take up senior positions in various agencies of the UN system. Thus when the Home Ministry invited in 1965, applications from IAS officers who wished to go on deputation to UN agency jobs, I submitted my application. Towards the end of the year I received an offer of appointment as member of a UN-OTC financed team of experts for preparing a 5-year development plan for Iraq. I applied for release from the Planning Commission to take up the post. When S. Tarlok Singh learnt about the offer, he was furious. How dare I apply for appointment to a UN job without requesting him and obtaining his approval. Therefore, he wrote on the file that since I was doing valuable work in the Commission, I could not be released. However on Prof.Thacker's advice, Mr. Ashoka Mehta, the then Deputy Chairman of the Commission overruled him and agreed to my release. Prof. Thacker had encouraged me to apply for a UN agency post in the first place.

The post in Iraq was cancelled because the government decided to postpone setting up the planning team. However, the local UN office asked me if I would like to be considered for the post of Professor of Planning in the newly established Institute of Economic and Social Planning in Kuwait — a small sheikhdom located at the head of the Persian Gulf (the Arabs called it Arabian Gulf) between Iraq and Saudi Arabia. When I read the pamphlet prepared by the UN office in Kuwait on living conditions, I was so discouraged that I would have refused the offer and waited for another post. The pamphlet mentioned the extreme heat and the blinding sandstorms which lasted often for two or three days. However one of Kamla's colleagues in Kamla Nehru College had a relative posted in Kuwait and she advised that I find out about living conditions in Kuwait before refusing the offer.

This gentleman, Dr Sen Gupta, a meteorologist working at the Kuwait airport, described living conditions in Kuwait in glowing terms. He mentioned that intense heat was not a problem because all houses and shops were air-conditioned and the sand storms were not as bad as the UN pamphlet had described. Furthermore, the Government provided to the UN experts and the experts recruited by itself a free furnished house. Consumer goods ranging from food and clothes to durables like refrigerators, air-conditioners, television sets and cars were so cheap that Kuwait could be called a 'shoppers' paradise'. There were several thousand Indians working in Kuwait, and Kuwaitis respected Indians because they had been trading with India for centuries. Many of them had married Indian women and maintained two establishments, one in India and the other in Kuwait. His letter so encouraged me that I sent my acceptance of the offer of appointment.

Pandit Nehru was still the Chairman, but he rarely attended its meetings. His health had deteriorated rapidly after the defeat of the Indian forces in the Indo-Chinese border conflict. The last two times I saw him in a meeting of the Commission and on the occasion of unveiling of a statue of Sardar Patel on Sansad Marg he was so pale and haggard that he looked like a living ghost. He had suffered a massive stroke in January 1964 and although it did not disable him, the weakness caused by it contributed to his death in May 1964.

Mr. Ashoka Mehta, the Deputy Chairman of the Commission was an ardent socialist who had been a successful labour leader in Mumbai. He believed that the 'commanding heights' of the economy should be controlled by the government. By 'commanding heights', he meant all heavy industries and control over large investments and foreign trade. This despite the fact that all the four steel mills and most of the industrial projects established by the government during the second and third five year plans had suffered long delays in becoming operational; their working was beset with major problems and they had not been giving even half the return on investment that had been expected of them. Agricultural output was stagnant and famine, caused by scarcity of cereals to meet the demands of a rapidly increasing population, could be averted only by large imports of wheat, which peaked at nine to ten million tons during 1962/63 and 1963/64 from the USA under the PL-480 programme initiated by it to get rid of its large surplus of wheat. There was rampant corruption in the ministries and offices responsible for issuing licenses for private investment in industry and import and export of goods.

Most of the large irrigation and power projects implemented during the first and second five year plans had also been completed after long delays, large cost overruns and were not yielding the benefits in terms of increase in irrigated area, generation of power, control of floods that had been expected of them.

Mr Anjaria, who had risen to become the principal economist in the Commission and the Ministry of Finance had resigned in 1961 because he did not want to be associated with the policy of allocating the major portion of public investment to heavy industries to the neglect of investment in other sectors, notably agriculture and infrastructure (power, roads, ports, etc.) The policy had been initiated during the second five year plan, on the advice of the Russian economists brought in by Prof. Mahalanobis and was going to be continued in the third plan. He felt that continuation of the policy would lead to economic disaster and he did not want to be a party to it.

The members of the Planning Commission continued to be persons of great ability and experience. They included besides Mr. Mehta, Prof Thacker, S. Tarlok Singh, Prof. V.K.R.V. Rao, (who held charge of Education and other social sectors), Mr. Chandulal Trivedi, who had a distinguished record of service as an administrator including a highly successful tenure as Governor of Punjab, and Professor Mahalanobis.

Discussions in meetings of the Planning Commission continued to be animated. However the Commission had lost most of the influence in policy making that it had achieved in the course of the 1950s. The Ministries of the government took decisions on various policies and programmes on their own and reference to the Commission for its approval had been reduced to a formality. The PEO had also lost the influence that it had in the 1950s. Instead of publishing annual evaluation reports on the entire range of the government's rural development programmes, it published from time to time reports on the working of individual rural development and employment generation programmes. It was headed by Dr. Mukherjee, a young Bengali economist.

After the death of Pandit Nehru, Mr. Lal Bahadur Shastri succeeded him as Prime Minister and Chairman of the Planning Commission. He fought a brief (3-week) but successful war with Pakistan. After his death in January 1966, Pt. Nehru's daughter, Mrs. Indira Gandhi became the Prime Minister. She did not care much about the Planning Commission and the decline in its influence was due partly due to her attitude. Economic policies were formulated by the Ministry of Finance, which was headed by Mr. T.T. Krishnamachari, an extremely able and efficient minister. I had an opportunity to see him several times in meetings of the Planning Commission and was struck by his encyclopaedic knowledge of India and his quick decision making capacity. Prof. Thacker had been appointed to oversee speedy preparation of the development plan for Calcutta primarily at his instance.

The few policy initiatives that Mr. Shastri took in the18 months before the war with Pakistan indicated that his top priorities were completion of projects that were being implemented and concentration of efforts to increase agricultural output. No new large project was started. The policy of increasing agricultural production, rapidly through use of new dwarf very high yielding varieties of wheat under conditions of adequate and controlled irrigation, intensive use of chemical fertilizers and pesticides and improved methods of cultivation that led to such dramatic increase in output of wheat that India became self sufficient in cereals by 1970/71 was initiated during his tenure. He gave adequate importance to the views of the Planning Commission and would attend as many meetings of the Commission as he could.

11

Kuwait, 1966-1970

When I arrived in Kuwait I found that the newly opened Institute had a UN-appointed Director and a Kuwaiti Co-director who were at logger-heads with each other. Relations between them were so bad that the Kuwait Government had written to UNOTC for a replacement for the director. None of the other posts in the UN team of professors had been filled. The director, Dr Charlesworth, an American economist, received me at the airport and took me to my temporary living quarters in a hostel for UN and other experts located about 16 km out of the city. This facility had been created by the government to house UN and other experts until family accommodation could be provided for them.

During the dinner in the evening of my arrival, Prof. Charlesworth poured his heart out and described the difficulties that he was having with the Kuwaiti Co-director, and why he was leaving in about three weeks. I found him to be a high strung man, with a mighty ego. I met him later when I spent a year (1971) at the University of Kentucky. He was a Professor of Economics there. But he was not a gentleman: I found that he had spoken against me to the Dean of Graduate Studies, that I was not fit to be a Visiting Professor in the Department of Geography because I had no teaching experience and had been hired only because I was a friend of the head of the Department, Prof. P.P. Karan.

The next day, I met the Kuwaiti Co-director, Mr. Sulaiman Mutawwa, one of the young western educated Kuwaitis who held the top ranking positions in various departments of the Kuwait government. He could be called a member of the young civil servant mafia which was ruling the country on behalf of the Amir (ruler) and his ministers. He described his own difficulties with Prof. Charlesworth and why he had asked for his replacement, preferably by an Arab economist.

During the next several months while the posts of the Director and other professors were being filled, I read extensively about economic development and planning. I found that although I had worked in the Planning Commission for almost 12 years, I knew very little about the latest literature on the subject. This period gave me an opportunity to fill this gap. Furthermore, I read enough about the economy of Kuwait and how it was being transformed from a small sheikhdom in the Persian Gulf to a modern city state that I wrote a short article on the subject which was published in *Economic Development and Cultural Change*, a highly respected economic journal published by the University of Chicago.

The new Director of the Institute, Prof. Mahmoud-al-Shaffie, an Egyptian economist, and other professors arrived in the next few months, and the Institute started its first training course in September 1966. The professors included an Indian statistician, Dr. S. Shivasubramanian, and an Egyptian industrial economist. Dr. El Shaffie was a very relaxed, amiable man and I developed good personal relations with him. Dr. Shivasubramanian was both a colleague and a neighbour because we were both allotted flats in the same two buildings during my four years' stay in Kuwait. He had two daughters, the younger one was of the same age as Jyotsna. The two became such close friends that Jyotsna would spend more time in their home than in her own. Mrs. Shivasubramanian took very good care of both girls.

Kuwait in the 1960s was a most interesting place. There was hectic construction activity as an old town of mud houses was being replaced by a new planned city built according to a plan prepared by a team of British town planners. The Plan provided for building a number of self contained neighbourhoods each with its own shopping complex and institutions such as primary and secondary schools for boys and girls, district hospitals, mosques and recreation facilities. A number of neighbourhoods had been built and were fully occupied by the time we left Kuwait.

The city had two very well equipped modern hospitals, staffed mainly by Egyptian and Palestinian doctors and para-medical personnel. The shops both in the central market just outside the old town and in the shopping complexes in the residential neighbourhoods were crammed with imported goods—American and European cars, consumer durables such as refrigerators, air conditioners and television receivers, western dresses and luxury goods of all kinds. All the food was imported—wheat and rice from U.S.A, beef from Australia and New Zealand and fruit and vegetables mainly from Lebanon, Syria and Palestine and to a small extent from India. Furthermore, imported goods were extremely cheap, in comparison with their prices in India. A small Fiat car was being sold in Delhi for Rs.12,000 or approx. $2500. In contrast, the prestigious Mercedes Benz 200 car, which only film stars and wealthy men could afford to drive in India was available for as little as $2800. And a one or two year old Cadillac car, the most expensive American car, unavailable in India, was being auctioned for approx. $850. Kuwaiti young men were very fond of buying new American cars driving them for one or two years and selling them to buy new ones.

The native Kuwaitis had been provided free housing built by the government and money to furnish it with basic furniture. Every Kuwaiti was provided a job. The educated Kuwaitis occupied administrative and technical jobs in various departments of the government. The uneducated ones worked as messengers, janitors etc. The number of persons employed by the government was far in excess of the requirement but they were employed because a job had been assured for every Kuwaiti. The government also employed a large number of Palestinians, Egyptians, Lebanese and Syrians. Indeed they performed all the technical and professional jobs in the various departments of the government. They virtually ran the economy. Most of the Indians and Pakistanis — there were about 15,000 of both — worked as shop assistants and artisans. Thus most of the washermen were Indians, while the tailors and barbers were Pakistanis. There were also a large number of nurses from Kerala and house maids from Goa. A few Indians ran their own stores. The biggest department store was run by a Sindhi whose father had come to Kuwait in the 1930s. The oldest clothing store was run by a Punjabi who had come to Kuwait immediately after World War II. We became quite friendly with owners of both of them.

All this prosperity had been built on the oil revenues of approximately $1 billion a year received by the government as royalty from the oil produced by the Kuwait Oil Co. which was owned jointly by British Petroleum and an American oil company, Gulf Oil.

Oil had been discovered in Kuwait in the late 1930s, but its production began only after World War II. It increased so rapidly that by the late 1950s, Kuwait was producing about 10 million barrels of oil a year. Production of oil was unbelievably profitable. Since Kuwait along with the adjoining areas of Iran, Saudi Arabia and Iraq were virtually floating on oil, the cost of production, estimated at four to six US cents per barrel in Kuwait of crude oil was very low. The sale price fixed by the consortium of the world's seven leading oil producing companies was $ 1.59 per barrel. The profits were fabulous despite the fact that, much oil was sold below the fixed price because the supply was more than the demand. These profits were shared equally between the Government and the oil company.

The formula of equal sharing of the profits between the oil company and the government of the host state had been agreed after a revolution in Iran in the early 1950s. Before it the companies paid a much lower royalty to the ruler of the host government and pocketed most of the profit themselves.

The royalty was paid to the ruler and not to the government. But the late Amir, Abdullah al-Sabah of Kuwait who ruled the state in the 1950s decided that except for a privy purse of 10 million pounds retained by him for support of his immediate family and those of the large number of cousins and other relatives, the rest would go to the government to finance an ambitious programme of providing social and welfare services and housing to the people of the state. The housing colonies and the social and welfare services were all financed by the oil royalties. Furthermore, large numbers of Kuwaitis were being sent to universities in Egypt, Lebanon, the U.S.A. and Britain to obtain degrees in the humanities, sciences and in technical and professional subjects. Thus Kuwait was steadily building its own cadre of administrative and professional personnel while the various services were being run by foreigners. The Co-Director of the Institute, Mr.Sulaiman al Muttawa, belonged to the first group of educated youth who were running the Government.

The Kuwait government was also keen on education of women and their employment in the government. The women took full advantage of this liberal policy. Girls outnumbered boys in the primary and secondary schools, and a number of Kuwaiti women had come home after obtaining degrees, mainly in the humanities from universities in the countries mentioned above. These educated women many of whom were working in the Government, were the leaders in modernisation of women and their coming out of the veil[1] Thus Kuwaiti society was undergoing economic and social change at break-neck speed. Kamla did a study about changes among the women of Kuwait with the help of a young educated Kuwaiti woman. The study was published in a collection of studies about changes among Moslem women of the Middle East, edited by two American sociologists.

The effects of these changes were both positive and negative. The first generation of western educated youth came to occupy the top positions in every ministry and department of the government. Those who came a few years after them found that although they had been given jobs in the government, they did not have much to do. This was demoralizing for them. Many of them took to wine and women.

There was a backlash against the rapid westernisation and steady erosion of traditional cherished Islamic customs and values by the older Kuwaitis. It found expression in strong protests against westernisation by the members of Kuwait's Parliament, most of whom represented the older generation of Kuwaitis. Although their protest did not have much effect at that time it resulted in Kuwait going back to traditional Islamic practices when Ayatollah Khomeini of Iran successfully led the protest against westernisation of the Middle Eastern society in 1979.

1. The veil called, *burquah* in India is a dress which covers the women from head to feet. It is the prescribed dress for Moslem women but is now worn only by the orthodox .

We lived in Kuwait until the summer of 1970. I wanted to stay another year so that the 5-year tenure would make me eligible for a UN pension. However in June 1970, the Kuwait Government suddenly asked for my reversion to India. I have never been able to figure out the reasons for this sudden decision. I have a suspicion that it was due to some back-biting by an Indian colleague who had joined the Institute a few months before my departure.

The Training Programme

The nine month training programme organised by the Institute included lectures by the faculty on various aspects of development planning and evaluation of projects, seminars and writing of term papers by the trainees. There were about 30 trainees in each course drawn from Kuwait, Iraq, Jordan, Saudi Arabia. North and South Yemen and Sudan . During the summer vacation Dr. El Shaffie would travel to the various countries which had indicated an interest in sending trainees to the Institute. The trainees were generally middle-level officials who had been working in planning organisations or development banks in their home countries. I learnt a lot about their home countries from the trainees who wrote term papers under me. One of them, an Iraqi, taught me enough Arabic that I could speak a few sentences in it. This knowledge helped me greatly during our travel through the Middle East and Europe in 1968. Another from North Yemen, told me that the pre-World War I Austrian dollar was still the currency of the country. Amazing!

Children's Education

On reaching Kuwait we were immediately faced with the problem of education of the boys. All the schools of the Kuwait government had Arabic as the medium of instruction. However, the Americans had opened an English medium school for education of their children and those of other expatriates. The boys were admitted to this school. The school was closed in 1967, because during the six-day war between Israel and the neighbouring Arab states of Egypt, Syria and Jordan in June 1967, two teachers of the school had written a

1-page article ridiculing the Kuwaitis for their insanitary habits. The article so enraged the government that it ordered immediate deportation of the teachers and closure of the school. Faced with the problem of continuation of their education, I wrote to the Chief Secretary of Rajasthan to recommend their admission to the Mayo College Ajmer one of the best public schools in India. He did and they were admitted to the school, and spent a year there before returning to the American School in 1968 when it reopened.

The Arab-Israeli War

The war which lasted only 6 days in June 1967, gave us an insight into Arab psychology. While it lasted, Kuwait radio and television were constantly broadcasting that the Arab forces would win the war and annihilate Israel, which had been created by the Jews illegally occupying Arab land. Like most other Arab states, Kuwait did not recognise the existence of Israel, so much so that any mention of Israel in American or British newspapers and news magazines was erased before they were allowed to be sold.

The Kuwait government sent a contingent of its small army to Jordan to join the Arab forces fighting Israel. However the war ended before it could join the Arab forces. As is well known, the forces of Egypt and Jordan did not put up much of a fight. The only serious fighting was done by the Syrians on the Golan heights on the border between Syria and Israel. The war resulted in large losses of territory to the Arab states. Israel occupied all the Egyptian land west of the Suez canal. Jordan lost all its territory west of Jordan river and Syria lost the Golan Heights. The Arab casualties were not large except for Syria When the loss was mentioned in the daily coffee meeting of the faculty, Dr. El Shaffie remarked that the Arabs would not let the Israelis rest in peace and would form a guerrilla force to constantly harass them. He was so right. Immediately after the war, a guerilla force, the PLO (Liberation of Palestine Organisation) was formed with Yasser Arafat as the Supreme Commander. Young men of the PLO continued to commit various acts of violence, such as bombing of Israeli buses and cooperative farms and killing of individual Israelis, despite severe reprisals by the Israelis.

Our 4-year stay in Kuwait was interspersed with considerable travelling. During the summer of 1967, after the Institute closed for the summer, we spent three weeks in Iran. We saw Teheran, a very busy metropolis with traffic jams which took hours to clear. Among the sights in Teheran we saw the museum, in which was located the *Takht-e-Tawoos* (the peacock shaped throne studded with gems) used by the Moghal emperors of Delhi which an Iranian invader, Nadir Shah, had brought from Delhi. We spent more than 2 weeks in holiday resorts along the Caspian coast. We found that all the villages along the coast were well planned and were provided with basic service facilities—primary and secondary schools, small hospitals, post and telegraph offices and banks. Iranian women were even more westernised than the young women of Kuwait.

The father of the last ruler of Iran, Raza Shah Pehlawi who had to abdicate in 1979, following the anti-western crusade led by Ayatollah Khomeini, hailed from a village along the Caspian coast. Raza Shah had spent liberally on development of horticulture in his home region and equipping all the small towns and villages in it with basic social and welfare services. We stayed in the old palace of the Shah which had been converted into a hotel. The new palace also served as a tourist hotel. However, an entire floor of the hotel was reserved for the Shah's visit.

II

TRAVEL IN THE MIDDLE EAST AND EUROPE

In 1968, after the Institute closed for the summer, Kamla and I decided that we would undertake a sightseeing tour of the Middle East, western Europe and England in about eight weeks in July and August. We had bought a Morris Oxford car earlier that year; and we hired an Indian driver to take us round. We prepared a very detailed itinerary for the tour to which we adhered by and large. We bought camping equipment and heavy woollens for our three children and ourselves so that we would not be cold when we camped during cold and wet nights in Europe. We decided to camp so as to keep our expenses down although the travel guides told us that we could rent rooms cheaply most countries.

In the eight weeks of our travel, we passed through fifteen countries—four in the Middle East and eleven in Europe. The travel was most enjoyable but not without incident. When we could not get a place to sleep in for the night in London, we slept in the car. In Florence, Italy, our driver got drunk and quarelled with a fellow drinker in a bar. I had to execute a personal bond with the police to get him out of jail. Another night, we slept in the attic of the house of an old German widow who had lost her only son in World War II. She did everything to make us comfortable but her frequent references to her dead son were pathetic.

We had planned to visit Budapest, after seeing Vienna. But the day we were to cross over, troops of the Soviet Union moved into the country and sealed the border so that no one could leave. We were saved an emparrassing situation in the nick of time.

The day we arrived in Baghdad on our way back to Kuwait, we found that the main streets were full of soldiers seated on personnel carriers. There had been a *coup d' etat* earlier in the day and the general who had been in power on our way up to Syria had been assassinated and had been replaced by another. However, the soldiers respected my status as a UN official,, and a diplomat by inference, and allowed us to spend the night in the small hotel in which we had stayed on our way up. We thanked God when we reached Kuwait the next morning.

We were lucky that none of us got sick, except for Virendra, who got a fever from the damp and cold of a camping site in Switzerland. But he recovered soon enough.

Among the European countries that we visited we liked Switzerland best. It was so clean and at the prevailing exchange rate of 4 Swiss francs to a US dollar not too expensive. The Swiss were fussy about sanitation but were otherwise efficient hosts.

Among the cities that we visited, Vienna was the most enjoyable. It was full of small cafes where one could sit for an hour or more sipping coffee and eating the most delicious pastries for less than $2 each. Another surprise was that while London was dirty, noisy and crowded, the English countryside was tranquil and clean. I got a glimpse of it on my visit to Cambridge at the initiative of a fellow of one of the colleges.

The tour was so enjoyable that Kamla and I decided that we would do it again. But such opportunities do not come twice in a lifetime.

III

HOME LEAVE TRAVEL, 1969

In the next 1969 summer holiday in the Institute we availed ourselves of our home leave and visited Delhi. Before our departure, Kamla shopped frantically for foreign goods which were much in demand by our relatives and friends in Delhi and which were not available in India. Since her mother wanted a TV set we brought one for her. Kamla brought about 100 Japanese nylon sarees for distribution to our relatives and friends. They were much in demand in those days as they did not crumple and lasted long. Furthermore, we brought gold ornaments for our relatives because gold was so much cheaper in Kuwait than in Delhi.

We spent three pleasant months of our home leave, dividing our time between stay with my parents and those of Kamla's.

As mentioned earlier I had wanted to stay five years in Kuwait so that I could get a pension from the United Nations. However, in May 1970, I was told by the Director one morning that since they had difficulty every year in obtaining agreement to extension of my deputation with the Institute from the Government of India, they had decided to replace me with an Arab economist. I was taken aback. I have written earlier about the probable reason for this sudden decision by the Director and the Co-Director. Thereafter, I wrote to UNOTC that I would be willing to be considered for another assignment in any country in which there was a post for a person with my qualifications and experience. I wrote also to an old friend, Prof. P.P. Karan, Chairman, Department of Geography, University of Kentucky, Lexington, U.S.A. that I would wish to spend a year or two as a visiting professor in his Department. Replies from both were encouraging. The UNOTC wrote back to say that it was sending my name for consideration by governments of four countries in Africa in which there were vacancies for experts with my experience and qualifications. Prof. Karan offered me an appointment as visiting professor in his Department for two years.

IV

RETURN HOME

Greatly encouraged by these letters, I returned to Delhi in July 1970—Kamla had come a month earlier—to stay for five months with my parents before leaving for Lexington, in January 1971.

We had to problem in transporting our personal and household effects and our car. The containers carrying our goods and the car arrived safely in Delhi within three weeks of shipping them from Kuwait. This was in sharp contrast to the difficulties that we had with transport of our goods from Boston which had mentioned in Chapter 17.

The Government of Kuwait used to provide to experts recruited by itself and those of the United Nations fully furnished accommodation and a chauffeur driven car free. The professors of the Institute were provided the same facilities. As a result, our monthly expenditure on food and clothing, etc., did not exceed one-fourth of my salary. At the end of my stay, I had enough savings to think of building the front portion of our house in which we lived from 1986 to 1994. Construction began in mid-December two weeks before I left for Lexington and was completed by March 1972. Construction was supervised by Kamla. She did prove to be an efficient supervisor. The boys were admitted to the American International School which ahd been opened primarily for children of Americans working in the Embassy and other agencies sch as the Information Service of the American government, but admitted a few children of Indians who had worked abroad and whose children had attended American schools there. Thus, there was no interruption in their studies.

The nearly two years (July 1970 – May 1972) that Kamla and the children stayed with my parents was a happy period for all of them. *Bhauji* enjoyed talking to Virendra — both of them were so fond of talking. *Beji* spent a lot of time with Jyotsna telling her stories from the epics Ramayana and Mahabharata. Arvind must have felt a bit neglected because of the attention received by Virendra and Jyotsna. But he did not seem to show it. It is only now that we understand how much influence this stay with their grandparents had on the children.

V

SOCIAL LIFE IN KUWAIT

Our social life was limited to spending two to three hours every evening at the house of one of the four Indian UN agency experts or professionals such as the engineers working for the Department of Telephones and Manager and officer-in-charge of Operations of Air India. The other three UN agency experts included my coleague and neighbour Dr. Shivasubramanian, Dr. Nedungadi a meteorologist who worked at the Kuwait airport and Mr. Varadan an engineer who was in charge of maintenance of equipment at the airport. The evening meeting usually would end with a dinner.

We were also quite friendly with two Indian merchants—Mr. Jashnmal, a Sindhi, who owned the biggest department store and Mr. Bhasin a Punjabi, who owned a big store which sold textiles and had a large tailoring department. Mr. Jashanmal's father had come to Kuwait from Iraq in the late 1930s. He used to tell us that before oil was discovered in Kuwait some of the *Sheikhs* (relatives of the *Amir*) were so poor that his father would send from time to time trays of specially prepared cooked food for their families. Mr. Bhasin had come to Kuwait to open his store in 1947. Both had been so successful as to become multi-millionaires. Mr. Jashanmal and Mr. Bhasin died years ago but their stores are still being run by their sons.

The older Kuwaities knew India very well because before the discovery of oil, Kuwaiti merchants had been going for centuries in their *dhows* (large wooden sail boats) carrying dates from Iraq to India and Indian textiles, spices and other goods to East African countries. However, we were surprised to notice that some of them called us *hindi maskeen* (poor Indians). What cheek! Calling poor the residents of a country by trading with which they had earned their livelihood for centuries! The older Kuwaities were however quite courteous in their manner in contrast to the younger ones many of whom were quite vain!

The four years that we spent in Kuwait were happy. The climate was healthy; and my work was not too heavy. Kamla and I had through our limited contacts with Kuwaities, some experience of a society in flux!

12

Back Home, July-December 1970

I was very encouraged by replies to my letters by UNOTC and Prof. P.P. Karan. But since I was a member of the IAS and had gone to Kuwait on deputation, I needed the approval of the Home Ministry for deputation to another assignment. Accordingly, I met the Establishment Officer, Mr. Virendra Kumar, who dealt with all cases of deputation of IAS officers to find out if the Government would approve of my deputation to another UN post if I was offered one. He assured me that the Government's approval would be forthcoming. I was greatly encouraged by this reply and was looking forward to going on another UN assignment. Having stayed abroad for four years, I was not too keen to work in India.

However, Mr. Virendra Kumar was transferred in August 1970, and an IAS officer, Mr. H.K.L. Capoor, was appointed in his place. He dug out an old rule which said that an IAS officer who had gone on one UN assignment could go on another only after five years. On learning that I could not go abroad, I met the Deputy Chairman of the Planning Commission, Prof. D.R. Gadgil, and its Secretary, Mr Ashok Mitra for a posting with the Commission. Both of them agreed and offered me the post of Joint Secretary (Rural Employment) which was falling vacant then. Mr. Mitra was kind enough to take the file personally to Mr. Capoor. But the latter insisted that I should go back to my home state of Rajasthan for some years before coming to a post in Delhi. This made me quite angry with him. On learning about his decision about my deputation, I felt that it was motivated by pure jealousy.

When the Rajasthan government learnt that I would be coming back to the state, it offered me the post of Member, Board of Revenue, at Ajmer. This increased my anger with the IAS system. I had been working on planning and development throughout my service in India and Kuwait and I was being posted to decide cases about rights in land and land use, when I knew so little about revenue law. I felt that the IAS system did not allow an officer to specialise in any field and was designed to produce mediocre 'generalists' who could be appointed to any job and expected to do it reasonably well. I recalled with regret Prof. Gadgil's remark when I joined the IAS, "Nath, you have converted yourself from a promising specialist to a second rate official".

The Rajasthan government, later changed its decision and created the new post of Development Commissioner, Chambal with headquarters at Kotha. There were serious problems of soil erosion and water logging in the area irrigated by the Chambal project which had been completed a few years earlier. Since the Rajasthan government was very concerned about them, it had requested the World Bank to field a team of experts to study the problems and suggest solutions for them. As Development Commissioner, I would work closely with the team and be the liaison officer between it and the Rajasthan government. The job was interesting and in retrospect I feel that I should have taken it. But at that time some personal considerations swayed my judgement. I would have to live in Kotha — away from my family since Kamla had taken up a job as lecturer in economics in the newly opened Gargi College for Women not far from our house in Lajpatnagar. The prospect of living alone in Kotah which was extremely hot most of the year and travelling frequently between Kotah and Delhi was very unattractive. I felt also that I might not keep good health living alone in a hot place and having to depend on food cooked by a Rajasthani cook who would never understand my food needs. I had a problem of high blood pressure besides the old problem of poor digestion.

Accordingly, I decided to resign from the IAS, go to the University of Kentucky as a visiting professor in the Department of Geography for a year or two and hope that a UN assignment would be available thereafter.

Arriving at this decision was not easy. I would be throwing away a permanent career in my own country for the uncertain prospect of UN jobs in different countries, mostly in Africa. Second, since I had not completed 25 years of service with the Government of India I would not get any pension, although I had contributed to a pension fund for the 20 years that I had worked with the Government. This was not a major consideration however, because the pension from the Government of India was very small in comparison with the emoluments of a UN job and a UN pension to which I would be entitled if I was lucky enough to complete five years as an UN official. I had not contributed to the UN Pension Fund in my assignment in Kuwait because I was on deputation from the Government of India and was contributing to my pension from the Government.

Within the family two people, *Baujee* and Kamla, helped me arrive at the decision to resign from the IAS. *Baujee* simply said, "*Kaka* (son) go wherever you are happy. You have not been happy in the IAS, so why stay in it?" Kamla also felt that a UN agency job was so attractive financially that it was worthwhile resigning from the IAS and becoming free to accept a job when one became available. However when my friend, Mr. R.D. Thapar, learnt about my decision, he laughed and said, "Don't be a fool, Does anyone resign from the IAS?" But when he learnt that I was firm in my decision, he said that he would help me in getting approval of the Governments of India and Rajasthan to my resignation.

Since approval of my resignation by the Rajasthan Government was essential, I went to Jaipur to secure it by meeting the Chief Secretary and the Chief Minister. My old friend, Mr. A.P. Dewan, fixed an appointment for me to see the Chief Minister Mr. Sukhadia, at 8:30 a.m. when he was shaving, because he was then alone and in a relaxed mood. When I told Mr. Sukhadia of my decision to resign, he smiled and said, "Why are you going? Don't you like us any more?" I was struck with the courtesy behind this remark. I replied that I had been very happy in Rajasthan and had great respect for him and the Chief Secretary, Mr. Mehta, but that I wanted to pursue an academic career and showed him Prof. Karan's letter. He was gracious enough to agree to my request and said that he would speak to the Chief Secretary about it.

Armed with these assurances, I tendered resignation from the IAS in December 1970; was very happy when it was accepted and telegraphed Prof. Karan that I would be joining his department in January 1971.

I may have been one of the first I.A.S. officers to resign from the service, but I have been followed by many others who have resigned to pursue an academic career or other studies or to join a business house. One of my young friends resigned from the service soon after his training, because he found the work boring. He loved Himalayan paintings and is now a distinguished professor and consultant on the subject in Punjab.

The Prime Minister and other ministers in the central government have as their advisers, people whom they know and who can best promote their political interests. Ministers have as their secretaries people whom they know and who would be prepared to bend the rules to serve their interests. Sudden transfers, when one incurs the wrath of a minister are frequent. As a Collector one has to be on the right side of the local M.L.A. (member of legislative assembly); otherwise one may be transferred to a most undesirable district. Finally, one cannot specialize in any branch of public service. One may work in the Finance department of the state government or the ministry in the Central government for a few years and then be required to work in the department or ministry of Education or Health.

As a result young men or women of even average intelligence coming from affluent or middle income families prefer to work in banks, Life Insurance or General Insurance Corporation, foreign and Indian companies like the Tatas which are known to be good employers. They pay well and promotion in their companies depends upon performance. The number of such firms is increasing rapidly as emphasis shifts from having family members to trained managers in key decision making positions. People of above average intelligence prefer an academic career to joining the I.A.S. In all these jobs security of tenure is as much as in the IAS. Furthermore, there is assurance of posting in one place, usually a large metropoltan city so that one can raise the family, put children through school and college without fear of being transferred suddenly. The Union Public Service Commission which has responsibility for recruitment to the I.A.S. and other all India and central services, writes regularly in its annual reports about the poor quality of the candidates who appear for recruitment to the services.

Finally the widespread feeling among the public that a proportion of the officers are corrupt lowers the prestige of the service.

13

Lexington, Kentucky, 1971

I left for Lexington in the first week of January 1971 so as to join my teaching duties at the University of Kentucky for the spring semester. On my way, I met the UNTOC officials in New York and told them that I had resigned from service with the Indian government and was now free to accept any UN assignment that was offered to me. They noted this with satisfaction and told me that they would get in touch with me as soon as an assignment became available.

My teaching duties—nine hours a week—were not heavy and left me enough time for personal reading and writing. I needed the time to acquaint myself with the latest literature in geography. There had been a revolution in geography in the 1950s and 1960s; quantitative techniques of analysis were being used increasingly in all branches of the subject. People like me trained in the 1940s or early 1950s were considered hopelessly out of date by young geographers. To get over this handicap, I devoted a great deal of time to reading the latest books and articles in journals and found that much use of quantitative techniques was superfluous, and most geographical facts could be explained just as well without them as with them. Among the courses that I taught there was one on urban geography. I found the literature on it extremely interesting and it gave me a lifelong interest in the problems of cities.

Lexington, the capital of Kentucky and the seat of the state University, is a small city with a population of about 200,000 in 1971. It is in the centre of Kentucky's blue grass plain where the best race horses in the USA are raised. Prof. Karan and I would sometimes visit the horse breeding farms and look at the fine horses that were being raised there.

My job as visiting Professor created some problems for Prof. Karan. The junior staff of the department seemed to resent my appointment as a full Professor, only because I was a friend of Prof. Karan. This did not bother Prof. Karan, but I did not like it, and began to feel that I had undermined his position by coming to the department.

During the four month(mid-May to mid-September) summer vacation at the university, I returned home. There were two reasons for coming home, besides the pleasure of living with the family. *Baujee* was ill; he had a tumour in his stomach, for removal of which he had undergone surgery at the hospital of the All India Institute of Medical Sciences. The surgery had made him very weak. Second, since the Vasant Vihar house was being built I felt that my presence would assist Kamla in supervising the construction. *Baujee's* health appeared to improve and I could oversee the construction of the house and make sure that the contractors did their work properly.

On my way back to Lexington after the summer vacation, I was told by the people in UNOTC that there was a job for me in Sierra Leone, a small English speaking country in West Africa, as a member of a 5-person team of experts which the UNOTC was going to send there to help the Government prepare its first 5-year plan for economic and social development. I could take up my appointment immediately, but I explained to them that I would do so only at the end of the autumn semester at the University. I had promised Prof. Karan that I would teach during this semester. They agreed and I joined my position in Sierra Leone in the last week of 1971.

The India-Pakistan War of 1971

During the first week of December 1971, there was a brief three-week war between India and Pakistan. The principal theatre of war was East Pakistan (now Bangladesh) where there was a rebellion against misrule by the Punjabi-dominated Pakistan army. As a result of the Army's campaign against Hindus living in East Pakistan, about 10 million of them had fled their homes and were living in the slums of Calcutta and other cities of West Bengal. When the Indian government's efforts to persuade the Pakistan government to end the anti-Hindu campaign of the Pakistan army so that the refugees could return home failed, Mrs. Indira Gandhi, who was then the Prime Minister decided to invade East Pakistan and defeat the Pakistan forces, with the aid of the large number of guerrilla forces and create conditions in which the Hindu refugees could go back. The Pakistan army surrendered to the Indian army after a three week campaign. Thereafter, the East Pakistanis decided to break away from Pakistan to establish an independent Bangladesh. Sheikh Mujib-ur-Rahman, the leader of the Bengali legislators in the Pakistan parliament was elected the first prime minister of Bangladesh.

Although the principal theatre of war was in the east, there was some fighting also along the Indo-Pakistan border in Punjab and Jammu and Kashmir and air raids on Indian cities including Delhi by the Pakistan air force and on Pakistani cities by the Indian air force. I followed the progress of the war with some anxiety and was greatly relieved when I heard from Kamla that there had been very few casualties in the air raids and all of them were well.

Mrs. Gandhi was a woman of great courage. Before the war broke out, President Nixon threatened her that if she invaded East Pakistan, he would send the Seventh fleet to bomb the Indian forces from ports such as Chittagong. However, she was not deterred by this threat, because caught between the advance of the Indian forces and the rearguard action of the guerrilla forces, the Pakistan army surrendered within three weeks. Almost 90,000 soldiers were taken prisoners and remained in jail until an agreement between India and Pakistan was signed in Simla early in 1975.

The war denied Kamla an opportunity to have a vacation which she had planned with me in Kentucky in December 1971 because all air travel was suspended during the war.

14

Sierra Leone, 1971-79

When I arrived in Freetown, the capital city of Sierra Leone to take up my appointment I found the city and the people so dirty that I wanted to run away from them. There was no underground sewerage system and open drains built on two sides of the main streets carried the waste water of the city to the sea. There were heaps of garbage everywhere. Although Sierra Leone was rich in natural resources—it was one of the largest producers in the world of gems and industrial diamonds and had besides rich deposits of iron ore, bauxite and rutile (the ore from which titanium, a metal used among other things for manufacture of frames of aircraft)—the people were very poor. Diseases like malaria, diarrhoea, dysentery, bronchitis, pneumonia and tuberculosis were common and caused an enormous number of deaths. The main streets were broad and well laid out and had well built official and commercial buildings; the other streets were narrow and dirty. Most people lived in *shanties* with corrugated iron roofs and unpaved floors. The roofs leaked constantly in the incessant rains during the 8-month (March-October) long rainy season. Furthermore, it was known as a country of thieves. Petty theft in the streets and robbery in houses of the affluent Sierra Leoneans, Lebanese and other expatriates were common.

Our office was located in four rooms in a First World War vintage building, which had not been painted or repaired for years. There were cobwebs in the staircases, leaking roofs and holes in the wooden floors of the rooms. Two Filipino experts, a financial planner, Mr. Arquisola, and an Infrastructure expert, Mr. Goyenechea, had already joined. Besides, five men and a woman—all graduates from small British Universities had been appointed as Sierra Leonean counterparts of UN experts. But since they had no work, most of them would be frequently absent from work; when they came, they would spend hours standing on the corridor outside the rooms looking at the sea or visiting friends in other offices of the Government.[1]

Seeing all this, my first impulse was to resign my post and go back to Lexington to complete the second year of my teaching assignment. But a few factors held me back. First, the salary and various allowances of the job were almost double my salary at the University. Second, Mr. Val Nylander, the Secretary of the Ministry of Development who had the responsibility for getting the First Five Year plan prepared, took an instant liking for me. He treated me with great courtesy and regard and considered me the best expert that the UNOTC had recruited. We had an extremely pleasant relationship throughout his 6-year stay as Development Secretary. Thirdly, I felt that by resigning what was expected to be a long-term UN assignment, I would be going to a 1-year teaching post after which I might not have any job for sometime.

Mr. Alfred Edwards, the UNDP Resident Representative, a Ceylonese, whom I had met in Colombo when I had gone to teach at the University—he was in the Ceylon Civil Service at that time - also treated me with such courtesy and regard that he wrote to the concerned officials in the UNOTC that my 1-year appointment should be extended to two years because the UN team was expected to stay for two or more years to help the Government formulate the development plan and oversee its implementation. It was extended.

I began to contribute to the UN Pension Fund on taking up my appointment. When I was assured a 2 year appointment, I requested the secretary of the Fund to include the period of my service in Kuwait for calculation of the pension. He agreed on condition that I pay the arrears of my contribution with interest in 48 monthly instalments. I was happy for his consideration in thus extending the period of my service for calculation of pension.

Since the first need of a UN expert after arrival and brief stay in a hotel is for suitable housing, I requested Mr. Nylander for assistance in obtaining a Government built house. He accompanied me to Cockrill, where the Government had built 24 houses for its senior officers and UN experts. We saw several houses, I liked one which was occupied by a German expert who was expecting to leave within a fortnight. He allotted it to me and ordered that it should be repainted and repaired immediately after the German expert had left. We spent four very happy years in that house; they were the happiest years of my entire stay in UN jobs.

Mr. N.S. Bawa was Civil Engineer posted as an expert on low cost housing with the Ministry of Housing. Two days after my arrival in Sierra Leone, when I was still living in a hotel, a Sikh gentleman came over, introduced himself and asked me to accompany him to his house for dinner. I was taken aback by his offer but could not refuse it because of his regard for another Indian expert. I spent a very pleasant evening with the Bawas. During it, he and Mrs. Bawa mentioned that their families had lived in villages in Sargodha district of Punjab before the partition of India and that their parents, like my grand parents had been traders-cum-money lenders. They told me also that there were about 40 Sindhi merchants who owned grocery stores in Freetown; three Indian lecturers in Fourah Bay College, one of the oldest colleges in Africa, and half a dozen other Indian experts. The Bawas were living in one of the 12 flats constructed by a Sindhi merchant. One room on the ground floor of one flat was being used as a *Gurudwara* (Sikh temple) where a religious service was conducted on every Sunday morning.

During the next 10 days, Mr. Bawa would come every evening and would take me to dinner at the house of an Indian family which had called fellow Indians for dinner. When I would protest that I did not know the hosts at all, he would reassure me that since I was an Indian I would be a welcome guest. Thus, through his help I got to know most of the Indian professionals and some of the owners or managers of the Indian business houses in Sierra Leone. Mr. Bawa also helped me in opening an account with the largest grocery store in Freetown – Choithram's. Its manager, Mr. Rajwani, a very nice man, became a friend. The Bawas had three children: a son who was settled in England, a daughter who was working as a resident in the hospital of the All India Institute of Medical Sciences in Delhi after taking her degree from it, and a son who was of the same age as Jyotsna and was living with them. He and Jyotsna were to become good friends and playmates.

Sorie Bangura : The best domestic servant that we have ever had

The day I was to move from the hotel to the house allotted to me, a young man come to me who wanted to be employed as a domestic servant. He said that he had worked earlier for an Indian FAO expert who had lived in the same house that I was to occupy and that he knew Indian cooking. The young man appeared to be honest and since I needed a domestic servant desperately to do the cooking, washing and other house jobs, I hired him on the spot. Thus, Mr. Bangura and I entered the house together. Little did I know then that he would stay with us throughout our stay in Sierra Leone.

Mr. Bangura and I were alone in the Cockrill house for four months, because while I had reached Freetown in the last week of December 1971 and had moved to the house in mid-January of 1972, Kamla and the children came only in mid-May. I found that although he knew the elements of south Indian cooking—the FAO expert for whom he had worked was a south Indian — he did not know north Indian cooking at all. I helped him learn to make *chapatties* and *curries* with little or no spices. But he was an efficient house keeper and whenever I would come home for lunch or after work, I would find that the house was spotlessly clean and all the housekeeping jobs including washing and pressing of my clothes had been done.

Although Bangura looked honest, he was not above petty theft. It was my habit to get Le 50 ($65 at the then prevailing rate of exchange of Le 1 = $ 1.3) from the bank for my household expenditure once a fortnight. When I would come from the office in the afternoon, I would hang my jacket and necktie on my chair at the dining table and go up to the toilet on the first floor. The toilets in the office building were so dirty that I did not like to use them. However I found that there would be only Le 48 in my pocket when I left for office. The first time this happened, I felt that I might have made a mistake in counting the cash when I got it from the bank. But when it happened a second time after I had counted the money very carefully at the Bank I was convinced that Bangura must be the thief. I found also that the contents of my coffee bottle were disappearing more rapidly than my daily in-take of 1 or 2 cups. So I told Bangura, "You are an efficient housekeeper and I am pleased with you. But you are not above petty theft. You have taken Le 2 twice from my jacket and you have also been using my coffee. I don't mind your taking the coffee; on the contrary, I shall pay you for buying a breadroll for your breakfast, but if you steal my money again you will end up in jail for petty theft". This direct confrontation had its desired effect. Mr.Bangura confessed his guilt and was so honest thereafter that we would leave the house to his care when we went on home leave and we would not find a pin missing when we returned.

Flappie, the dog

Due to the widespread prevalence of house thefts, other UN agency experts advised me that it would be good to have a dog. Luckily for me, a Canadian expert, who was leaving Sierra Leone had two six-week old pups to give away. He gave me one. For the first two weeks of his stay in the house the puppy was so scared, that Mr. Bangura had great difficulty in feeding him. But slowly he got so used to his new surroundings and proved to be such a good dog that we never had a theft in our house. His bark was sufficient to drive away any petty thief. He stayed with us throughout our stay in Sierra Leone and the Ghanaian expert to whom we gave him when we left had great difficulty in keeping him. He would run away from their house to the one in which we were living when we left Sierra Leone. Eventually, he ended up living with the Chowdhuries, our good friends in Sierra Leone, who had looked after him during our home leave periods; we had looked after their dog.

Work on formulating the First Five Year Development Plan of Sierra Leone, 1974/75—1978/79, began in right earnest only after Dr. M. Mesaric, a Yugoslav economist who had worked as the Assistant Secretary in the planning ministry of his own country and had been appointed the leader of the UN team of experts arrived in Freetown in May. Pending his arrival, Mr. Steven Tanzil, an

Indonesian-Chinese economist working in UNOTC was sent over as Acting Project Manager. He was a nice, but high strung man, who quarrelled with the Resident Representative during his short stay. At the end of his tenure he recommended that I should work as acting Project Manager I did. The Filipino experts were not pleased but were clever enough not to show it. My appointment as acting Project Manager was not liked also by Mr. Okuosa, a Nigerian who was the Deputy Resident Representative. He felt that because of my friendship with Mr. Edwards, I was not showing him the deference due to him because of his 'high' office. I explained to him that I never meant any disrespect to him and if I showed it inadvertently I was sorry. This mollified him. I mention him because there are so many super-egos in UN posts that one has to be very sure not to offend any of them, if one wants to stay in a post.

The Economy of Sierra Leone

During the four months between my arrival and that of Dr Mesaric, I read all that was available locally in books and reports written by earlier experts on the economy of Sierra Leone. The country was very rich in natural resources. Besides there were large forested areas in the interior. Because of high rainfall and fertile valleys, it could produce enough rice to feed its population and export the surplus. But the country was a net importer of rice, partly because the local produce did not reach the capital, on account of transport difficulties, but more so because the politicians and officials of the Rice Corporation, which had responsibility for import and distribution of rice in Freetown were interested in the money to be made in its import and sale. The waters off the coast of Sierra Leone were teaming with fish, and fishing was the principal occupation of the people living in villages along the coast. But the Government had given the contract for fishing off the coast to a Russian company whose trawlers fished so close to the coast, that the fishermen's catch started dwindling very rapidly. This led to discontent among the fishermen and also among the poor in Freetown, as fish, an essential item in their diet, was becoming so expensive.

Gems and industrial diamonds were the principal export of

Freetown. Most of them were found on the surface, in the bed of the Sierra Leone river and its tributaries, in Kono district in the northwest of the country. Others were found underground in mines.

Before Sierra Leone became independent in 1961, the British government had given the exclusive right to exploit the diamond field to the Sierra Leone Selection Trust (SLST) a British company, which had close links with De Beers the Dutch company which controls most of the production and marketing of diamonds in the world. The SLST employed modern machinery to exploit its concession and as the surface resources began to be depleted, it took to mining of underground deposits.

In addition to the SLST, tens of thousands of Sierra Leoneans were engaged in panning the river sands for diamonds. They worked during the night in order to escape arrest by the guards employed by the SLST. Most of them would get a few small stones fit only for industrial use, sale of which yielded them a bare subsistence. But occasionally one of them would strike it rich and find a large gem worth a hundred thousand dollars or more. It was this hope which kept (and still keeps) tens of thousands of them busy in panning the river sands. The valuable stones were sold generally to Labanese merchants who exported it at a price which was double or more of the price they had paid for it.

Soon after Sierra Leone became independent, the Government nationalised SLST to form DIMINCO (Diamond Mining Corporation) in which the Government had 51 percent share and SLST had 49 percent share, but the responsibility of managing production and export of diamonds rested with the officers of the SLST.

The formation of DIMINCO did not please the directors of SLST, and they decided to exploit the best part of their concession as fast as possible and get out. This they did and after record production and exports in the late 1960s to mid 1970s, production and export of gem diamonds began to decline rapidly. The rich revenues from the export of diamonds should have enabled the Government to establish an adequate and efficient system of social services and alleviate if not eradicate, poverty and hunger. But it did not do it for several reasons. First, the best stones were smuggled out of the country, mainly by the Lebanese, but also by Sierra Leoneans in high positions. The Government knew this but chose to look the other way. The social services were not only not improved, they were allowed to deteriorate because of decline in financial allocations in real terms for their maintenance and operation. There was a similar decline in infrastructure services - transport and supply of electricity.

Sierra Leone had a narrow gauge railway which connected the capital with the most productive oil palm and cocoa producing areas in the interior. It was dismantled in the late 1960s and the first two years of the 1970s on the advice of the World Bank, because its operation was causing heavy losses to the government. The Bank recommended that the railway be replaced by a system of roads to connect Freetown with the principal towns in the interior. But construction of roads was proceeding slowly because of the high cost of their construction and maintenance. Furthermore, with dependence on motor transport imports of petroleum products increased rapidly, which caused a heavy drain on foreign exchange.

Electricity supplies in Freetown and the principal towns in the interior also deteriorated steadily. Generating capacity in the power stations was not increased adequately to keep pace with increase in demand on account of increase in population of Freetown and of principal towns in the interior. Maintenance of power stations was so poor, that generation much below capacity was the norm and breakdown of the stations became increasingly frequent, resulting in large areas of the city not having any power supply for several hours and sometimes for two or three days.

Whenever there was a major breakdown, engineers and the needed spare parts would be flown in by the German company which had supplied the generating machines. The telephone and telegraph services functioned quite well, however, because they were being operated by the British telecom giant, Cable and Wireless, which used to operate these services in most British colonies.

The value of the Sierra Leone currency, the Leone, began to decline rapidly after 1974-75 when the diamond exports began to decline. The balance of payment was always negative, because expenditure on imports was higher than the earnings from exports.

When I arrived in Sierra Leone, the Leone was worth $ 1.3 as mentioned earlier, but by the time I left it in March 1979, the exchange rate was 8 Leones to the dollar. Later, when I visited Sierra Leone as a short-term consultant in 1985 and 1987, one could get several hundred leones for a dollar on the flourishing black market.

An Accident and a Lesson

The ambition of most Indians after they got a UN job in those days was to buy a Mercedes Benz car. I had wanted it in Kuwait but later changed my mind and bought a Morris, on the advice of friends who said that there was very heavy import duty on Mercedes Benz cars in India and besides their maintenance and operation in Delhi would be very expensive.

When I was assured a 2-year stay in Sierra Leone, I lost no time in ordering a Mercedes Benz 200 car. It was available at the time for about $ 4500, which I could pay easily out of my savings. I took delivery of the car, in the first week of March. The same evening I drove it to the beach for my daily walk and swim. After the swim, as I was putting on my street clothes, a black young man hit me on the head with a glass bottle filled with sand, searched the pockets of my trousers and ran away with the few Leones that were in it. I fell down bleeding profusely. A kindly passing motorist helped me get up and opened the car for me to drive home. On reaching home, I asked Bangura to clean the wound with surgical cotton, bathe it profusely with after shave lotion and put a clean cotton bandage on it. The cotton and the bandages formed part of the first aid kit, which along with anti-malarial and anti-diarrhoea pills are supplied by the Medical Service of the UN to every expert working in the field. I bathed the wound with after shave lotion because I argued to myself that since it was mostly alcohol, it would prevent any infection of the wound until I could see a surgeon. After this first aid, I went to my neighbour, Dr Eleady Cole, the Chief Cardiologist at the biggest hospital in Freetown, for advice on any further action including taking some antibiotic pills that I should take. But he curtly told me that being a cardiologist he could not give me any advice. I was taken aback by his reply because an Indian doctor would have readily given me his advice.

Next morning, I went to the surgeon in the Hill Station Hospital, which was meant only for senior officials of the Government and expatriate experts and showed him the wound. He was very pleased with the quality of the first aid on it, dressed the wound and asked me to come daily for changing the dressing until it healed. I reported the incident to the Resident Representative next morning, who arranged for the police to register my complaint and arrest the culprit. I do not know if they took any action, because the culprit was never arrested.

This incident taught me two lessons: never to go alone to the beach and to expect no help from the police if there was any incident on the beach or a petty theft. Thereafter I would always take Mr. Bangura with me when I went to the beach for my evening walk and swim.

Bauji's death

In the first week of March 1972, Kamla informed me of *Bauji's* death due to cardiac arrest. He and Virendra had been walking together in the drive way of our Lajpatnagar house in the evening of March 6 - he was very fond of talking to Virendra because both of them were such good talkers-when he suddenly fell down. A doctor was called immediately but his attempts to revive him failed. Bauji had been suffering form high blood pressure for many years and had become weak and anaemic after the surgery for removal of the tumour in his stomach. The news came as a shock to me. I felt that I had been orphaned. I was not only very fond of him but greatly respected him for his courage and vision. But I felt that it would be useless for me to go home to mourn his death because all the post-cremation rites like the visit to Hardwar for immersion of his bones in the Ganga would be done quite well by Virendra and Kamla. Virendra has never forgotten the heart-rending experience of lighting the match for his grandfather's cremation.

Kamla and the children arrived in Freetown in the first week of May. I was very happy to see them. Both Virendra and Arvind had grown to be 6 footers and Jyotsna who was 9 was also growing up to be a tall and beautiful girl. Kamla took an immediate liking to Freetown, because of its sea and the greenery that she saw all around. She had been used to living in small towns and did not mind the filth of the city because our house was located in a clean suburb from which we got a good view of the sea. The house was quite comfortable and its two bed rooms would be adequate for our needs, especially because Virendra had been admitted to the University of Michigan in the USA in the Department of Industrial Engineering and would leave at the end of August. She did not like Sorie Bangura at first; considered him slow as he never spoke much and rarely smiled. But I told her to be patient with him and to see his work for a few days before making any judgment on him. She agreed. Soon she was impressed with his efficiency and habits of personal cleanliness and began to like him.

The Bawas introduced her to the circle of Indian friends; their son Pammi and Jyotsna became happy playmates because they were of the same age. Jyotsna was admitted to the International School, a primary school run by a British lady which prepared students—mostly children of expatriates living in Sierra Leone—for admission to secondary schools in Sierra Leone and Britain.

Dr. Milan Mesaric, the Project Manager, also arrived early in May and was allotted the house next to ours, so that he and I were both colleagues and neighbours. Kamla and Mrs. Mesaric became good friends and the friendship grew during the four years that we were neighbours. Three other experts — a Norwegian, Mr. Kaare Rund, arrived to take up his post as Manpower Planner; an Egyptian, Mr. Sami, joined as Social Planner and another Filipino, Dr Quintana, joined as Agricultural Planner. Thus the team was complete and the work of formulating the Five Year Plan of Sierra Leone began in right earnest at the beginning of June. It lasted two years. The plan included all the development projects that were in operation and others that were needed to achieve the goals of economic and social development of the country and formulated recommendations on better utilization of its natural and human resources.

After the Plan document was published, UNOTC fielded an Evaluation Mission to make recommendations relating to continuation of the project. The Mission had two members. Mr. M. Edward, a lecturer in Economics in a college in London, and Mr. Dan Hartstein, an economist working in UNOTC. The mission heard two conflicting opinions on the work of the team. The Secretary and the Minister of Development were all praise for it and the quality of the plan document that had been produced. On the other hand, Mr. Nikson, a young Britisher who had been working with the team as an Associate Expert and Mr. Abdul Noman, the Assistant Resident Representative in the UN office, pooh-poohed the work of the team and advised Mr. Edward that the project should be terminated. When we learnt this, Dr. Mesaric and other members of the team, were furious because our hard work was being pooh-poohed instead of being appreciated.

In the evening before the departure of the Evaluation Mission, Dr. Mesaric held a reception for its members at his house. At this reception, I had a long and heated argument with Mr. Hartstein in which I vigorously defended the work of the team and the quality of the plan document produced despite the enormous difficulty of collecting reliable data on various sectors of the economy of Sierra Leone. The argument had its desired effect. Mr. Hartstein stoutly defended the achievements of the project team and strongly recommended its extension for another two years in order to oversee implementation of the Plan and to prepare annual plans, while Mr. Edward recommended that the project be wound up.

The UNOTC rejected Mr. Edward's recommendation since he had no experience of planning and extended the project as recommended by Mr. Hartstein. Another result of my argument with Mr. Hartstein was that we became good friends. I would always see him whenever I went to New York on official business.

During the next two years, the principal activity of the project was to oversee implementation of the plan, prepare annual plans and conduct a training seminar in which the UN experts gave lectures to their Sierra Leonean counterparts and officials dealing with implementation of projects in various ministries of the government on the elements of formulation and implementation of economic development plans. The work was not heavy and all of us had considerable time on our hands. I could have used it to do some serious reading and writing on planning and economic development but could not do it because of the absence of a good library in Sierra Leone.

UNOTC fielded another evaluation mission in 1977 to review project activities in the previous two years and to recommend further extension, if any. One member of the Mission was Dr. Subhash Dhar, my old friend and colleague in the Planning Commission. He had joined UNOTC after spending a few years with the International Atomic Energy Agency in Vienna. This mission also recommended a further extension of the project by two years. However since it was becoming apparent that the government was not following the recommendations of the plan either in implementation of projects or in economic policies, another evaluation mission was fielded by UNOTC, early in 1978. This was a 1-man mission consisting of Mr. Hartfelt a relatively junior officer of UNOTC.

By this time, Dr. Mesaric, Mr. Ruud and Dr Quintana had left the project. Dr Mesaric retired in June 1977, after completing five years of service with UNOTC. He was tired of the government ignoring the recommendations of the Plan, and selecting projects recommended by Lebanese merchants. The worst example of this was a project for preparing uniforms for Sierra Leone police for which a Lebanese merchant gave a loan to the Government at 18 percent per annum.

On Dr. Mesaric's recommendation, I was appointed Acting Project Manager. Thus Messrs Goyanachea, Arquisola and I were the only three members left of the original 6-member team. Mr. Hartstein recommended that my post should be terminated in August 1978, while Mr. Goyanachea and Mr. Arquisola should continue for another 2 years. I was surprised by this recommendation, because it showed a clear religious bias. Mr. Hartstein was a staunch Catholic and had recommended that only the jobs of the two fellow Catholics should be extended. The Ministry of Development did not agree with Mr. Hartstein recommendation, however, and insisted that I should continue till February 1979 in order to prepare a 3-year (1978/79—1981/82) programme of economic adjustment in Sierra Leone. Preparation of such a programme was insisted upon by the World Bank and the IMF. The Bank, which is a major donor for implementation of projects in LDCs (less developed countries), had never believed in five year plans, arguing that in the rapidly changing economic situation of the late 1970s. five years were too long a period for formulation of economic and developmental policies and that a shorter period of three years was more appropriate. Being the only economist on the team, I had to prepare the programme. I completed it before leaving Sierra Leone in March 1979.

During 1978 and in the first two months of 1979 I had considerable mental tension for several personal reasons. I had wanted an appointment at another duty station, and the office of personnel offered me a post in South Yemen. However I was advised not to accept this appointment.

Another source of tension was that Jyotsna was in her tenth grade and needed to stay in Freetown until January 1979 so that she could appear for the 'O' level examination conducted by the London University for overseas students. By passing this examination, she could continue her studies at a British school which prepared students for the 'A' level examination, after passing which she could enter a University. When extension of my assignment in Freetown up to February 1979 was assured, Miss Dilsworth, the Headmistress of St. Joseph's Convent, the high school that Jyotsna was attending, advised me that she should leave school, and that I should arrange for her coaching in different subjects by tutors.

In the last week of February 1979, Mr. Friscic came to Freetown with the news that my appointment as Project Manager and leader of the team of experts which would assist the Ministry of Development of the Government prepare the Second Five Year Plan of Economic and Social Development of the Gambia, had been approved and that I could join my duties after taking two months' of the home leave due to me. I was very happy to hear this, because Banjul, the capital of the Gambia was known to be a healthy place. Furthermore, the Gambia had a stable government which treated experts from the UN and other international organizations assisting it very well. Thus relieved of my anxiety about my posting, I applied for leave and decided that we would all go to Ann Arbor because both Virendra and Arvind were studying there at the University of

Michigan, which had a good teaching hospital. By staying in Ann Arbor we would be with the boys and Kamla would be treated at the University hospital.

We left Freetown on 6 March 1979. Sorie Bangura, was one of the persons who saw us off at the airport. Meanwhile, Kamla had arranged for his employment with the Manager of the British Caledonian Airways. Since he had served us so well for seven years we were keen that he should have a good job when we left. He mentioned to Kamla that he wanted a job with a European family because the Europeans paid and treated their servants well.

One of the things that sustained us through our long stay in Sierra Leone was the active social life among the India-Pakistan-Sri Lanka community. A dozen or more professionals and Sindhi merchants would get together for dinner on Saturday and Sunday evenings and often also for lunch on one of these days. Drinking and eating of 'small chops' would start about 8 p.m. by which time the Sindhi merchants whom the hostess had inivited would had arrived after closing shop. Dinner would be served at around 11 p.m. In between there would be singing of songs to the accompaniment of the harmonium or other musical instruments and exchange of prices. On Sunday mornings, a large number of couples would assembled at a temple where there would be readings from the Sikh scriptures, singing of devotional songs, followed by a brunch which one of the women would prepare.

In the cool season (November to March) there would be picnics on Sandays, on a beach 20 km. from Freetown. Men, women and children would get together at the beach by noon and for four to five hours, would go swimming, playing bridge or other card games and having lunch and then tea, before returning home. These meetings also allowed us to make friends with several doctors who worked for the Government and were very useful when either the children or we ourselves full sick.

Uncertanity of Tenure

The Bawa case illustrates the perils of working in a UN agency job. Mr. Bawa had established very good relations with the Permanent

Secretary (PS) of the Ministry of Housing to which he was attached. He was a competent engineer, had a cheerful and friendly disposition and since the Bawas were good hosts, the P.S. a woman and her husband were frequent guests at their home. But this 'cordial' relationship came to a sudden end when Mr. Bawa requested the P.S. for leave to go to Delhi to celebrate the marriage of their daughter and the P.S. refused. Putting his duty as a parent above his job, Mr. Bawa applied for 2-months' leave and sent in his resignation at the same time. After celebrating the marriage in March 1974 and getting their leave, the Bawas had to return to Freetown because Mr. Bawa's contract was up to June. The P.S. was so angry with Mr Bawa's defiance of her wishes, that she did not allow him to attend office after his return from leave. She must have given him a very bad report because Mr. Bawa never got a UN job again. From Freetown, he went to Zambia, where he worked for the Government for several years before his return to Delhi, where he built his house and started his practice as a civil engineer.

Postscript

Sierra Leone has been in the midst of a civil war for some years the end of which is nowhere in sight. This was the predictable end result of the process of bleeding white the fabulously rich natural and human resources of a small country by an unholy alliance between rapacious Lebanese merchants and a corrupt government. The British and the United Nations are now trying to restore peace and order. Even if they succeed, it will be many years before the people of Freetown can get enough food to eat. Reducing illiteracy and disease will remain a more distance objective, achievable only with large technical and economic assistance by various agencies of the U.N. system and western donors.

NOTE

1. Freeetown had been built by the British government early of in the nineteenth century to settle slaves living in Britain and those captured by British ships on the high seas. Its hinterland which constituted Sierra Leone was conquered gradually during the course of the nineteenth century. Several schools were opened for educating the children of ex-slaves and a hospital was built for providing medical care. The Fourah Bay College, the oldest in Africa was established in 1824, primarily for training missionaries for work within Sierra Leone and neighbouring countries. The freed slaves, all Christians called themselves Creoles and claimed to be superior to tribal people whom they considered savages. Freetown has one of the finest harbours in Africa, which was used as a naval base during World War II.

15

The Gambia, 1979-83

After leaving Sierra Leone in March 1979, we went to Ann Arbor to be with Virendra and Arvind and for Kamla's medical treatment. Her sickness proved to be much less serious than we had feared. All that was needed was a small operation which required her stay in the University of Michigan hospital for two days. On our way to Ann Arbor, we visited Malvern College for Jyotsna's admission. She did very well in the interviews and was accepted for admission. Since her course was to start in September, Virendra hired an apartment close to the University for our stay from March to September. I stayed in Ann Arbor for two months (March to May 1979) and went to join my post in The Gambia early in May, but Kamla and Jyotsna stayed there till mid-September. Virendra, who was already working for a small company continued to stay in his small apartment but Arvind moved in with us. He had by then got his Bachelor of Science degrees in chemical and mechanical engineering and was studying for his Master of Science degree in the latter.

The Gambia is a very small country with a total area of about 10,000 sq.km. It had a population of about 600,000 in the early1980s. The country consists of a narrow strip of land on both sides of the river Gambia. It is surrounded on the north and the south by Senegal and has the Saharan desert country of Mali on its north western border. It was made famous by Arthur Hailey's novel, *Roots*. Hailey, a black American journalist and author claimed, on the basis of evidence which is highly suspect, that his ancestors had lived in the small village of Juffure on the north bank of the river, before being captured by slave traders in the eighteenth century and brought to the US as slaves. The book, which is extremely well written sold in millions and the TV show based on it, which was watched by about 80 million Americans every week made Mr. Hailey a multi-millionaire. He visited the Gambia during my stay there with a party of about 30 black American journalists. I accompanied him to Juffure. He and his party were state guests.

Mr. Hailey promised that he would finance building of a small electricity generating station which could supply electricity for homes and water for irrigation. The promise, which had been made earlier also, was never fulfilled, and all that the villagers got out of his visit was about 30 head-ties (turbans) worn by the women.

The Gambia is an agricultural country with groundnut as its principal export crop and rice grown in swamps along the river and sorghum and millets grown on the uplands as the principal food crops. There was no industry except a few small workshops which repaired motor vehicles and electrical appliances and a government owned mill which decorticated groundnuts for export and made groundnut oil for consumption within the country. Import of goods for smuggling to Senegal where import duties were much higher than in Gambia was a principal source of income for its merchants. The Government of Senegal was very unhappy about the smuggling but could do little to stop it because the imported goods could be carried as head-loads by people living in villages along the border between the two countries.

The Gambians are tall and well built and are far more intelligent and enterprising than the people of Sierra Leone. A major source of employment for The Gambian young men and income for the government was tourism. Tens of thousands of tourists from Scandinavian countries, Germany and Britain visited the Gambia in winter. The warm dry winter and excellent beaches provided the tourists a welcome escape from the damp cold of North European winters. However, tourism had also led to male prostitution. Most of the tourists were single Scandinavian women.

On reaching Banjul, the capital of the Gambia and its only city, I stayed for some months in a hotel before moving into a house after Kamla arrived. Mr. Ruud who was earlier in Sierra Leone helped me find a house. Another friend who welcomed me was Mr. Moinuddin, a Pakistani expert in agricultural credit who had worked in Sierra Leone for two years before moving to the Gambia as a member of a team of FAO experts. His office was located in the same building as mine. He introduced me to Dr. Langley, the Secretary of the Ministry of Development and other officials.

Mr. Friscic, who had arranged for my transfer to the Gambia also visited Banjul within the first week of my arrival. His visit helped me greatly in establishing good relations with Dr. Langley and his colleagues.

The planning team was assembled over the next few months. Mr. Mikko Eklin, an official working in the Ministry of Finance of Finland, joined as Financial Planner in June. Mr. Ruud, designated as a Manpower Planner, also looked after health, education and welfare of women and youth. The fourth member was an American, Mr. Michel Chirman. He had resigned his permanent post with UNOTC in New York and had come to the Gambia because he and his wife – they had no children – were tired of living in New York. The fifth member of the team was a young Dutchman. He worked as an infrastructure planner. The FAO agricultural experts were to provide the advice needed for agricultural development. An industrial planner was also not needed because there was hardly any industry in the Gambia and the prospect of industrial development was also very limited in the absence of mineral or forest resources and the tiny local market. The government had built an industrial estate in a suburb of Banjul. But most of the units located in it were sale-cum-service shops for motor vehicles and other machines or units packaging for local consumption, goods imported in bulk from abroad.

During the first year of my stay in the Gambia, I participated as a member of the Gambian delegation in discussions with the Senegalese on construction of a bridge-cum-barrage over The Gambia river where there was a highway linking the northern and southern parts of Senegal. The Government of Senegal was keen on construction of the bridge because crossing the river by ferry boats was very time consuming. However, the Gambia Government wanted construction of a bridge-cum-barrage, as a result of which the inflow of salt water up the river from the Atlantic ocean at high tide would be checked, and the swamp lands located upstream of the barrage would be available for production of rice. A feasibility report on the project had been prepared by an American consulting firm. The discussions, held in Dakar, Banjul and a small border town in Senegal extended over a year but were inconclusive. Construction of the bridge was economic because the toll on motor vehicles (mostly trucks) using it would provide an adequate rate of return on the investment. But construction of a bridge-cum-barrage was not economic because the benefits from it in additional production of rice did not justify the enormous expenditure.

Banjul, was a small city with a population of about 100,000 in the early 1980s. It was divided into two parts, the old town and the suburbs about 15 km from it. The President's palace, the offices of various ministries of the government, the small port and most of the big stores were located in the old town. The suburbs were mainly residential. Like most expatriates , we lived in Fajara, a suburb which was very close to the beach and the tourist hotels.

The Gambia had a radio station, but no television station. It did not have an army, but only an armed constabulary of about 500 men mainly for maintaining internal security.

There were very few Indians. In contrast to Sierra Leone, where there were about 40 Sindhi merchants there were only three Sindhi merchants. The number of Indian experts varied between four and six. Thus we missed the active social life within the Indian community that we had in Freetown. Our closest Indian friends were Arun and Usha Banerjee. Arun, a senior official of the Researve Bank of India was an IMF-appointed adviser to the Bank of the Gambia; and his wife, Usha, was a charming Gujarati lady, whose brothers were among the biggest cotton merchants in Mumbai. I had met Arun briefly in the early 1950s, when he was Secretary to the Governor of the Reserve Bank of India and I was working in the Planning Commission. Our close friends besides the Banerjees and Moinuddins were three families with whom we played bridge and had dinner once a week.

Two of them, Mr. Gretsinger, a Canadian, and Mr. Jefford, an Englishman were UNESCO experts recruited to build a school for training technicians in the Gambia. Of the third couple, Mr. Keen, an Irishman was the manager of the local office of Cable and Wireless the British company which operated telephone and telegraph services in most of the former British colonies.

Among our other expatriate friends were an American couple, Steve and Ann Fitzgerald and a British couple, Chris and Joan Collins. Steve, an employee of the Centre for Disease Control in Atlanta, Georgia, was working for a US-AID project for immunization of Gambian children against polio, diphtheria and whooping cough; Chris Collins was the Representative of the European Union in the Gambia. We have kept in touch with the Gretsingers, the Fitzgeralds, the Collinses and two of my colleagues in the project — the Eklins and the Ruuds — through exchange of letters at Christmas or New Year.

I cannot help mentioning here an incident which gives an interesting insight into human behaviour. Mrs. Moinuddin was a devout Moslem and an ardent Pakistani. However, one night when Mr. Moinuddin was away on a 1-week consulting mission to Ghana, there was a quarrel between their two watchmen culminating in the murder of one by the other. After an enquiry by the police and a court case, the murderer was sentenced to death. But during the two days between the murder and Mr. Moinuddin's return, his wife came to stay with us. They had a number of Pakistani friends, but apparently she had more confidence in us than in them! During this stay, she told us that while the Hindu and Sikh migrants from Pakistan to India had suffered no discrimination in India, the Moslem migrants from India to Pakistan were discriminated against by the native Sindhis, particularly in Karachi, and that there were frequent attacks by the Sindhis on affluent migrants from India, who had occupied high positions in the civil services, and professionas or had beema wealthy businessmen. This conflict between the two communities in Sindh became serious in the 1990s and is an important part of political life in Pakistan even today.

Another friend in Banjul was Mr. Lele, an agricultural statistician who retired from the FAO after nearly 25 years of service at the end of his assignment in the Gambia. I had met him in Delhi in 1954 when I was working with the P.E.O. and he was working with the Central Statistical Organisation.

Small places provide a much better environment for making friends than a metropolis like Delhi. We have been living in Vasant Vihar for more than 14 years but have made few friends!

The Gambia had a large number of young men and women working for agencies such as the Peace Corps (American), V.S.O. (Voluntary Service Overseas of Britain) and CUSO (Canadian Universities Services Overseas). They would live and work in Banjul or large villages for one or two years before returning home.

Some of the young men and women fell in love with each other and married. A number of volunteers of the peace corps and other agencies taught English in schools in Banjul and the larger villages; others taught the villagers the basics of improved agriculture. The young women taught Gambian women the basics of nutrition, child care, personal hygiene, and measures for prevention of diseases.

Our principal interest in the Peace Corps was that it showed American movies at its headquarters. English movies were also shown occasionally at the Fajara Club of which we were members. Most of the members of the club were Britishers, working in the High Commission and other expatriates. The club had a small library, courts for playing tennis and badminton and a sandy golf course. Since I played no game, our interest in the club was in using its library and watching the movies.

Various other unofficial aid agencies like the Catholic Relief Service (American), CARE (Corporation for American Relief Everywhere), Freedom from Hunger Campaign (German) and Action Aid (British) were also active in the Gambia. The Catholic Relief Service distributed free food for the children and pregnant mothers and taught the mothers the basics of personal hygiene and child care. CARE, FFHC and the World Food Programme of the FAO had a number of projects in which balanced food was given to men working on projects such as construction or repair of approach roads to villages, reclamation of swamps for production of rice, construction of sanitary drinking water wells. Action Aid was a British agency which concentrated on agricultural extension and teaching villagers construction of sanitary drinking water wells through voluntary labour. Its Director, a young Englishman, became quite friendly with us and showed us some of the projects executed by Action Aid. SOS (Save our Souls), an American aid agency, ran a residential school for orphan children. While living in the school the students were given primary education and taught crafts like carpentry and masonry so that they could earn a living after they left school.

Work on formulation of the Second Five Year Plan of Economic and Social Development began in earnest in August 1979, after Mikko Eklin and Michel Chirman joined the project. It extended over two years and was completed by the end of 1981. As mentioned earlier, Mr. Friscic's visit had greatly facilitated my establishing good relations with my Gambian counterparts. Dr. Langley, the Secretary of the Ministry, was so nice to me that in one of the meetings on finalisation of the Plan document, he humorously remarked "you are one of us, and henceforth I shall call you 'Pa Nath'". He was as good as his word; Pa (lit. father) was a word used for any respected elder. Because of his attitude, his two principal deputies, Mr. Abdou Njie and Mr. Alieu Ngum, also treated me very well. Dr. Langley, a scholar of Gambian history, was in his late forties while the other two were in their early thirties.

My relations with the members of the UN Team were also cordial. Excepting the young Dutchman, the other three were not only competent professionals but also thorough gentlemen. An additional source of satisfaction of working in the Gambia was that in contrast to Sierra Leone where the government ignored the Plan and implemented projects initiated by Lebanese merchants, who had the ear of the President , the Government of the Gambia would follow the recommendations of the Plan both in economic policies and implementation of projects.

Mikko Eklin was the ablest of my colleagues. In the last two months of formulation of the Plan, he asked me one day to allow him to work at his home for three days to produce the macro-economic model for the Plan. I readily agreed and at the end of the three days, he produced a set of tables in which every figure relating to the Plan had been meticulously worked out. Because of his ability and pleasant disposition, he was invited by the Ministry of Development to work for two years after I left the Gambia.

The Abortive Coup – July 1981

One morning when I had almost reached my office, I learnt that there had been a *coup d' etat* and all government offices were closed. The rebels led by a sargeant of the armed constabulary had occupied the President's residence-cum-office and taken prisoner his favourite wife, Lady Chillel. The President, Sir Dauda Karamba Jawara was away in Britain for his normal summer golfing holiday. The rebels were in the process of blocking the road that linked Banjul with the suburbs, and I was advised to go back home as fast as possible. Hearing this, I rushed immediately to the office of Cable and Wireless, to send a telegram to Jyotsna, who had gone to Sierra Leone to visit a friend there, not to return home until normalcy had been restored in the country. The rebels had not captured the office of the company yet although I could hear rifle fire from the President's house located next to it.

After sending the telegram I tried to return home but found that no vehicle could pass the bridge on the river Gambia on which the road linking Banjul and Fajara passed. In desperation I sought refuge in the house of Mr. Mathew one of the two Indian teachers in the Gambia high school who lived just outside the city. I tried to telephone Kamla to tell her that I was safe in Mr. Mathew's home but could not reach her because by then the Cable and Wireless office in which the telephone exchange was located had been captured by the rebels. I spent six hours in the Mathews' home hearing gun fire in Banjul all the time. Around 4 p.m., my driver came and informed me that the rebels were allowing vehicles to pass the bridge and that we should go home. There were soldiers with guns on the bridge and at several other places along the road including the entrance to the building housing Radio Gambia but they respected my diplomatic status, and allowed me to go home.

Kamla was greatly relieved when I reached home. So was Mr. Ayala, the Assistant UNDP Resident Representative, who had been deputed by the Resrep to go to the houses of all experts living in Fajara to find out whether they were safe. After the *coup* had failed and normalcy had been restored, he remarked with a twinkle in his eye, at a meeting called by the Resident Representative, "I was counting my chickens and was worried to find that one of them (Dr. Nath) was missing! So I was greatly relieved when I got a call from him that he was back home."

The *coup* had been organised by a group of disaffected members of the Gambia's armed constabulary. They had raided the armoury which was located about a kilometre from our house very early one morning, captured all the arms, and had by 8 a.m. captured the airport, Radio Gambia and various offices of the government. By 10 a.m. they had captured the President's residence-cum-office, the port and Banjul city. The leader of the coup was Sargeant Samba. In his first broadcast to the people of the Gambia, he declared himself President, explained that he and his colleagues had seized power in order to eradicate corruption, inefficiency and tribalism in the government and to work for the welfare of all the people of the Gambia. He belonged to a tribe which was a minority in the Gambia and was denied all positions in the government. He accused the President of corruption and inefficiency, who had massed great wealth and was more interested in golf than in leading a government which eradicated poverty, illiteracy and disease in the country and provided gainful employment to Gambian youth.

The *coup* came as a complete surprise to all the expatriates, officials of the government and most of the people of Banjul. For about two months, before the '*coup*', we had seen on walls at various places writings accusing the government of inefficiency and corruption and the need for a change. But we had ignored them because the Gambia had a stable government which had been in office since it had been granted independence by Britain in 1965, and going by African standards, it was well governed.

Hearing of the *coup*, the President, Sir Dauda Jawara, rushed to Dakar and appealed to the President of Senegal, Mr. Abdou Djouf to send the Senegalese army to recapture Banjul and restore his government. The President of Senegal agreed on condition that Senegal and Gambia would join to form the Senegambian Confederation of which the President of Senegal would be President and the President of the Gambia would be Vice President. The Confederation would have the responsibility for defence and external relations while internal governance of the two countries would continue to be the responsibility of the two governments. The Government of the Gambia would take all measures needed to prevent smuggling of goods from the Gambia to Senegal which was causing an enormous financial loss to the government of Senegal. The two countries would have a single army, the two constituents of which would have responsibility for both external defence and internal security. When both Presidents had signed the document constituting the confederation, the President of Senegal sent in his army which defeated the rebels in two days.

The abortive *coup* lasted 10 days in which several large stores in the city were burnt. More than 100 Americans, employees of the Embassy, volunteers of the Peace Corps and experts working for various aid agencies had crowded in the house of the American Ambassador, which was located near the beach, so that they could be airlifted by helicopters to land on a ship which was ready to take them home. No other foreign diplomatic mission had made such arrangements. However, there was no need for this because the *coup* ended in 10 days. Its last two days were most dangerous for us because our house was located on the road between the Senegalese Army on one side and the rebels on the other. I give below a diagram to illustrate the location.

Senegalese army on Pipeline Road

Cross fire A Our house

Rebels in the Armoury

On the last day of the coup, we heard the cross fire between the soldiers of the Senegalese army mounted on personnel carriers on the pipeline road and the rebels concentrated in the armoury from about 9 a.m. In order to escape being hit by a bullet, Kamla and I lay on the floor of the passage connecting our two bedrooms. We chose the passage because it had a solid wooden door on the side facing the road and was protected by the bedroom on the side facing the armoury. Besides, the danger of being hit by a bullet there was the danger of being attacked and looted by a fleeing rebel. About noon, a soldier did come to the house. We were scared, but he only wanted a drink of water from our gardener, who gladly provided it. By about 1 p.m. the firing seemed to have died down and we took our lunch. But as soon as we lay on our beds for rest after lunch, a bullet whizzed through the room and hit the wall. Thanking God for this providential escape we went back to the mattress on the floor of the passage and lay there till 4 p.m. when the BBC broadcast the news that the rebels were fleeing to escape being taken prisoner by the Senegalese army. Most of them did manage to escape; a few were taken prisoner. Sargeant Samba, their leader, committed suicide.

During 10 years of living in West Africa I had become an addict to listening to the African service of the BBC. It provided news and comments on various events in Africa and the world and music ranging from pop songs to symphonies of great composers like Mozart and Beethoven. But I was impressed by the efficiency of its news service that afternoon as I had never been before. The news of the end of the coup was broadcast by it at 4.15 p.m. within minutes of the event.

On hearing the news and finding that the cross fire had ceased, we got up and went about the house and its large yard to find out how many bullets had hit the house or were lying in the yard. We found that half a dozen bullets had hit the house and a similar number were lying in the yard. The seven hours of lying on the floor in the passage between our two bedrooms, listening to the BBC and praying for our safety was the most harrowing experience of our 12 year stay in Africa. And we had to go through it in the Gambia which was supposed to be a most peaceful country in Africa; where nothing ever happened. "Truth is stranger than fiction" is an old adage, but the truth of it was brought home to us that day as never before.

During the next few days, each one's experience in the coup was the topic of conversation among our friends. No one was hurt, but Arun and Usha Banerjee told us that they had a miraculous escape because several bullets had passed through their drawing room.

Donor Agencies

As in Sierra Leone, delegations from the IMF and the World Bank would visit the Gambia every year in the cool season. The IMF delegation would review the economic polices of the government and the foreign trade and balance of payments position of the Gambia; the World Bank delegation would review progress on projects that it was financing in part. Both delegations would go back generally satisfied because the government had followed the policies recommended by the IMF and progress on implementation of projects financed by the Bank was satisfactory considering all the constraints of manpower and infrastructure.

I would attend the discussions with these delegations generally held in the Bank of the Gambia on behalf of the Ministry of Development. The discussions convinced me of the power of the two organisations. I found that no western donor would finance a project which had been considered uneconomic by the World Bank. Furthermore, the western donors would urge the government to give up economic policies on which the IMF had expressed reservations. The headquarters officials of the governments of the donor countries working on aid to the Gambia would also visit in the cool season to review progress on projects being financed by them. We would often joke that all these officials descended on the Gambia in the cool season in order to have some relief from the bitter cold and damp of the northern European and American winter and that their visits were in fact brief working vacations.

Work on formulation of the Second Five Year Plan was completed by the end of 1981. In the following two years, the work of the UN Team consisted mainly in reviewing progress on the implementation of the Plan through preparation of annual plans. I retired from UN Service in December 1983, five months after I had reached the mandatory retirement age of 60 years for experts working in the field.

Donors' Conferences

In 1983, the UNDP and the principal western donors to small African countries decided that there was need for greater coordination in their aid to these countries, so that duplication of aid by different donors for projects with similar objectives was avoided and the aid given had the maximum benefit. By this time, it was becoming apparent also that in the nearly 20 years, since the African countries had become independent, the level of living of the population had not risen. On the contrary, there were increasing problems of very rapid population growth, increasing unemployment among African youth, millions of whom were leaving their villages to flock to the cities in search of jobs, and rapid degradation of the environment because of deforestation and overgrazing on grasslands.

In order to achieve these objectives it was decided that the UNDP should organise 'a Donors' Conference once in three or four years for every small African country, in which representatives of the principal donors would meet, review progress of their aid programmes and work out strategies and policies for future assistance. The Donors' Conferences would be similar to the development fora which are organised by the World Bank annually for coordinating assistance to large developing countries like India and Pakistan.

UNOTC asked me to prepare the agenda paper for the Donor's Conference. I accepted the assignment on condition that I should be allowed to continue working on it after I left the Gambia to go to Boston and would complete the document only by the end of February 1984. UNOTC agreed to these conditions, and I completed the document by the agreed date. Discussions on finalising the document were held in New York in May 1984 and a successful Donors' Conference was held in Banjul in December 1984.

I was happy to return to the Gambia, a year after I had left it. A major change had taken place in the top personnel of the Ministry of Development. Dr. Langley had left to become Secretary to the President, the seniormost position in the civil service and his senior deputy, Mr. Abdou Njie, had become the Secretary of the Ministry.

Appreciating the high quality of the Background Document on the Gambia and the success of the Donors' Conference, UNDP asked me to prepare a similar document for Sierra Leone for which it planned to hold a similar conference in December 1985. I accepted the assignment and spent the first five months of 1985 in Freetown preparing the draft document. On return to Sierra Leone more than six years after leaving it, I found major changes in the economy and in the UNDP office. With greatly reduced foreign exchange earnings from export of diamonds and other minerals and rapid increase in the cost of imports, Sierra Leone was facing serious problems of rapid inflation and large balance of payments deficits. The value of the currency was falling rapidly, and there were occasional shortages of essential goods such as rice, sugar, kerosene oil and petrol.

The UNDP Resident Representative was a highly efficient lady, Mrs. Mary Chennery Hesse, who treated me with great courtesy. The Minister of Development was so courteous that he would often come to my office or call me to his house on Saturdays or Sunday mornings in order to finalise some portions of the document. This courteous treatment by the top official in the UNDP and the Minister of Development made working on the document a pleasant task and helped overcome in large part the loneliness of living away from Kamla and Jyotsna.

The Background Document was received in New York in July 1985, after which it was decided that a small delegation led by the UNDP Resrep, and consisting of two officials from UNDP, New York and I should visit London, Paris and Bonn for personal discussions with the headquarter officials of the principal western donor agencies to Sierra Leone, and prepare the ground for the success of the Donors' Conference scheduled to be held in December, 1985.

Among these visits, I enjoyed particularly the one to Bonn, then capital of West Germany, which I had not seen before. It is a small, but very clean city situated along the bank of a small river which could be seen from most streets in the city.

The Donors' Conference was not successful, however, because the donors were very critical of the government's economic management which had led to rapid deterioration in the economy and tardy implementation of projects assisted by them. Furthermore, they could not get any assurance from Sierra Leone officials of either better economic management or more rapid progress on implementation of projects in future. The failure of the Conference left a feeling of frustration in my mind because all my hard work on preparation of the Background Document had proved to be a waste.

Travels within the Gambia and Southern Senegal

One of our pleasures was to drive about 100 km west of Banjul on a Sunday to have lunch in a small but very clean restaurant, run by a Swede. He had built the restaurant along the river about 3 kms from the road. He had his house there and had kept also a few animals and a variety of fish in a small pond. It was a pleasure to have lunch and spend a couple of hours in sylvan surroundings and walking along a well maintained beach.

Another pleasure was to spend a weekend in a small but very clean hotel located near the beach in southern Senegal about 120 km from Banjul. The hotel consisted of a number of one or two bedroom chalets with mud floors and thatched walls and roofs which had electricity and running water and were kept spotlessly clean. The hotel served excellent French food. The principal pleasures were to drive to and from it through tropical forest and to walk along the beach. Swimming was not advisable because of the danger of sharks.

During the four months, May to September 1979, between my arrival in Banjul and Kamla's, I had traveled throughout the country. The road from Banjul to the western border of the Gambia with the Saharan desert country of Mali was well maintained but there were only three towns along its 400 km stretch. It was interesting to see the progressive change from tropical vegetation near Banjul to the dry sands near the border. There was considerable smuggling of imported goods from the Gambia to Mali. Kamla made many visits to a village on the north bank of the river, where women made salt from the water of the river. She wrote a paper based on the work which was much appreciated by officials in the UNIDO (UN Organisation for Industrial Development).

The Gambia Revisited

I returned to the Gambia in the late summer of 1987 to assist in finalising the Background Document for the Second Donors' Conference scheduled to be held in December 1987. The document had been prepared by the Ministry of Development with assistance from members of the UNOTC project team. The project of which I had been the manager was being continued; its manager was an amiable Cypriot economist. I developed excellent relations with him. Mr. Alieu Ngum had risen to be the Secretary of the Ministry, while Mr. Abdou Njie had been promoted as Governor of the Central Bank of the Gambia. Dr. Langley had been transferred to Washington as representative of the Gambia to the I.M.F. Thus the three top officials of the Ministry with whom I had worked closely were regarded so highly by the President that they had earned these promotions.

Mr. Ngum and Mr. Njie welcomed me warmly; it was a pleasure to revisit Banjul where we had spent four pleasant and rewarding years. Work on finalisation of the document was easy, because a high quality document had already been prepared by the ministry.

The economy of the Gambia was doing well. The exchange rate of the currency, the Dalasi, was stable. Progress on the projects approved as a result of the Donors' Conference of 1984 was satisfactory and the Conference scheduled to be held in December 1987 was expected to be successful.

Smuggling of imported goods from the Gambia to Senegal had continued much as before, despite the solemn assurance of the President given to the President of Senegal at the time of formation of the Senegambia confederation to minimize it.

The tourist industry was booming. Besides one new large 400–bedroom hotel, owned by a prestigious French hotel group, a number of small hotels, owned by the Gambians, had come up. The Gambians had also established a number of small restaurants. They were no more than shacks with mud floors and thatched walls and roofs, located under a few palm trees. They served, however, good traditional Gambian or continental food to the accompaniment of one or more musicians playing traditional Gambian music. These small but clean restaurants gratified the tourists' craving for authentic Gambian food in an African setting.

Among our old friends, the Pattakanaiyas — Mr. and Mrs. Pattakanaiya were both teachers in the Gambia High School — were still there. The Mathews, whom I have mentioned earlier, had returned to their home in Kerala. We had known the Pattakanaiyas in Freetown, where Mr. Pattakanaiya had spent several years teaching at the Government High School. They invited me for lunch several times during my stay.

I learnt in November 1998 from Mr. Lele, that the Pattakanaiyas are now settled in their home in Mangalore in Karnataka.

My last visit to Banjul was between December 1989–March 1990. I had undergone coronary-by-pass surgery in March 1989, but the cardiologists at the Escorts Hospital where the surgery was performed, considered me fit enough to undertake this consultancy mission. I was pleased and enjoyed the return to Banjul, as I had done three years earlier. Mr. Ngum was still the Secretary of the Ministry of Development but was appointed Secretary of the Ministry of Finance soon after my visit. Dr. Langley was still in Washington and Mr. Njie continued to be Governor of the Bank of the Gambia.

I do not remember the precise terms of reference of this mission but I recall vividly that the changes in Banjul and the Gambian economy were markedly less in the three years 1987 – 90 than during 1984 – 87.

I do not know how the Gambia is doing now. However, from the absence of any news about it, I conclude that it must have a stable government and a moderately good economy. Kamla and I shall always recall our stay in the Gambia as generally pleasant and professionally rewarding, but where we had also our most harrowing experience of my 16 years' stay in UNOTC assignments.

16

Boston University, 1964–86

We arrived in Boston on 4 January, 1984 to take up our positions as visiting research scholars at the University of Boston, Boston, Mass. in the U.S.A. I had visited Boston in September 1983 on my way back to the Gambia from New York where I had been called by the UNDP for discussion on preparation of the Background Document for the Gambia. During this visit, I met Prof. Gustav Papanek, Professor of Economics and Head of the Centre for Asian Development Studies to explore the possibility of spending a year or two at the University as an honorary visiting scholar in the Centre. Prof. Papanek was most encouraging and offered me the position of an honorary Research Associate at the Centre for two years. Since Kamla had written some papers on economic activities of Gambian women, and wanted to do further work on the subject, I saw Prof. John Harris, Head of the Centre for African Studies of the University. Prof. Harris, a well known economist offered for her the position of an honorary Research Fellow for two years in his centre.

I had wanted to stay at a research centre in an American University before returning home so that I could write on economic development and planning in developing countries. After writing numerous reports on these subjects in Sierra Leone and the Gambia for 12 years and lecturing on economic development and planning in Kuwait for four years, I was anxious that I should do some writing on my own. Stay at a research centre in an American University would provide the time and congenial environment for such writing.

The offers of Prof. Papanek and Prof. Harris were most attractive. We would be provided offices within the buildings of the centres. We could attend seminars held in the centres and discuss our writings with the professors and other research scholars there. The positions were honorary; we did not have any obligation to work for the centres. Prof. Papanek also arranged for my being allotted by the housing office of the University a two bed-room flat owned by the university at a moderate rent . It was within walking distance from our offices.

Besides our desire to write on economic development and planning in developing countries, there were other reasons for our going to Boston. Virendra and Arvind were both in the U.S.A. and we felt that by living in Boston, we could help them settle down. I remembered that in 1977/78, when Virendra was having trouble with his professors in the University of Wisconsin, I had successfully persuaded him to return to the University of Michigan, where he had spent four happy years. He was happy to return, passed his M.S. examination, securing good grades and got a job immediately afterwards as a Consultant with a small company. He had been in Honolulu for nearly four years working as an adviser on materials management in the Queen's Medical Centre, the largest hospital in the city. However, he was feeling frustrated because he was not being promoted on account of in-fighting among his superiors. He was thinking of starting his own computer data entry company. We felt that we could help him settle down with his friend namely Mckowsky.

The stay in Boston was enjoyable in many ways. We attended dinner seminars organised on Friday evenings once a fortnight, jointly by the Boston University and the Massachusetts Institute of Technology. The seminars would be held alternatively within the campuses of the two universities. After a sumptuous dinner, there would be a talk by one of the professors of either university or by a distinguished visitor. One of the visitors was Mr. T.N. Kaul, Indian Ambassador to the U.S.A., who spoke on Indo-U.S. economic and political relations. The talk, which was followed by an hour of questions was most interesting, because Mr. Kaul tried to answer criticism by American economists of India's economic policies. Both of us greatly enjoyed the lectures.

Long walks after lunch along the Charles river on summer and sunny winter afternoons was another pleasure.

We attended lectures on Sunday mornings at the Ramakrishna Centre, located within the campus of the university about 1 ½ km. from our flat. Swami Sarvagathananda, who was head of the centre, was a good scholar and an excellent speaker and his hour-long lecture made me forget our problems. The half hour tea after the lecture gave us an opportunity to meet about 40 Indian professionals, mainly technologists working in the Boston area and settled there. The university had a number of Indian students in its economics, political science and sociology departments. Our social life was limited, however, to having lunch or dinner once a month at their houses or ours with Bhim and Sheila Mahajan. Bhim, an old friend from Lahore and Delhi had retired from a long tenure of service with the UNOTC—FAO and was spending a year in Cambridge before returning to Delhi in order to provide a home to their son, Rahul, who had joined the Harvard University as an undergraduate student in Economics.

Another pleasure was joining one of the short trips into the Atlantic Ocean to see whales in July or August. The whales, which migrate from the Arctic Ocean to the Caribbean sea during the summer, could be seen near Boston during these two months.

Despite the facilities offered by the Centre, I could not do much writing on my own. This was due only partly to my being busy with work for UNDP. A more important reason was that despite working in planning organisations for nearly 30 years, I was not as well equipped to write on economic development and planning in developing countries as I had thought I was. I wrote one paper, "Urbanisation in India: Retrospect and Prospect, 1950–2000". It was very well received. It was included in the book, *Asian Urbanisation*, published by the University of Akron in the U.S.A., which remained the authoritative text on the subject in American Universities for many years. It was included also among occasional papers of the Centre for Asian Development Studies. After returning to Delhi, I published a revised and up-dated version of it in the *Economic and Political Weekly*, Mumbai.

Consultantcy Mission to Nigeria – June – July, 1984

During June-July 1984, I went to Nigeria on a 6 week consultancy mission on behalf of UNOTC. The leader of the mission was a Canadian – Japanese economist, teaching in a University in Vancouver, Canada. The object of the mission was to evaluate the progress of UNOTC assisted projects in development planning in the six states of northern and central Nigeria. The visit was interesting and professionally rewarding.

In Lagos, we stayed in the hostel for UN experts, which had its own security guards provided to the experts and consultants in order to assure them a safe stay. The population of Lagos had increased several times since the country became independent in 1961. Infrastructure facilities particularly supply of electricity and water were not expanded enough to take care of the needs of the greatly increased population of the city and gainful employment could not be provided to hundreds of thousands who were flocking to Lagos and other cities. This had made the frustrated youth take to violence.

UN officials were required to travel from the UN complex to the airport and back between 4.30 am and 7.00 a.m. in order to escape being attacked and robbed. The UNDP Representative was Mr. Demeska; he had been promoted quickly as Representative in his own country, because of his good work in the Gambia. We hired a taxi to go from Lagos to the capitals of the six states and return to Lagos. The driver had strict instructions not to drive after 4.30 p.m. while passing through the central part of the country in order to minimize the risk of being attacked and the car being taken away by robbers. There had been a military *coup d' etat, a* few months earlier and the General, who had taken over as the president, was slowly consolidating his position.

The northern states were peaceful however and one could travel safely through them. After we reached Kaduna, capital of one of the states, we divided ourselves into two groups, with the leader and I visiting three states each. The ministers and secretaries of the ministries of development and economic planning of the states were most courteous and treated us very well. I remember vividly meeting these tall, well built men, dressed in light blue or white, ankle length flowing robes and small white skull caps. Except the head-dress, their dresses were so much like the dresses of old Kuwaitis. Among the cities that I visited the most interesting was Kano, capital of one of the states. It was a large city with a population of about 1 million located on the border between Nigeria and Niger, a country which formed part of the Sahara desert. Most of the houses had light brown mud plastered on their brick walls and roofs in order to keep them cool during the long , hot summer. With its numerous mosques and turrets on all its public buildings, it appeared very much like a Middle Eastern city. However, in contrast to Lagos, which was bursting at the seams it was uncrowded, because it was spread out over a large area.

Among my other memories is of a visit to Jos, capital of one of the states of central Nigeria. Located at an altitude of about 3000 feet, it was cool and resembled a hill station in India. One of the officers, who had worked under me in the P.E.O. had spent 10 years in it as a UNOTC expert in development planning and was still remembered by the officials of the ministry of development for the good work that he had done. He did not appear to be too bright while working in the P.E.O. but apparently his talent had blossomed in Jos.

Although Nigeria received large revenue from export of a large output of petroleum, there was such wasteful expenditure by the Government that there was a flourishing black market in its currency, the Naira, in the border states. One could get 6-8 times of the official rate of the (the Naira) for one US dollar.

Departure from Boston

We left Boston in March 1986; Jyotsna and I returned from Boston to New Delhi after staying for two days each in London and Paris. The stay in London allowed me to visit the office of Merill Lynch to review my investments. The stay in Paris, was enjoyable. Jyotsna liked Paris with its wide boulevards and numerous tourist attractions. She felt it was a real city while London was an overgrown town. Kamla who left Boston a couple of days later joined us in Mumbai. We stayed two days in Mumbai to see some of our friends before returning to New Delhi on 17 March, 1986.

17

Back Home, 1986-2000

We moved to our own house in Vasant Vihar on 28 March after a 10-day stay at the India International Centre. The date and time of our entry into our house had been indicated as auspicious by our friend, Mr Ramanan, an FAO expert on agricultural credit, whom we had known in the Gambia. He was a devout Tamil Brahmin, who, we believed, had a fair knowledge of astrology. However his advice on the auspicious date and time of entry into our house proved to be completely wrong, because we had no end of problems during the first year of our stay in the house. I have never believed in astrology, and this experience strengthened my disbelief.

During the 14 years of our stay abroad after the house was built in 1972, it was let out to foreigners. The tenants during the first four years were two Colombian diplomats. Thereafter, it was rented out to some Germans. The occupant in 1985 was a Mr. Hanseleit, a German economist who was the Representative for South and South East Asia of a German Trade Promotion Organisation. In order to persuade him to leave by March 1986 - his lease was to run for another year I travelled from Boston to India in December 1985 via Cologne, where he was spending his Christmas vacation. At our meeting the Hanseleits reluctantly agreed to vacate the house by 15th March 1986. They were reluctant because they had greatly enjoyed the three years that they had spent in it and did not relish the prospect of moving to another house for the remaining few months of their stay in Delhi. Mr Hanseleit was due to be transferred from Delhi by December 1986 after finishing his four year tenure.

There were two other reasons for my travelling to India in December, 1985. I wanted to explore the possibility of working as honorary research professor at one of the several institutes of research that had come up in Delhi during the previous ten years. Second, Kamla was very keen that I should go and see Sai Baba to seek his blessings for the health and happiness of the family.

I have never believed in the healing powers of holy men. But I went nevertheless to Sai Baba's headquarters in Puttaparti, a small town in Andhra Pradesh, because of Kamla's insistence. My first objective was achieved. Dr. S.R. Sen, a senior colleague in the Planning Commission suggested that I join the Centre for Policy Research, which had been established in Chanakyapuri by Dr Pai Panandiker. I had known Dr. Pai slightly when he had worked in the Planning Commission as a Consultant on Public Administration in 1965. I met him and we agreed that I would join the Centre as an honorary visiting professor immediately on return to Delhi.

But the visit to Puttaparti was fruitless. I travelled to it via Bangalore, where I stayed both on my way to and return from Puttaparti with the Nedungadis, our friends from Kuwait. The late Dr. Nedungadi, a meteorologist, had been posted for two years at the Kuwait airport when we were there. They were one of the four Indian families with whom we spent our evenings.

The Nedungadis were very pleased to see me, after 18 years; they had left Kuwait in 1968. They had not gone back to their ancestral homes in Kerala after Dr Nedungadi retiring but had decided, like many other South Indian UN agency experts to settle down in Bangalore. It is a modern city with a congenial climate, in which live a number of retired experts of various agencies of the UN system with whom they could interact. I was greatly impressed with the quiet efficiency with which Mrs. Nedungadi ran her home. As soon as I entered the house, I had the experience of peace and tranquility. But Dr Nedungadi's assessment of Sai Baba was not very good. He mentioned that his healing powers were greatly exaggerated; furthermore, all his devotees were affluent or middle class Indians or foreigners and that the poor had no place in his blessings. Dr Nedungadi however, arranged for a taxi which would take me to Puttaparti and bring me back after an overnight stay.

When I reached Puttaparti after a five-hour drive on a hot morning — the road was fairly good but it was hot even in December—I found that it was extremely difficult to get a room for the overnight stay. The officer-in-charge of allotting rooms gave me a place to sleep in one of the several large tin sheds in the Ashram (lit. abode of a holy man). When I protested that I had come to seek Baba's blessings all the way from Boston and not being used to Puttaparti's heat would fall sick under the tin shed, he relented, and gave me a room which had an attached flush toilet and a tap under which one could take a bath, but no furniture, not even a makeshift bed. So I had to sleep on the floor, with two bed sheets and a small pillow that I had brought from Boston, as my sleeping kit. Fortunately for me, the toilet was in good working order and there were few mosquitoes in the room. I got only about six hours of sleep that night because from 5 a.m. groups of devotees passed through the streets of the Ashram singing devotional songs or those in praise of Baba for his miraculous healing powers.

Lunch and dinner were served in the complex with diners seated on the floor in long rows and rice or *chappaties*, curd and hot curries served to them by the bearers. As I was not used to eating hot curries, I had to content myself with eating *chappatties*, curd and a curry which did not have chillies (hot pepper). For my afternoon tea I went outside the Ashram to one of the several small cafes. This allowed me to see the bazaar (main street) of the small town. At about 5 p.m. the devotees, including all the visitors were seated in long rows in the area earmarked for Baba's *darshan.* The devotees sat on white cotton sheets spread on the ground or on the bare dusty ground itself if they could not find a seat on the sheets. They would sit in this position until Sai Baba appeared from his office at 6 p.m. sharp. He would pass by all the assembled persons, bless them and give them his *vibhuti* (sacred ash) which is supposed to have magical healing powers. Occasionally, he would have a few words with a devotee, Indian or foreign, who had come so often to the Ashram that he recognised him or her. The darshan lasted for about 45 minutes after which the gathering would disperse. The exercise was repeated at 8 a.m. in the morning, immediately after the devotees had had their breakfast.

Sai Baba was a short very dark man, with a mass of bushy hair on his head. He reminded me of some of the aboriginal austroloid people of India. He was dressed in an ankle length scarlet robe. His appearance was not at all impressive. Although ardent devotees saw a halo of divine light around his head, I saw no such glow. He was however a smart businessman. From the large contributions received from his devotees, he had established a trust which managed several institutions — a degree college, a technical training institute, high schools for boys and girls, and a well equipped hospital in Puttaparti. The trustees were mostly retired government officers and executives of companies; their managerial experience ensured that the contributions were well spent, and there were no serious financial irregularities. The Ashram also had a library which contained scriptures of all religions, several collections of Baba's teachings, and books written by his devotees, containing his teachings and also in his praise.

I looked at some of the books and found that Baba had like many other Hindu holy men, put the teachings of the Srimad Bhagwad Gita and other Hindu scriptures in words, which modern educated men and women in India and abroad could understand and appreciate.

I came away with the impression of Baba as a smart holy man, who had managed to satisfy the craving of modern educated men and women for a spiritual experience. Any healing powers attributed to him were all due to the devotees' own belief. Those who got well, did so because of their own faith — their auto-suggestion.

Before we moved to our house, Mr Hanseleit told us that the house was fairly clean, every thing was in working order and that we should move into it as it was, and carry out any changes that we wanted, after we had lived in it for a few months and after the long hot summer of Delhi was over. But we did not heed his advice and decided that the house should be repainted and the floors which had a few oil spots on them should also be cleaned. Secondly, we decided to cut some of the bougainvillea bushes that the Hanseleits had planted all around the house to keep it cool. Mr. Lava Pratap advised us that we should rent the furniture that we needed from a furniture renting company until the furniture that we had bought in Boston for our use here arrived.

We ignored both pieces of advice and suffered immensely. In retrospect, Kamla and I regard the first six months of our stay in our house as the most uncomfortable period of our stay in Delhi. We engaged a painter to paint the house. He promised to complete his job in ten days, but took seven weeks to do it. Indeed, we had to literally throw him and his men out, after we had grown sick of living with the nauseating smell of fresh paint in all our rooms. Secondly, we decided to cut some of the bougainvillea bushes to have more light in the rooms. We did get the light but also the full blast of the scorching heat of Delhi's summer.

During these trying months of 1986, my only relief was my position at CPR. Because of it, I could escape from the difficulties at home and spend six to eight hours on week days reading and writing in my office, and attending the seminars given at least once a week by one of the faculty members, or by a visiting lecturer. The lecturers included Mr. I.K. Gujral, who became the Prime Minister of India for several months in 1997. Early in 1987, I joined on the advice of an old friend a newly formed Rotary Club, which gave me an opportunity to meet with fellow professionals and young businessmen once a week.

UNDP invited me to undertake a two-month consultancy mission to the Gambia to revise the Background Document for the Second Donors' Conference which was to be held in 1987. The document had been prepared by a consultant recruited by UNDP in collaboration with the leader of the UNOTC Project on Assistance to the Ministry of Development. I enjoyed going back to Banjul, where we had spent four happy years. The UNOTC project of which I had been the Project Manager had been extended and had as Project Manager, a Greek Cypriot economist. He was an amiable gentleman and we got along very well.

There had been major changes in the top personnel of the Ministry of Development. Dr Langley had gone to Washington as the Gambia's representative to the IMF. Mr. Abdou Ngum, was now the Development Secretary, Mr Abdou Njie, who was Deputy Development Secretary in my time had become the Governor of the Bank of the Gambia after a one year stint as Development Secretary.

Abdou Ngum welcomed me and I spent two happy months in Banjul. The town had not changed much, nor had the Gambian economy. The bridge-cum-barrage on the Gambia river had not been built because it was considered uneconomical by the World Bank and no western donor had come forward to finance it.

The Gambian economy was doing well. Inflation was low and the Bank of the Gambia was able to maintain the foreign exchange value of the currency. The number of tourists had increased and in addition to a new large 400 -bed French-owned hotel, located along the beach, a number of small hotels and restaurants had been established by the Gambians themselves. These served traditional Gambian food on tables placed under palm trees with musicians playing traditional West African music and were very popular with the tourists. However, dancing by groups of men and women, dressed only in reed skirts, which was so popular in Sierra Leone, was taboo because the Gambians were devout Moslems.

With the beginning of 1987, our initial problems of settling down had been largely solved and we began to lead a normal life. Through the assistance of an old friend Mr. O.P. Mathur, who was heading the National Institute of Urban Affairs, I got a contract for preparing a long-term plan for financing implementation of a 12- year (1988-2000) programme of development of the National Capital Region (NCR), prepared by the NCR Planning Board (NCRPB). The principal object of the programme was to reduce the very rapid growth of economic activities and population in Delhi, by encouraging dispersal of industries and service activities to 6 cities in the Delhi metropolitan area (DMA) and eight growth centres located in neighbouring states of U.P., Haryana and Rajasthan. The DMA towns/cities were located within a 30-km. radius of Delhi and the regional growth centres were located at distances of 60-160 km.

NCRPB sanctioned Rs. 200,000 for preparing the financial component of the programme over a 2-year period. I was to work as honorary director of the project; the funds would finance recruitment of a stenographer and two research assistants to conduct economic surveys of the 14 DMA towns/cities and regional growth centres. I recruited a stenographer and two research assistants. They had all worked with me in the P.E.O. The researchers were conscientious and able workers, who could make a fairly good assessment of the economic structure, development trends and growth potential of the DMA towns/cities and the regional growth centres. The project was completed in 27 months instead of the 24 months allotted to it; the three month delay was due to my illness. NCRPB accepted the report, but took no action on it because it had very little funds of its own and could only persuade the three member states of the Board to undertake the development projects included in the 12-year programme. The state governments implemented the projects which they considered most essential and which they would have implemented even without the preparation of the programme.

The project enabled me to travel to the 14 towns and cities, see the developments in them, and assess their problems and potential. I greatly enjoyed the travel.

In the late summer of 1987, I was asked by UNOTC to under take a two month consultancy mission to Sierra Leone to revise the Background Document for the Second Donors' Conference which was expected to be held in December 1987. I was one of the two consultants — the other was a Nigerian — recruited for this job. This was an unhappy mission for several reasons and at the end of it I resolved never to go to Sierra Leone again.

Sierra Leone had changed greatly in the two years since my last visit. With continuing decline in export earnings from diamonds and other minerals, and a large balance of payments deficits due to wasteful expenditure by a corrupt and inefficient government, the value of the currency was falling by the day. Prices of essential goods like rice, kerosene and petrol were rising rapidly and there were increasing shortages of these. President Siaka Stevens, who had ruled the country since it got independence in 1961, had retired. He had been succeeded by a soldier, Col. Momoh, who was addicted to drinking and was most inefficient.

The revised document that I prepared was severely criticized by the UNDP Resident Representative and the other expert, both Africans, recruited for the job. I deeply resented their criticism because most of it consisted of trivial comments about the wording of sentences, placing or omission of a comma or a semi-colon in a sentence.

On this mission I had my first heart attack. As I was returning from my evening walk along the beach I experienced severe chest pain, and perspiration on the forehead and all over the body while climbing the hill. On reaching the hotel, I telephoned Mr. Rajwani and one of the Bangladeshi doctors whom I had known during our seven year stay in Sierra Leone. They came over immediately. The doctor gave me some medicines which provided immediate relief. He came again next morning to see how I was doing and was satisfied that I had got over the attack. But he advised me not to climb the hill again. After returning home, I mentioned this incident to my physician, Dr Kutar. He gave me a through physical check-up and declared me fit. but asked me to continue my hypertension medicine.

Honolulu, 1988

In the summer of 1988 I spent three months in Honolulu to escape Delhi's scorching heat. Virendra hired a two-bedroom flat in which he would come to sleep at night, while spending the day in his own flat and his office. He had set up a data entry company early in 1985 in partnership with Nancy Makowsky with whom he lived. His business was doing well and was steadily expanding, and he felt very happy about it. I would spend a number of hours every day in the library of the East-West Center of the University of Hawaii. Much of what I wrote there was never published, but I enjoyed reading books and articles on subjects of interest to me and attending seminars and lectures given by the faculty of the Centre or visitors.

During this visit, Virendra and I visited two other islands, Maui and Hawaii, of the Hawaiian archipelago. Honolulu is located in Oahu , one of the smaller islands of the group. Maui is known for two things; sunrise at Haliakala, a 10000 ft high peak in its mountains, and its harbour which was one of the ports from which American whaling ships went out to slaughter whales in the Pacific in the nineteenth century. Virendra and I went out one early morning to see the sunrise. Seeing the sun rising above the mountain, resplendent with no air pollution to mar its glory is an experience which is etched deep in my memory. It reminded me of the description of Usha (sunrise) which I had read in some of the Sanskirt texts in college. The Aryans being sun-worshippers, their scriptures and early Sanskrit books are full of descriptions of the majesty and beauty of Usha.

The island of Hawaii, the biggest in the archipelago, is known for its live volcanoes. Seeing them and walking over fields of freshly solidified lava was a memorable experience. But what I enjoyed most was the one-day tour round the island. In this tour, we passed from lush tropical forests, through grasslands in which large herds of cattle and horses grazed, to desert. I was amazed to see this transition from tropical forest to desert all in the space of about 160 km. Contrary to what one would expect, the desert part of the island is liked most by the tourists. Some luxury tourist hotels had been built along it; others were planned. The tourists come here in the winter to escape the damp and cold of eastern and mid-western U.S.A.

But it was during this visit that I had my second and third attacks of chest pains. The next attack, much less severe, but equally unexpected, came at the Singapore airport when I lifted my overnight bag for inspection by the customs officials. I forgot all about it until December 1988, when I experienced severe chest pain one evening immediately after dinner. By this time I had started keeping with me some pills which I took and they did relieve the pain, but I called Dr Kutar as a precaution.

He advised me that since these attacks were recurring, I should go for a thorough medical check-up to the newly opened Escorts Hospital which specialises in the treatment of heart disease.

The next attack came early in March 1989. Virendra was visiting us at the time. Dr Kutar was called and after some emergency treatment, underwent an angiography to determine if surgical intervention was required. After the angiography, the Surgeon, Dr Naresh Trehan, advised that a coronary artery by-pass surgery was essential. I agreed readily to the operation.

The coronary by-pass surgery was performed successfully on 17 March 1989 and I stayed in the hospital for three weeks thereafter to recover fully from its after effects. A fellow patient at the hospital was M.F. Hussain, one of the best painters that India has today. After the surgery I recovered well enough in two months to resume my work on the NCR project.

Nandi's death

About two months after my surgery, on 31 May 1989 my only brother Narendra Nath, who was 11 years younger than me, and whom we always called Nandi, died suddenly of a heart attack. He had left our house in Lajpatnagar, where he was living with his family after retiring from the Army, in the morning for Hardwar for a dip in the Ganga. But as soon as he went into the icy cold water of the river, he suffered a massive heart attack. He came out immediately and lay on the stone pavement of *Har Ki Pauri* (the steps of Lord Shiva) a place where a bath in the Ganga is supposed to wash off all sins of the bathers, according to traditional Hindu belief. His son, Prafulla, who was accompanying him rushed immediately to fetch a doctor but before the doctor could arrive, he was already dead.

His death came as a rude shock to all of us. Being the youngest among the four children of our parents, he was the baby in the family. It was an irony that he was the first to pass away! His widow, a son and two daughters live in our house in Lajpatnagar.

Construction of the house

In early December 1988 two weeks before my third heart attack, we had started construction of the back portion of our house. The construction extended over a period of about 21 months and was completed in September 1990. We were lucky in getting a good architect, Mr. S.G. Pradhan, to prepare the plan, get it approved, and to take full responsibility for overseeing it. I could not do much for the first six months of the construction because of my illness. Later, when I got better, my principal role was to keep accounts of the expenditure, and ensure that there was no interruption in the construction.

After the house had been completed, I got a taste of the increase in corruption among officials who deal with the public in the eighteen years since the front portion of the house was constructed in 1971. At that time we could get the completion certificate from the Municipal Corporation of Delhi and electricity, water and sewerage connections by paying nominal gratification to the concerned officials. But this time, I had to pay a sum of Rs. 25,000 to the inspector of the Municipal Corporation who came to inspect the house before issuing a completion certificate! I never got the certificate because the inspector was suspended for corruption in the week following his acceptance of the bribe. When I mentioned this to Mr. Pradhan, he bluntly told me that I should not have paid the bribe, because the Corporation is bound to issue the certificate within 60 days of receipt of the application for it, and if it did not issue it within this period, the house owner can assume that the certificate had been issued. We have not got the certificate until today.

The second lesson was in getting the electricity connection. All the concerned senior officials of the Delhi Electric Supply Undertaking (DESU) approved our application for the supply of electricity. However the inspector who was to authorize the connection of the house with the supply source of DESU and provide the meters for recording consumption of electricity would not do so on various pretexts. Finally, on the advice of the contractor who had done the electrical work, I had to pay him Rs.18,000 before I could get the connection and the meters. I was disgusted by the increase in corruption among public servants between 1971 and 1989.

Since the increase in corruption has continued and even a former Prime Minister of India, some chief ministers, many ministers of both the central and state governments and many top bureaucrats are accused of corruption, the lower level functionaries of various departments of the Government which deal with the public, have a free hand in lining their pockets undaunted by any fear of punishment.

After construction was completed, Kamla was getting restless because she didn't want to devote all her time to being a housewife and mother. She began to contact the women scholars who had been doing studies on the economic activities, social status and problems of Indian women. But, she was not successful in her efforts to attach herself to an organization undertaking such studies until after we returned from our 10-month long stay in Honolulu during 1992-93.

Jyotsna got her B.A. (Hons.) degree in English literature early in 1991 and started working as a proof reader-cum-editor in the Oxford-IBH Publishing House, Delhi which specialises in publishing books on the natural sciences. She continued working there until we left for the U.S. in May 1992.

Papaji's Death

In May 1990 Kamla's father died after suffering for a year from paralytic stroke as the age of 88. He was extremely popular in the neighbourhood, Rajouri Garden, in West Delhi, where he had lived after retiring from government service. He was a good doctor and was also socially active. Until his stroke he would spend four hours every morning at the hospital, which he had built up from a small charitable dispensary to a hospital which had eight specialists and was well equipped with X-ray machines and other diagnostic aids. After retiring as Deputy Director of Medical Service of Punjab in 1957, he had established a successful practice as a physician in his own house. He was also a patriarch in the true sense of the term. Neither his wife, who had died in 1971, nor any of his seven children dared disobey him; his word was law in his house. One of his sons, who had been living with him for several years, spared neither time nor expense on his treatment during the one year that he lived after his stroke.

I had a feeling of great personal loss on his death. He was our last surviving link with the older generation. Second, I felt extremely sad that a man who had relieved the suffering of thousands, both in his service and after retirement, should have to suffer so much before leaving this world. I felt that if there was God, he was not just because while many sinners die a painless death he had to suffer so much.

Honolulu, 1992-93

In May 1992, we went to the U.S.A. for what proved to be a 10-month long stay; we returned in March 1993. I had not been keeping good health. Virendra advised us that I would get much better treatment for my complaints at the Queen's Medical Centre, the hospital in which he had worked earlier for four years, than in Delhi. On our way to the U.S. we stopped in London for a couple of days for discussion with officials of Merrill Lynch, the company in which I have invested all my U.S. savings.

On our way to Honolulu, we stayed for four days in Albuquerque, New Mexico, as house guests of my old friend, Dr. Bob Campbell. He had cancer of the knee and I was anxious that I should see him before he passed away; he died six months after our visit. Bob was leading a retired life, except that he taught a course in Human Geography at the University. He was 76 and knew that he would not live long because he had cancer of the knee which caused him great pain. But this did not reduce his zest for life, or affect his warm, friendly temperament or his love for good food. He took us to the best restaurants in and out of town. He was a good cook himself and one evening he cooked for us on excellent chicken dinner. His flat roof house made of mud bricks with a fountain playing in the small yard reminded me of houses in the canal colonies of West Punjab.

One day Bob and Elinor, the lady with whom he was living gave us a 300 km tour of a part of the state. Starting at about 10 in the morning, we stopped for lunch at a Spanish restaurant located in an old Spanish castle, a few miles from the highway which served excellent food. After lunch, we drove past Los Alamos, the U.S. Government-owned laboratory where the first two atom bombs, which were dropped on Hiroshima and Nagasaki in Japan in August 1945 were built. In the afternoon, we stopped for an hour to look at the relics of one of the villages of Pueblo[1] Indians. Elinor, had specialised in the study of these people, who form a significant proportion of the population of the state. She told us many interesting facts about their economy, based on cultivation of maize, their life style, religious beliefs, family and community organisation and other aspects of their culture.

New Mexico and several other states of south western United States including California were under Spanish rule and formed part of Mexico for three centuries before they were occupied by the United States in the middle of the nineteenth century. New Mexico is the state in which Spanish influence is most evident. People of Spanish descent, American Indians and Mestizos (progeny of Spanish fathers and American Indian mothers) form the majority of the population. White Americans are a decreasing minority, because there is continuous in immigration, legal and illegal, from Mexico to the United States.

I reached Honolulu on the 31 May 1992; Kamla and Jyotsna followed a couple of days later because they wanted to see San Francisco, which I had already seen. Virendra had hired a 3- bedroom, fully furnished, airconditioned apartment for our stay, which was very close to his own apartment. He had also obtained the names of the best urologist and surgeon for treatment of my complaints of an enlarged prostate gland and haemorrhoids.

While I was in Honolulu, Dr Pai Panandiker wrote to me that he would not extend my association with the Centre for Policy Research because they wanted to recruit younger people at the Centre. On reflection, I felt that he was fully justified in his decision because I had been at the Centre for six years and had not produced much, except a few articles, and the report on the project funded by the National Capital Region Planning Board. However, I decided that I would continue my writing work at home as long as my health permitted.

The year 1993 was not a happy one for me. My health was causing me auxiety. Suffering was an absolute necessity. The post-operation recovery was slow but steady. For about a month I was so weak that I would lie in bed listening to broadcasts from the All India Radio and staring at the roof through day and night. Even the friends and relatives who came to see me and enquire about my recovery, had to see me in my bedroom. However by October, I was well enough to resume my reading and writing. I contributed a paper on 'Integrated Rural and Urban Development - A Strategy for Spatial Development in India', to the Fourth Asian Urbanisation Conference scheduled to be held in Taipeh (Taiwan) in January 1994, and felt fit enough to attend the Conference. The visit was most enjoyable. It enabled me to see Taiwan about the rapid economic growth of which I had read so much. Furthermore, meeting geographers and specialists on urban affairs from South, South East and East Asia, Europe and the U.S.A. was a pleasant and intellectually invigorating experience. The University and the Government of Taiwan and the city government of Taipeh showed their hospitality by arranging receptions, lunches and dinners for the delegates to the Conference.

On our return from the U.S.A, Kamla was successful in getting a position as Consultant to the Centre for Social Research, a non-governmental organisation (NGO) which is engaged in research on economic, social and political status of women and is also conducting several projects in Delhi and Uttar Pradesh for uplift of poor rural women. Kamla greatly enjoyed the job because it fulfilled her deeply felt wish to do some academic work. She and the Director of the Centre, Mrs. Ranjana Kumari, became good friends.

Kamla's association with the CSR, brought her in contact with Prof. Anand Kumar, Professor of Sociology at the Jawaharlal Nehru University. He helped me locate Mr. Amarendu Jha, a young journalist and research scholar in JNU who was working for his Ph.D. degree in sociology under him. Mr. Jha assisted me in writing my autobiography over a 15-month (December 1994-March 1996) period. He would visit me two to three times a week; we would sit together for about two hours, in the basement of the house, where we would not be disturbed. During these sessions I would talk about all the events in my life and my work. Mr. Jha would listen patiently, raise questions to ascertain the facts more precisely, make comments on my talk and prepare drafts which would be of greater interest to the reader than the draft of my personal monologue.

However this arrangement came to an abrupt end in September 1995. Mr. Jha left and soon afterwards I had a fall.

In September 1995 a few days after Kamla had returned from Beijing, I fell down twice in the house which must have been due to my losing consciousness for a second or two. The first fall did not do much harm, but in the second I suffered a fracture of the left forearm. Within a few days of the second fall, I had an attack of ventricular failure as a result of which I had to be rushed to the Escorts Hospital for treatment.

The vertigo and the ventricular failure were secondary complications. They also X-rayed my left arm and explained to me that the orthopaedist who had tried to repair the fracture before putting the forearm in a cast had not done a good job so that a slight deformity of the left forearm would remain after the cast came off. However, the deformity would not be so serious as to affect my using the left arm for minor activities like shaving and so on.

The stay at the hospital had one unexpected benefit; I began to gain weight and strength. Kamla was extremely pleased; she had got tired of seeing me as a skeleton. So she decided that I must get the same diet that I had at the hospital. The gain in weight and strength have continued and have enabled me to reduce the period of lying in bed during the day to the minimum, and to devote a large part of my day reading and writing. During the evenings I would spend a couple of hours playing bridge at the Vasant Vihar Club, or attending a meeting of my Rotary Club in Ashoka Hotel or attending a lecture or seeing a performance of music or dance at India International Centre. But because of my health constraints I was not comfortable on a long drive or a plane journey. My last plane journey was to Pondicherry in January 1995; it may be long before I feel strong enough to undertake another.

As the new year dawned, (1998) I prayed that there would be no more injuries and I would be able to continue my reading and writing for the few years that I had to live without any future mishap. However, this was not to be. In February, I had a fracture of the hip joint which required hospitalisation for six weeks. At the end of it, I was so weak that I could not walk without a walker and with somebody accompanying me. However, I am well enough now to be able to walk with a stick, with the strength provided by exercises done with the help of a physiotherapist.

In the evening of my life, I can only say, "What will be will be; man does not know what the next day will bring". Let me do what

I can, as long as I live, for my own good and that of my fellow humans.

I still walk with a stick and with someone taking me from bed room to the dining table and back. But I can read and write for 4-5 hours a day, Kamla has helped me write this story and editor friends of various journals have encouraged me to publish several articles on urban, regional and industrial development. A physiotherapist is determined to help me walk with a stick and has prescribed homeopathic medicines which enable me to have sound sleep at night; I could never do that earlier. As a result both my health and concentration at work are better.

NOTE

1. A Pueblo is a 1-2 story mud house built by Indians in south western United States. The residents are farmers who grow corn (maize) the staple on which they subsist, on tiny farms around the Pueblos. The American Indians are desperately poor and ignorant; illiteracy, disease and superstition are rife. The programmes undertaken by the U.S. government for their welfare are a complete failure. However in recent years, their young men have started to get educated and get low level jobs such as clerks and thus join the mainstream economy. One of their principal sources of income is sale of bracelets, necklaces and other trinkets made of blue stones which are found in the area. These are sold on Sundays in towns like Santa Fe. Sunday is the market day for the Indians. We visited Santa Fe on a Sunday and were delighted to see the market and a dance performance.

18

Reflections

I have devoted the conclusion of this story to reflect on various periods of my life and the influences that have contributed to my development as a human being. The personality of any human being is influenced first by the love and care (or lack of these) that he or she receives from parents and siblings and the attitude and behaviour of friends in childhood. As he or she grows from a child to an adult, teachers and friends in school or college and the social economic and political environment in which he or she lives are important additional influences on development. In youth and middle age, when he or she works, job satisfaction and security, the nature and behaviour of the spouse (if he or she is married), and the attitudes of colleagues and superiors in the job are important influences. They influence not only job satisfaction but also his or her self perception. Another influence is development of his or her children because it influences his or her self perception as a parent.

I was exceptionally lucky in the influences that contributed to my development from a child to a teenager. Being the first born and a son, I received more love from my parents than did any of my three siblings. The birth of the first son is celebrated in Hindu families because it ensures the continuity of the family. Furthermore, as is well known, there is great preference for sons among middle class Hindus; (and indeed among most groups irrespective of caste or religion in Indian families). Since I was a good student, my parents were proud of my academic success. So were my teachers.

I grew so used to the pampering at home and in school that I greatly missed it in college and this contributed to my sickness after two years of college. The Government College, Lahore, which I attended, was one of the best colleges in India. It produced some of the best graduates, sportsmen and athletes in Punjab. Many of the teachers had post-graduate degrees from Oxford, Cambridge or London universities. But they were government servants; they did their assigned duties well but took little interest in the welfare of the students. Furthermore, they could provide to the students no guidance on selection of a career. Indeed, in the situation of acute unemployment among educated Hindu youth in the 1930s, because of the economic depression, it was difficult to give such guidance. When World War II started in September 1939 and a large number of students of the college joined as officers in the armed forces, service in the forces seemed to be the best career. Unless the young man suffered from some physical defect, being at student of the college was enough for selection as an officer in the armed forces. I did not wish to join the forces. I hated the need for constant flattery of higher officers and obeying without question their orders which are required for success as an officer.

On my father's advice I left college after two years because of ill health. I had also not done well in my examination held at the end of two years. However, I felt sicker after leaving college on account of being extemely bored at having nothing to do.

As soon as I rejoined college, my health began to improve so much so that I passed the M.A. examination in geography, standing first in a class of about 30 students. Immediately, thereafter, I received an offer, which I accepted, of a fellowship for post graduate studies at the University of Wisconsin, Madison, in the U.S.A. I stayed in the U.S.A. for three years, 1946-49, and obtained a Ph.D degree from the University of Maryland, located in a suburb of Washington D.C. I have written in Chapter III about Prof. Baker, my adviser for the dissertation. He was a much respected geographer. Besides, I have yet to meet a man who was more concerned about the welfare of his students than he. He gave me as a parting gift a certificate in which he wrote that I was the best student that he had ever had.

The Influence of the Economic Depression

When I was growing up in the 1930s, the world was experiencing the severest economic depression in living memory. Millions were unemployed in Europe, the U.S.A., Canada and many other countries including India. Unemployment among educated Hindu young men in Punjab was so acute that the newspapers carried reports every day of one or two young men committing suicide because they could not get a job.

The depression contributed to my developing a pessimistic outlook on life, which I have not been able to shake off, despite all the opportunities for travel and work in India and abroad on UN-OTCD (Office of Technical Assistance for Development) assignments. I would worry that after I graduated from college, I might have much difficulty in getting a job.

Nobody had an inkling in the 1930s that the job situation would change radically with the outbreak of World War II. Unemployment among educated youth disappeared. Tens of thousands, including half the students of my class in Government College joined as officers in the armed forces. As late as the winter of 1945, a few months before I passed my M.A. examination, the only visible job prospect was of teaching geography in a college in the Punjab or western U.P. The war had ended; thousands of officers were being demobilised and the Government of India had decided that first preference would be given to them in recruitment to the superior services of the government or other jobs in the government.

I have always worried about the prospect of getting a job. Yet, I have not been un-employed for a day in 34 years of professional work. Despite this experience, I have not learnt the simple lesson that worry about job, health, happiness as a spouse or as head of a family is not only useless but destroys a part of one's being; it greatly reduces one's chances of being a happy and successful human being.

The Movement for Independence and My Attitude Towards the British

In the 1930s and the early 1940s, we witnessed the movement for Independence of India from British rule and attempts to suppress it by the Governments of India and of the various provinces. The British were so firmly entrenched as the rulers of India that until the beginning of World War II, we the common folk, could not believe that Independence would be achieved in our life time. This belief affected our attitude to the British living in India. They were so aloof that a person of the middle income group had no occasion to meet them. The governments of the provinces had thrown tens of thousands of participants in the movement for independence in jails; besides thousands had been injured and hundreds had been killed while defying the orders of the government against participation in the various movements launched by Gandhiji. They were considered to be ruthless but highly efficient administrators.

This impression changed completely when I met a few British professors in the Government College. I learnt all that I know about English poetry from an Englishman who taught us for three months. He was the Head of the Department and an outstanding art critic. But this position had not made him arrogant. Another professor, a fresh graduate from Oxford, was more tolerant of the pranks of his students than any Indian professor. An Irish lady, who was the principal of the government college for women and taught a course to us when we were studying in M.A. was more considerate to the students than most of the Indian professors.

Although I read with great interest the progress of the movement for independence through the 1930s, and up to the end of World War II, I never believed that it would be achieved during our life time. As late as the summer of 1942, Mr. Churchill, the Prime Minister of Britain during most of World War II, had declared, "I have not become the King's first Minister to preside over the liquidation of the British empire". India was the crown jewel of the Empire, and he knew that grant of independence to India would mean the beginning of the end of the empire.

Yet barely five years later, his successor, Mr. Clement Attlee, announced that India would be given independence and would be divided into two parts on the basis of religion, with areas in north western and north eastern India in which the Moslems were in a majority forming part of Pakistan and the remaining parts, in which the Hindus were in a majority forming part of the Indian Union.

The largest and bloodiest migration in human history which followed the partition of the country in which an estimated 12 million people—Hindus, Sikhs and Moslems—moved and hundreds of thousands were killed or wounded and countless numbers of women were kidnapped and converted to the faith of their captors was totally unexpected by the leaders of both the Congress and the Moslem League or by the Government of India and of the affected provinces. The measures that were taken to minimize the casualties in the migration were decided from day to day.

I know of no study of what suddenly turned friendly and peaceful neighbours into frenzied demons.

My parents and siblings were among the migrants from Pakistan to India; I was away studying in the U.S.A. They migrated safely before the partition. But Kamla's family who followed a few weeks after the partition, narrowly escaped being massacred.

When I went to the U.S.A. I found a country whose people were fabulously rich by Indian standards. However, my fellow students in the University, most of whom had been soldiers in World War II, were friendly and anxious to know about India and its people. Madison, where the University of Wisconsin was located was a very friendly city; wherever I went, I was greeted with a smile. I learnt concepts and techniques of research in my subject, about which I had been totally ignorant. My spirits soared; I felt that I was like a flower which was slowly blooming into its full potential. I had been afraid that I might not keep good health in the bitter cold of Madison. But I have never been healthier than in Madison. The five week motor tour of central and western United States in which four fellow students and I saw a large part of the country including its most scenic national parks was an unforgettable experience. Yet, it was planned only a few weeks before we made it.

My second job after returning from the USA was in the newly established Planning Commission of the Government of India. Me first, was in Sri Lanka. I worked in it for eight years 1950 – 58 and have always looked upon the period as a very happy period of my professional career. Living with my parents and seeing my father regain his middle income status which he had in Lahore was a pleasure. I had an opportunity to observe and comment on the community development programme—a programme of providing basic services to the villages: approach roads, drinking water wells, primary and secondary schools and basic health care centres and teaching farmers methods of improving agriculture and animal husbandry and better farm management. The job provided also an opportunity to tour extensively and see the immense variety in the ethnic composition, and life styles of the people of different regions, and the variety of landscapes that India has. I saw in some regions, people who were desperately poor, but in most other regions, incomes and level of living of the rural people were improving steadily partly as a result of the programme.

In a later job in the Commission, I had an opportunity to see the increasingly difficult problem of providing housing and essential services to the people of India's rapidly growing large metropolitan cities. This job has given me a life long interest in study of the problems of large metropolitan cities.

The attitude of my superiors contributed greatly to my satisfaction in these jobs. Most of them, while appreciating my work, were willing to overlook my mistakes!

I have worked in Un jobs for 16 years in 3 different countries. The jobs have many advantages. They provide to the experts an opportunity to observe and appreciate the values and life styles where are very different from their own. The emoluments are quite attractive. And if the expert serves for 5 years or more, he or she becomes entitled to a pension, which provides him or her financial security for life.

But there are serious disadvantages also. There is extreme uncertainty of tenure; one's job may be terminated at any time;

contracts are renewed from year to year and often from quarter to quarter. In many places there are no suitable facilities for high school or college education of children, so that they have to be sent to the expert's home country, to a country in Europe or to the USA where there are such facilities. Furthermore, children have to learn to appreciate values and life style very different from those of their parents. This is not easy for growing children and even adolescents.

Kuwait

In Kuwait, I saw a traditional, poor Islamic society experiencing economic and social changes at a speed which is difficult for any society to absorb. Exploitation of its vast resources of crude oil had brought to the government fabulous revenues. A benign and far sighted ruler decided that the bulk of the income would be used for the welfare of his people. The old city of mud houses and narrow winding streets was being replaced during our four year stay by a planned modern city with a large number of self contained residential neighbourhoods each with its own shopping complex, primary and secondary schools, health centres and mosques. Every Kuwaiti was provided a house and basic furniture and a job, the pay in which enabled him to live in modest comfort. Thousands of young men and hundreds of young women were sent to Universities in Egypt, Lebanon, Iraq, Britain and the U.S.A. for education in public administration, the humanities, education, science and technology. The first young men from these universities came home to occupy the top administrative positions in various departments of the government. They ran the government with the help of technical assistance provided by experts recruited by the government or provided by the agencies of the U.N. systems. The young women graduates, many of whom worked in the government, led Kuwaiti women to discard the veil (the women wore) educate their children and adopt a western life style.

However, the negative effects of this too rapid westernization began to be seen soon. They were voiced by the elderly Kuwaiti members of parliament their protest against too rapid westernization did not have much effect in the 1960s, but it did in the 1980s when Ayatollah Khomeini of Iran successfully led a revolution against rapid westernization and consequent loss of traditional Islamic values of Middle Eastern societies.

One of the ill-effects was demoralisation and consequent over-indulgence in wine and women by the young graduates who came home a few years after the first group.

Sierra Leone

In Freetown, capital of a small country in West Africa where we lived for seven years (1972-79), we saw the systematic plunder of the riches of the country by an unholy alliance between a corrupt political executive and rapacious foreign merchants. When we reached there we found that most of the people were poor and lived in *shanties* (huts made of mud bricks with walls and roofs of corrugated iron sheets). The population of the city was increasing rapidly with influx of thousands of young men and hundreds of young women who were fleeing the villages in search of jobs. There was little discontent. Everyone could get the basic food -- rice and fish and employment as unskilled workers, domestic servants, watchmen etc. A large part of the foreign exchange earnings from export of gem and industrial diamonds and other minerals was appropriated by the political executive and the merchants. Despite this, there was enough to pay for import of rice and other essentials. Waters off the coast were teaming with fish.

Conditions were radically different by early 1979, when we left. There were recurrent shortages of rice and fish and other necessities such as kerosene and petrol and increasing unemployment. Earnings from export of diamonds, the principal export had declined because of exhaustion of reserves. Fish had become scarce, because the trawlers of a company which had been given a contract for deep sea fishing had in fact concentrated on fishing near the coast.

Such impoverishment of the people, led to a succession of coupsd' etat in the late 1980s and to a civil war in the 1990s, the end of which is nowhere in sight.

Gambia

In Gambia, where I was posted from 1979 to 1983, I saw a traditional Islamic society which was being modernised slowly, at a pace which it could sustain. A major source of income for the country and employment for its young people was tourism. Thousands of young men were employed as guides for tourists and as workers in hotels and restaurants that catered to the tourists. Most of the tourists were unmarried young women from Scandinavian countries, and Germany or men and women from Britain. In the early years of growth of tourism, there was much male prostitution because sex with a ycung and virile Gambian was a source of great satisfaction for unmarried Scandinavian women. But the government had effectively suppressed it. The economy was not dominated by foreigners as that of Sierra Leone was. While the first hotels had been built by the Swedes, later on the Gambians themselves had built and were running successfully small hotels and restaurants that catered to the tourists.

Gambia lacked the rich natural resources of Sierra Leone. It had no minerals and earnings from its principal export crop, ground nut were barely adequate to pay for essential imports. The people were poor but they were content because their traditional Islamic institutions and simple life style had not been seriously disrupted by tourism.

The economic and social changes in the countries which are very different in their economic conditions and cultures have one thing in common. Most people are happy when the social and economic changes experienced by them are not disruptive of their traditional institutions and values and when they are not being impoverished. The latter has led to a civil war in Sierra Leone. But as the example of Kuwait shows even sudden inflow of unbelievable riches can be socially disruptive.

Living in the USA and Sri Lanka has added further to my understanding of the human conditions in different lands and what makes people happy or unhappy. The U.S.A. was during the late 1940s and early 1950s just waking up to its status as an economic and military super power. The arrogance that comes with perception of this status was already evident among the members of the American Congress, but it had not percolated to the Universities and to residents of small cities like Madison.

Most people were happy. There was little unemployment and income levels were rising. The depression years during which millions were unemployed were best forgotten. The two basic institutions – marriage and the family were stable. There were few divorces. However, nearly 40 years later, when we went to live in Boston during the mid 1980's, we found a major change. At the University itself there were many divorced, lonely and unhappy middle aged men and women. Similarly, we saw several old people unhappy because their children did not allow them to live with them and shower their love on their grandchildren. A sizeable black middle class had come up but unemployment among black youth was so acute that the black-dominated areas of the inner cities were crime-ridden ghettoes.

A comprehensive system of welfare had ensured that every one could have education, health care, social security which provided a living wage during limited periods of unemployment and an adequate pension after retirement. Highly subsidized food was provided by the government to the poor. Thus there was no material want; but large numbers of people were unhappy because their emotional needs were not being met.

In Sri Lanka, where I worked immediately after return from the U.S.A., I saw the people of this extremely beautiful island enjoying the first fruits of independence. There was no poverty; a system of distribution of rice at low prices ensured that every one had enough to eat. The economy was booming because prices of its principal export crops – tea, coir and rubber were high. Since malaria, the great killer, had been eradicated by the early 1950's, there had been a great improvement in the health of the people and increase in their life span. Furthermore, thanks to a network of primary and secondary schools, there was little illiteracy. Tension between the Sinhalese and the Tamils that were to result in violent conflict between them from the 1980s was barely perceptible.

Political, Social and Economic Changes in India

When India became independent, the Prime Minister and the Chief Ministers of most of the large states were either Brahmins or belonged to the other high caste—Kayasthas, traders or Rajputs. The most important ministers also belonged to the high castes.

Fifty years later, the position has been reversed. The Chief Ministers of almost all the major states belong to one of the dominant cultivating castes, the Chief Minister of Bihar belongs to one of the other backward castes. Furthermore most of the other important ministers in their cabinets also belong to the dominant cultivating castes or other backward classes or the Scheduled Caste.

The political leaders of the Brahmins and other high castes have not resisted this change. They have accepted it as inevitable in a country in which the high castes form a minority of the population and the dominant cultivating castes, the other backward castes and the scheduled castes form the majority.

Social Change

Major social changes are accompanying the political change. The slow disappearance of untouchability in villages of a district of Rajasthan which is a comparatively backward state has been mentioned in Chapter IX. Furthermore, I saw in the small towns of the district, emergence of a class of educated scheduled caste youth, who were entering the lower rungs of public service, as teachers , secretaries of panchayats and cooperative societies and village level workers of the community development programme and as clerks in government. A recent report of the Union Public Service Commission indicates that an increasing number of entrants to the Indian Administrative Service and other central services are from the rural areas and belong to castes other than the high castes. The ministers and officers belonging to the scheduled castes use their political and administrative positions to raise the economic and social status of the people of their castes.

The ministers have to do it in order to get reelected. Furthermore, the provisions in the Constitution of India that 25 per cent of members of Parliament and the state legislatures must belong to the scheduled castes and the scheduled tribes and that 25 per cent of jobs in the government should be reserved for them ensure that their economic and social advance receives increasing emphasis in policies and development programmes of the governments at the centre and in the states. Since most people of the groups are poor, illiterate, in poor health and live in villages or slums of the large metropolitan cities, there will be greater emphasis than hitherto in eradicating poverty and illiteracy among them, improving their health and providing them suitable housing in the cities.

Such emphasis should accelerate economic growth. The examples of China and other countries of East and South East Asia which have achieved high rates of economic growth in recent decades indicate that a literate and healthy population is the first requirement of rapid economic growth.

Land Reforms: When India became independent, in large parts of the country, the farmers had to share their produce with zamindars. They had been appointed by the East India Company to collect land revenue from the farmers, but became in course of time virtual owners of land. However, in the first 15 years after independence, *zamindari* and similar systems of land tenure, such as *jagirdari* in most of the princely states were abolished and full rights of management of their lands were conferred on the farmers. This change has contributed not only to improvement of the economic condition of the farmers but also provided them with powerful incentive to increase production by adopting improved methods of production. Partly as a result of the reform agricultural output has increased more than 3-fold during the half century 1950-2000. The former *zamindars* and *jagirdars* as well as the farmers have accepted the basic change in their condition as in centers.

Rise in Education and Power of Women

Just over a century ago, education of women was taboo. Most of the women in villages were illiterate. The few who were educated in the villages and the towns had studied upto the primary level. But education of women has spread so rapidly that there is a rapidly growing class of high school and college educated women in the urban areas who have taken up jobs in the government, the companies and the professions, particularly education and health. The rate of female literacy is still low in some states but has risen rapidly in most others in recent decades. The levels of education and health of the people, rates of increase in per capita income, and rise in level of living of the people are appreciably higher in states with higher levels of female literacy than in the states with low levels.

Women are playing an increasingly important role in representative institutions of rural development. Reservation of 1/3rd of seats in these institutions has been made mandatory under an amendment to the Constitution and similar reservation in the Parliament and the state legislatures appears to be a near term prospect. The women members of institutions of rural development have used their power as well as or better than the men. Since survival in health of their children, their growing up as productive farmers or citizens and their own survival and of their husbands is the prime concerns of women. The women representatives in rural institutions have given emphasis to eradicating illiteracy and providing primary education and basic health care to all. There is little doubt that these emphases in our national development programmes will increase with increase in number of women members of the state legislatures and the Parliament.

There is great variation in rates of female literacy in different states. However, it is noteworthy that both the rate of economic growth and rise in level of living of the population is higher in state with high levels of female literacy than in those with low level of literacy. Furthermore, acceptance of family planning is significantly higher and the rate of population growth is lower in the states with high female literarcy than in those with low literacy. There is little doubt that rapid increase in female literacy in the lagging states will contribute to faster national economic growth, and rise in level of living besides slowing rate of population growth.

Economic Change: In the half century before independence, growth of agricultural output and of gross domestic product was less or marginally higher than the increase in population. However, in the half century after independence these rates have been significantly higher than the rate of increase in population which itself has been much higher than in the pre-independence half century.

The Hindu rate of economic growth of 3-4 per cent per annum during 1965-80 has been replaced by rates of 5-7 per cent during the 1990s. And while population has increased 2½ times between 1951 and 1991, food-grain output is 3½ times larger. The fact that an estimated 1/3rd of the population does not get enough calories to maintain health is due mains to maldistribution. The undernourished people are concentrated in hilly and forested areas in which communications are poor and in states like U.P and Bihar in which large numbers of people are too poor to buy enough food.

Against this depressing statistic, there is rapid increase in the size of the middle class in towns and villages of many states and rapid increase in consumption of protective foods – milk, vegetables, fruit and cooking oil and of articles needed to improve personal hygiene – soap, hair oil and of consumer durables – radio and television receivers and use of liquefied petroleum gas instead of cow dung or firewood from forests for cooking in the richer states – Punjab, Haryana, Gujarat, Maharshtra and several southern states. The level of living of the large majority of the population has increased significantly in all these states. With more rapid economic development in the backward states–U.P., Bihar, Madhya Pradesh, Orissa and Rajasthan in which the poor are concentrated, through actions of determined government there should be rapid decline in number of the poor, the illiterate and the sick in the cell.

Alongside these highly desirable political, social and economic changes there have been others which can only be considered deplorable and to minimize which effective measures must be taken urgently. These include, increase in corruption in all branches of the civil services and at all except the highest levels of the bureaucracy. It has penetrated also to an extent in the armed forces.

There has emerged a strong nexus between corrupt politicians, bureaucrats businessmen and criminals. Its emergence was inescapable in a system of parliamentary democracy in which elections to the state legislatures and the parliament cost very large sums of money and institutional finance of the expenses—by political parties, by business houses, or by the government is either non-existent or is grossly inadequate. The sources of institutional finance must be adequate, so that the candidates selected by the major political parties do not have a strong incentive to resort to corruption in order to recoup their election expenses.

Some remedial action has been taken by the Election Commission and the major political parties. A determined Election Commissioner, took effective measures in the mid 1990s to eradicate violence during elections to state legislatures and the Parliament. As a result, there has been little violence in the elections to Parliament during 1996-98 and a minimum of violence in elections to state legislatures held in 1998. The statutory limits for election expenses have been greatly increased to take into account the rise in prices. The Election Commission is now busy in ensuring that the expenses are not exceeded and also that persons against whom there are criminal cases in the courts are debarred from contesting the elections. Major political parties are cooperating.

Conclusion

This brief review of development in different periods of my life and work in different countries has taught me, I have seen through living and work in India and in foreign countries that most people are happy when their economic and emotional needs are being met. The example of Sierra Leone has shown that steady impoverishment of a people is socially disruptive. That of Kuwait shows that suddeen prosperity is equally socially disruptive.

The brief references to social and economic changes in India during the half century 1950-2000, convinces me of the resiliece of

Indian society and its capacity to make far reaching social changes without violence. The steady accelaration of economic growth and rise in levels of living of the majority of the people in several stages during this period, gives me the hope that India could in the next two decades be a land in which poverty, illiteracy and disease are much less than at present, and that most people belong as in most developed and many developing countries, to the great middle class. I trust that this hope does not prove to be a chimera.

INDEX